T0292961

Embracing Chaos

Embracing Chaos: How to deal with a World in Crisis?

BY

JAN ROTMANS

Erasmus University Rotterdam, The Netherlands

And

CO-WRITTEN BY

MISCHA VERHEIJDEN

Co-operative Re-story.be, Belgium

TRANSLATED BY

MICHAEL GOULD

United Kingdom – North America – Japan – India – Malaysia – China

Emerald Publishing Limited
Emerald Publishing, Floor 5, Northspring, 21-23 Wellington Street, Leeds LS1 4DL

Copyright © 2023 Jan Rotmans and Co-Writer Mischa Verheijden.
Published under exclusive licence by Emerald Publishing Limited.
Translation by Michael Gould. The moral rights of the translator have been asserted.
Copyright © 2021 Jan Rotmans en Mischa Verheijden.
Original title Omarm de Chaos.
First published in 2021 by De Geus, Amsterdam.

Reprints and permissions service
Contact: permissions@emeraldinsight.com

British Library Cataloguing in Publication Data
A catalogue record for this book is available from the British Library

ISBN: 978-1-83753-635-1 (Print)
ISBN: 978-1-83753-634-4 (Online)
ISBN: 978-1-83753-636-8 (Epub)

INVESTOR IN PEOPLE

Table of Contents

Introduction: The Turmoil in Ourselves and the World

It's not surprising if you feel uneasy right now. In fact, it would be strange if you didn't. It's very turbulent in the world, and it feels like we are in a series of permanent crises. The restlessness in the world reflects the restlessness in ourselves. We are living on the cusp of a new era, in which everything that we took for granted is being called into question.

Transformative change of this kind is far more drastic, difficult and threatening than 'regular' change. Transformative change is deep change and it's about thinking, acting and organizing the world in a quite different way. This places an almost impossible pressure on us: to let go of the tried-and-tested while embracing the new and the unknown.

Instinctively, we prefer not to. Our evolutionary development means that our brains are geared to stability and continuity, but that's the one thing we lack today. And yet a lack of this kind sometimes indicates a new direction. Chaos and unrest are inherent in the development of complex systems, such as our society and its economy. And no less importantly, they are inherent in us humans. In complexity theory, chaos is the transitional situation between two periods of equilibrium. It's the in-between-period, the time between 'it is' and 'it will be'. Chaos is a necessary precondition for a transition, and then it literally creates scope for the birth of something new.

We are now in just such a time: our social systems, the economy and we ourselves are changing in fundamental ways. Searching for equilibrium, we must choose a new path in this period. 'Time no longer has any direction' is how Korean philosopher Byung-Chul Han puts it. This in-between-period has no clear beginning or end and so lacks direction, which people sense. Many people find this confusing.

This lack of direction is the cause of our unrest and has hugely increased since I published my book In het oog van de orkaan (*In the eye of the hurricane*) in 2012. In the eye, it's windless and cloudless, while outside the storm rages. Depending on where you are, you experience one or the other. Many people were in the eye of the hurricane in 2012: they didn't see the storm raging through society. But, as I wrote at the time, it was a question of time before they would experience it. Much

Embracing Chaos, 1–9

has happened in the last 10 years, and many of those who escaped unscathed at first have felt the effects of the tempest first-hand. Now that the covid storm has been raging across the world since early 2020, many of us have come to realize that we as a society have reached a tipping point.

Three Developments

In 2014, I highlighted three developments in my book *Verandering van tijdperk* (*Change of Era*) explaining that we aren't in an era of change but in a change of era.

(1) *A new societal order is taking shape.* Vertically ordered, centralized, top-down society is evolving into a horizontal, decentralized, bottom-up society with connections, such as communities, cooperatives, and virtual and physical networks.
(2) *A new economy, with other foundations, is coming into existence*, which is distributed, digital, sustainable, glocal and circular.
(3) *A change of power is taking place*, globally with a shift in economic and political power from West to East and underlying a shift from established and destructive power to innovative and transformative power. A new power that has the capacity to change the way resources are distributed.

That these three developments and the material changes they produce are fundamental, are found in practically every area of society, occur simultaneously, and reinforce each other, means they are harbingers of a change of era – the birth of a new era. It's high time because the covid pandemic and the war in Ukraine have made us face the facts and shown that society is vulnerable to disruptions. Moreover, it has become even clearer that we humans are not living in equilibrium with nature, and many of us now think that we can't continue like this any longer.

But you have been telling the same story for 20 years, my children sometimes say. How can you be such a bore? They are right: I *have* been telling the same story for 20 years, but I keep updating it. And I constantly use the lessons I learn to deepen the story. It has evolved from highly analytical and academic to something increasingly human.

In the preceding years, I had come to realize that transitions are the result of work done by people. It's ultimately people who determine the course of transitions, naturally subject to and in interaction with a complex web of technology, markets, institutions, policies and culture. But when push comes to shove, a system transition requires a personal transition. It's only possible to embrace chaos and overcome fear by looking more deeply into ourselves to discover who we really are. Only then do we make the connection between head and heart and only then is a sense of unity possible. The big challenge for all of us is developing that connection. Once we have done so, the process is irreversible. And that's what we need.

Alongside this personal aspect, the world is facing a multifaceted systemic crisis that deeply affects our vital systems, such as trade, food, energy, mobility, healthcare, education and democracy. For 10 years, the world economy has been muddling through and it's now moving towards another recession. There is also an ecological crisis, which is fundamentally influenced by humans and is ruining the earth. But the systemic crisis is at its most profound level a moral crisis. We have internalized the systems, and they pervade our norms and values, our attitudes and behaviour. But these vital systems have passed their expiry date: they no longer meet the standards we set for them.

Europe in Polycrisis

Europe is confronted with an accumulation of crises that can partly be traced back to decades of failed policy. Where other world powers such as China and the United States have been working on energy and raw materials policy for a long time, Europe has been hesitant and naive for too long. Only now, shaken awake by the war in Ukraine, is Europe realizing that energy and raw materials are being used as modern weapons in a global power struggle. The geopolitical dimension of the energy transition is becoming increasingly important and with it the pursuit of energy autonomy. In the urge to quickly become independent from Russian gas, Europe is forced to fall back on fossil alternatives such as buying gas elsewhere, importing liquefied gas and using coal for longer, thereby further fuelling the climate crisis. With this emergency package, with a bit of luck, there will probably be just enough gas reserves to get through the coming winters. However, that is not the real problem. The fossil reset will make Europe even more dependent on gas and oil in the next 5–10 years and will literally pay the price for this. Gas and oil prices will probably not remain as high as they are now, but fossil energy will no longer be really cheap. We can expect sharp fluctuations in a volatile fossil market with medium high prices. This also means that the climate targets are further out of sight, which will further increase instability. This is bad news for European citizens: the next 10 years will be rough, with prices for energy (both gas and electricity) remaining high, even if caps are set. And in the meantime, accelerated efforts must be made to increase sustainability, which also costs hundreds of billions of euros, and the user will also have to pay for this in part. This calls for a social emergency plan to provide European citizens with long-term support, because not only the vulnerable are at risk of financial problems, but also the middle class. A social crisis is imminent and a social uprising can no longer be ruled out, because it is already germinating in England and France.

The accumulation of crises constitutes a polycrisis, a concept introduced in 1999 by the French systems thinker Edgar Morin, who described it as intertwined crises that cannot be traced back to a single cause and carry systemic risks, thus posing a potential risk to people and planet. The polycrisis in Europe is an almost inextricable tangle: Covid-19 and the Ukraine war have led to food and raw material shortages and a deep energy crisis, which is fuelling the climate crisis, which in turn leads to drought and water shortages, which leads to the deterioration of nature, which is exacerbated by the agricultural and nitrogen crises, which also have adverse consequences for construction (housing shortages, infrastructure). Weather extremes due to climate change threaten the energy supply again, partly due to low water levels, which means that insufficient cooling water is available for nuclear power stations and inland vessels can transport less coal and gravel. On the other hand, the energy crisis leads to rising inflation and interest rates, fuelling an economic recession and resulting in growing energy poverty, which can lead to a social revolt. Because not only energy is becoming more expensive, raw materials, water, food, care and groceries are also becoming more expensive, to such an extent that it threatens to become unaffordable for many people.

On this basis, I think that in Europe we are heading for a prolonged period of social unrest. Perhaps comparable to the second half of the nineteenth century, when the industrial revolution brought about social and economic inequality and plunged many workers into poverty. This led to major social unrest that forced the government to intervene radically in several areas. Legislation and regulations were introduced to protect vulnerable citizens, trade unions were formed to protect workers, housing associations were founded for affordable workers' housing, education was designed to elevate the social underclass and the power of large steel, coal and railway companies was broken by splitting them up.

Translated into the current transition period, it is quite conceivable that the government would initiate a similar structural recovery programme as part of a series of radical measures needed to tackle the related crises. Short-term emergency bandages no longer help. We can no longer avoid a thorough agricultural reform. And that applies to all transition domains. Because we have failed to really intervene for decades, we have to cut through the pain. Only more than ever this has to be done together with citizens, otherwise the social unrest will become much greater. The covid crisis has taught us that it is crucial to offer citizens perspective and to communicate clearly. Telling the honest story to citizens: we are facing difficult times, it will ask a lot of us, it will cost a lot but it will yield much more. Such as a new and clean energy supply that is ultimately affordable for everyone. Or circular agriculture that goes hand in hand with sustainable nature restoration. This does, however, require authentic leadership from people who stand firm in the storm. Who do not continue to muddle through with poldering, but who dare to make radical choices. Who consistently work on a reform programme based on a vision that we want our country to achieve. It is now or never, otherwise a social uprising of citizens, fuelled by populists, threatens to have a disruptive effect on our society.

For this reason, we must focus on the core of the problem, which is deeply anchored in the capitalist system we have created. Together we have created a society that bases its assessments on extremely hard values: efficiency, returns, effectiveness, cost/benefit. These are all harsh masculine values. We have gone too far; the human dimension has been lost. A society ordered in terms of efficiency – which I call a 'spreadsheet society' – can function well in rational terms but is in fact ailing and makes people ill. The most prevalent diseases these days are anxiety disorders and depression, which are increasingly prevalent, especially among young people.

Spreadsheet society has not only resulted in our loss of trust in each other but also in social systems, large companies, and their CEOs, and in government. The Edelman Trust Barometer is an annual study of the level of trust in governments, media, NGOs and business. For many years, this barometer has shown a decline in trust.

We can see an example of this distrust in healthcare, where there has been an accumulation of distrust. Everything is about returns and efficiency, and everything must be measured, checked, and controlled according to protocols. This is based on fear and distrust. In itself, there's nothing wrong with efficiency: replacing a worn knee with a prosthetic must be done efficiently. But every knee belongs to a person. Nobody only wants to be treated efficiently. You also want to be treated with affection. I experienced this first-hand when I had a bike accident. I saw many different surgeons because I had sustained injuries to so many parts of my face. Technically, they all gave me excellent assistance, each in their own area of expertise. But oddly enough, no one ever looked at the composition of my face as a whole or asked me about the mental harm, which was at least as great as the physical damage. No one, apart from the nurses. They treated me with concern and affection and were my real heroes.

This human value will predominate in the era ahead. Humans will again be the central focus: in healthcare, in education, in fact everywhere. Nonetheless, there are still many people, especially in the establishment, who are still in the eye of the hurricane and want to return to business as usual, life before corona, the 'old normal' as soon as possible. The authorities are still quite capable of protecting existing resources: knowledge, money, lobbying power, fossil fuels, infrastructure, and so on. But for how much longer?

More people will now accept the idea that the Covid-19 crisis has cleared the way for substantive changes. The transformation to a new social order, another economic basis, and a change of power will be the irreversible and ineluctable result of the in-between-period we are living in now. That goes for the Netherlands, Belgium, the rest of Europe, and in fact the entire western world.

Making a Difference

A period of transition does not occur in everyone's lifetime, so you and I are fortunate to experience one. Fortunate because every individual and every initiative counts in this transition. You can make a difference right now. Yet we humans have a deep-seated fear of far-reaching change. Our brain is conditioned in such a way that if the change is too great, too fast, and too dramatic then we are more inclined to take a step backwards, fearing for our livelihoods and loss of status, income, power, and identity.

We would prefer change based on positive energy and inspiration, but we are obstinate in our behaviour, so a reset is needed. Crises often go hand in hand with a great deal of personal pain, but they also have a cleansing effect. We seem to need these crises to make us aware that we are heading towards a dead end. This is why I see a crisis as a *blessing in disguise*. If something that happens to you deeply affects you then you are more likely to think: what am I doing with my life? That's why people who have been through a personal crisis more often undergo radical change. They are people with the courage to deal with chaos – people who overcome their fear because something else is more important to them: a mission, a vision another perspective. That way you can put aside your fears. That makes you a real leader in my eyes, and I see far more of this kind of leadership in society than in politics.

The Illusion of Powerlessness

Wonderful things are taking place in many areas, such as food, energy, construction, mobility, healthcare and education. People see these examples but fail to make the connection with themselves. They go to a school or hospital and are pleasantly surprised to find that people really are the focus there. Then they go home and think up all sorts of reasons why that's not possible in their situation. I call this the illusion of powerlessness.[1] People can't imagine that another system is possible.

That is a common misconception. People make systems and systems form people. So, it works both ways: structures partly determine people's behaviour, but people can change systems too. Behaviour (people) and structure (systems) are intertwined and co-evolve. That is the crux of Giddens' structuration theory. In periods of chaos, systems become unstable, and people's actions can lead to rapid change. In addition, the indirect effect of an action is at least as great as its direct effect: those who think in stationary terms underestimate their power to affect change, whereas those who think in transformative terms use this potential. The direct effect of what you do might not be so great, but the indirect effect is. That is transitional thinking.

Take the indirect effect of the Urgenda lawsuit which was filed in 2015 against the Dutch State for its failing climate policy. The case attracted attention in many other countries. There are currently nearly 2,000 climate lawsuits against governments and companies. These may not be comparable to the Urgenda lawsuit, but many cases refer to it. The number of lawsuits has exploded in 8 years.

The Urgenda lawsuit also led to a climate lawsuit against Shell, brought by the same lawyer, Roger Cox. He won this case too, and its indirect effect is hard to overstate. It will reverberate for a long time across the whole oil supply chain. Comparable oil giants such as BP and ExxonMobil can expect lawsuits, and other multinationals such as Tata Steel will also have to adjust their fossil-fuel strategy.

These climate lawsuits exert a great deal of pressure on the entire fossil-fuel system: on its structure, legislation, culture and funding. Ultimately, this will certainly contribute towards system change. The timing is crucial. A climate lawsuit would not have made much difference 10 or 20 years ago, but it does in

---

[1]The term was coined by Flor Avelino, one of my PhD students.

this period of chaos. Policy failure has made governments and companies far more vulnerable now, and the whole fossil system has become fragile.

A great many breakthroughs in history started with something small. Something small can become big, and something big can crumble and become small. Think of the rapid rise of global movements such as MeToo, Black Lives Matter, and the climate movement. They heavily influence our social norms and are an important driving force in system change. From a transition perspective, there are countless examples of people initiating system change. And this period of chaos helps something small become something big.

Personal Transition

Back to leadership. The new version is no longer based on ego. A large ego always seemed to be related to great leadership, but those days are over. People see through that more quickly nowadays. I prefer the leadership we have in ourselves: far more connective and based on authenticity. This starts with connecting with yourself, without which you can't connect with others. What you feel and how you act must be the same. That is the authenticity we need – without which you will fall flat on your face in no time at all. Making a career for yourself is interesting, but it may serve to muddy the waters and distract from the essence of life. Appreciating this requires humility and is the start of a personal transition. It's all part of your path, along which you may accept that you are but a small part of a greater whole.

In my case, I came to this realization after my children suffered from serious illnesses and after my bike accident. At one time I had been, at 31, the youngest professor in the Netherlands. I was successful and had my own research institute. But I didn't connect with people at all; I thought and acted purely from my mind and the knowledge I had. Only when I had a serious bike accident and couldn't do anything for a year did I think: am I doing what I want to do, and do I want what I'm doing? Only months later did I realize that I wasn't really doing what I wanted, which was painful. While the entire world thought I was successful, I considered myself a failure. I had disappointed myself. It was not what I had promised myself as a little boy. When I was 5 years old, I had exclaimed: 'Make the world better!' But, after my accident, I thought: your impact is not great; you reach perhaps a thousand people at most. Who do you share all your knowledge with? Only with academics. You have little impact, and you are successful in a small world. That was, apart from my children's illnesses, the most difficult moment in my life. And it showed me the way forward.

From that moment I became more of an activist and started sharing my knowledge in society. I founded Urgenda with Marjan Minnesma, and we started a lawsuit against the Dutch State for its climate policy, forcing it to reduce CO_2 emissions in line with the Paris Agreement. Doing so might have cost me some academic authority but I gained social authority. There are now hundreds of activist academics in the Netherlands and thousands worldwide. Young people, in particular, write to me saying that I have been an example to them. I appreciate this – another example of the indirect effect – because I have been through many difficulties and have often wondered why I do it all. People have hurled insults at me and threatened to burn down my house and my institute; a major Dutch newspaper, *De Telegraaf*, featured me alongside several prominent politicians on its front page, labelling us 'green villains;' people have said they hope I get Covid-19. I have been jeered at and threatened but I have always thought what I'm doing feels good, it feels right. I'm doing what I really want to do.

I grew far more connected with myself, and only then was I able to connect with others. I used to mainly show off my knowledge, which doesn't make you connect with others. It's more likely to create distance. I started delivering lectures in a different way, more from my heart so that I touched people at another level. Now they react far more emotionally, sometimes even crying. When I first started telling people about my accident or my children, my eyes would also brim with tears. It always embarrassed me until someone said that it was good seeing me with the courage to show my vulnerable side. I wanted to be strong. Until I realized there's strength in showing your vulnerability.

I had this realization again during the Covid-19 crisis. In the beginning, I was unsettled. I was also angry, but I didn't know with whom. All my work had ground to a sudden standstill; I was in a panic. I kept my head down for a while as I had not yet clearly worked out what was happening. That would surprise many people because they think I know all the answers as a professor of transition. Well, I was unsettled. Until my wife Inge said: 'This is what you're always talking about, a period of chaos, which we must embrace'. She had hit the nail on the head, but I couldn't yet deal with it.

Until more and more journalists called me wanting an explanation because this was *the* time of transition. My confidence in publicly expressing my opinion grew a bit, and I was able to analyze it more keenly. After the first unsettled month, it sank in and I calmed down because I thought, as my wife had said, I must embrace chaos and show leadership. As a social counterbalance to the Outbreak Management Team, the Dutch government pandemic commission, whose members were all from the medical profession, I founded the Break-out Team: a group of engaged thinkers and doers who examine the effects of Covid-19 on society, the economy and democracy and develop ideas for a post-Covid-19 society. This is necessary because we must view this crisis more broadly than from a purely medical perspective so that we come out of this better together.

Connectors and Demolishers

Years ago, I said that we needed more frontrunners: inspired people who create space. Frontrunners are content-driven; they see *the* solution and can't imagine that other people do not understand. This means that they are often too far ahead of the pack. Just in the Netherlands, there are thousands of them right now. But frontrunners aren't good at connecting – when they look back, they discover nobody is following them. This is why we need connectors. The coming decades will be the era of those who link ideas, projects and people, who connect the old and the new. This will create a new web, a new ecosystem. Connectors will make the new structure less vulnerable because new things are always vulnerable.

Then you need builders and demolishers: people who build new things and people who demolish existing structures. We prefer building to demolition because people enjoy creating new things. Demolition is less popular and has a negative connotation. Moreover, as a rule, new things lead, and old things follow. Building something is, relatively speaking, faster than demolition, and when you build something new it becomes clearer why the old must go. Without demolition, the old still occupies all the space. Laws, rules, and institutions must be demolished, and once that happens, things can go swiftly. But a single crisis will not change everything. Every crisis helps a little because every crisis changes the way some people think – at most 5%–10% of them. Once sufficient people reach that stage (about 25% is enough) we will reach a tipping point at which the remaining 75% will go along with things relatively easily. The Covid-19 crisis has accelerated this process, but we aren't there yet. I think the climate crisis, which is already starting to affect us, will become much more severe and demand far more of us. This could become the tipping point.

Embracing Chaos

Realize that this chaos is bringing us to a new equilibrium, after which we can continue in a different way. Let's learn to embrace chaos. Let's learn to view chaos and crisis in a different way: do not immediately see it as a problem but as an opportunity to really do things differently. We can use our uncertainty and unrest for growth and development. That will give our brains, which are focused on stability and continuity, equanimity. Really, there is something new on the horizon, and that's hopeful. The demolition of the old creates space for something new, which we have yet to get used to. New connections, new values, new communities, new economic activities, increasing awareness ...

In this book, I present the perspective from which I view the world in transition. That will help you realize where the unrest in the world – and in ourselves – comes from. You'll have the tools you need to identify the signals our society is giving. I hope this gives you a sense of direction, which will create the equanimity needed to embrace chaos. Not that you can then sit back and relax. Rather, I hope this book spurs you to action because there are two possibilities in this crucial chaotic phase of complex systems: dying off or breaking through. In the latter case, the system is able to reinvent itself. Let's go for the breakthrough together.

Chapter 1

Transition Lenses: Seeing in a Different Way

Understanding transitions starts with looking at them differently. This is why, over the years, a number of transition lenses have been developed to look at (deep) changes in time, scale and nature. These lenses provide insight into what is going on and how things can change. This insight provides reassurance, and it is the prime reason for writing this book par excellence: we crave reassurance in this time of chaos. Nowadays, so much is changing in all kinds of areas that people lack insight and an overview. Once you have deeper insight, you see and understand that we do not live in an era of change, but in a change of era. Then you start thinking differently, feeling differently and ultimately acting differently.

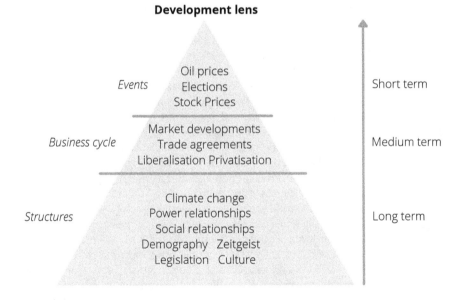

Embracing Chaos, 11–25
Copyright © 2023 Jan Rotmans and Co-Writer Mischa Verheijden
Published under exclusive licence by Emerald Publishing Limited. Translation by Michael Gould.
The moral rights of the translator have been asserted. Copyright © 2021 Jan Rotmans en Mischa
Verheijden. Original title Omarm de Chaos. First published in 2021 by De Geus, Amsterdam
doi:10.1108/978-1-83753-634-420231002

The development lens is inspired by the three layers of time – structures, conjunctures and events – identified by the French historian Fernand Braudel, who has been a source of inspiration for me. It is a lens through which you can look at developments in time differently. What Braudel did for history, transition researchers like me do for transitions. The essence is to look through time and beyond the short term. Like Braudel, the development lens distinguishes between the short, medium and long term. In the short term, it is about everyday events such as elections, stock market prices or the price of oil. In the medium term, it is about slow-moving cyclical developments such as market developments, liberalization, privatization and trade agreements. In addition to economic developments these can also be of a social nature, such as travel and food behaviour. In the long term, we look at structural developments, or fundamental changes lasting decades. This is the undercurrent, and the structural changes in the undercurrent take place insidiously, under the surface. That is why they remain invisible for a long time, but the fundamental changes they cause are inevitable and irreversible once visible. These include power shifts, cultural changes, laws and regulations, climate change, social norms and demographic developments. If you look through the development lens, you see the connection between short-term (daily), medium-term (annual) and long-term (decadal) developments. You make a jigsaw puzzle, as it were, of these timepieces and see how they fit together.

Where, for example, did the gilets jaunes (yellow jackets) in France suddenly come from? That is not an isolated event. It's a movement that is embedded in cyclical developments: market forces in almost all economic and social sectors. Healthcare and education have also become markets. Everything is geared towards efficiency and effectiveness. In combination with globalization, this has led to greater inequality between rich and poor. In several European countries, people, especially those in the middle class, have not seen their real incomes increase for decades, while on the other hand, they have seen the elites become richer. This creates a subcutaneous tension, and a certain trigger, an event like an increase in fuel prices, can make this tension visible. The rise of populism can also be explained in this way because the middle class, in particular, who feel disenchanted and not seen, follow populists. If you look closely, this has been going on for decades in the undercurrent, and then it is just a matter of time until it comes to the surface, forms a wave and ignites in the form of an event. Similarly, the terrorist attacks of recent years are more deeply rooted in shifting power relations in the Middle East, the United States, Russia and China. The colonialism, elitism and superiority of the West have sown a great deal of hatred, and it is only a matter of time before this manifests itself (not that I am condoning these attacks, on the contrary.).

So, you have to look right through the events to recognize how they are embedded in the undercurrent. Events, such as the yellow jackets protests and terrorist attacks, are important in themselves. They can set things on fire, but they can never do so if there is not a peat fire raging at the structural level in the undercurrent. Otherwise, the effect would be very short-lived, and it would disappear again. But if the event is embedded in such a peat fire, it will keep coming back.

To stay with fire: decades ago in Australia, you had ordinary bushfires. Now they are larger in scale, more intense, last longer and are directly and indirectly linked to climate change. As a result, there is a lot more commotion now than decades ago when they were ordinary forest fires, coincidental. The same applies to the floods in July 2021 in Limburg, Belgium and Germany. That was the result of an extreme amount of precipitation that fell for days, but it was intensified by climate change. We can therefore expect more of these types of weather extremes in the coming decades.

In the chapter on the systemic crises, I make it clear that events with a small chance of occurring but high risk – so-called black swans or blind spots – are not coincidences, nor bad luck. They have been 'in preparation' in the undercurrent for decades, and then suddenly they surface and become a wave. So, a transition is not a sum of events, as many people think. You can, of course, list a series of events and then you will see certain developments, but you will not see what lies behind them.

Events are therefore embedded in cyclical developments and these, in turn, are embedded in structural developments. These overlapping developments can reinforce each other and thus accelerate a transition. It is essential, however, that the developments go in the same direction. If the climate were to get colder, the forest fires in Australia would never be linked to it. In any case, the Australian Prime Minister Scott Morrison, who is known as a climate denier, now reluctantly admits that the forest fires in his country are linked to the long-standing peat fire called climate change. In the Netherlands, too, Prime Minister Mark Rutte reluctantly agrees that there must be a connection between the floods in 2021 and climate change.

Understanding the underlying structures, the undercurrent, is essential to understanding what is going on in the long term. It also provides peace of mind when you understand what is happening. In fact, in the daily news, you should be informed about the various time layers, whereby for each event you get an interpretation of the underlying economic and structural developments. If you constantly embed eventualities in the cyclical and structural developments, you cannot really be surprised anymore. Of course, you can still be surprised by the moment itself and the way in which it happened (think of 9/11). After all, nobody has a predictive crystal ball, including me. It is not always easy to interpret point-by-point, but a kind of logic and order emerges, which increases our understanding of why events happen. As the great footballer Johan Cruijff put it: 'You only start to see it when you get it'. Or in my own logic of transition: 'Those who don't look closely are always surprised, whereas for those who look long and hard, it makes sense'.

The most current event is the Ukraine war and in particular its geopolitical consequences, which made us realize in Europe that we have become far too dependent on Russian gas. We have been naïve and that brought us in a vulnerable position, where we should have shifted much earlier to renewables to avoid this energy crisis.

And, of course, Covid-19, the virus is an event in itself and the reason for the crisis we are experiencing. The underlying cyclical development is the exponential multiplication of covid through globalization. The cause – the structural development – lies much deeper in the undercurrent. The root of Covid-19 is the way we treat animals and nature: the interaction between humans and animals under poor hygienic conditions. Wherever you put so many animals close together and bring them into contact with people, there is a risk of transmission of these kinds of diseases. You can point to China, to the unhygienic markets in Wuhan, which are an ideal breeding ground for the spread of infectious diseases. But Covid-19 could also have occurred in De Peel in Brabant in the Netherlands because intensive livestock farming is the breeding ground for the next pandemic. If we do not take drastic measures, we will be waiting for it to go wrong again. I will come back to this in the chapter on the systemic crises. First, I will present some other transition lenses that will help you look at things differently.

Time Lens

The time lens shows the various phases of a transition: a pre-development phase, a tipping point, and then the further development phase, which is nicely represented in an s-curve. The time lens also indicates that a transition never has an absolute beginning and end.

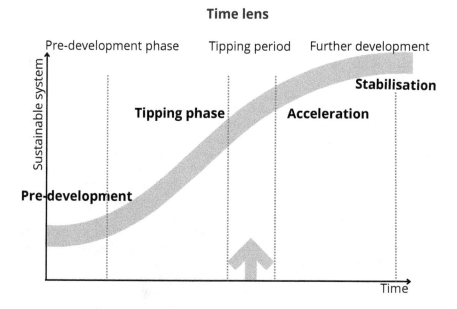

That S-curve is a stylized form. In reality, transitions are much more capricious, with many shifts and shocks (the events) and fluctuations in the underlying cyclical and structural developments.

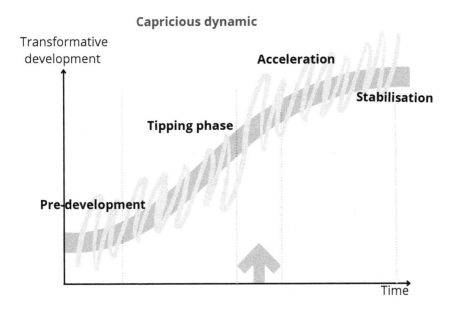

What people often fail to realize is that many transitions tend to get stuck and only succeed in part or perhaps not at all. The optimal outcome is the exception rather than the rule. In reality, a transition often remains stuck in a sub-optimal state, a lock-in. The mobility transition is in just such a lock-in: we have not succeeded in solving the traffic jam problem for 50 years. We are avoiding radical solutions such as road pricing and are too focused on car mobility. Even if we switch to electric transport, we will still be stuck in traffic jams – albeit cleaner. Even with the current energy transition, it could be that we continue to use oil and gas for a long time and that we reach the sub-optimal situation of not achieving the objective of the Paris Climate Agreement of staying well below a 2°C increase in temperature above pre-industrial levels. Three-quarters of our energy would be renewable by 2050, but not all of it. That is why it is so important to take drastic measures in the current tipping point phase.

We could also end up in an *overshoot collapse*, where we end up even worse than where we started. This is what the Club of Rome warned against in its 1972 report *Limits to Growth*. In their model, they made causal connections between the growth of the world population, industrialization, depletion of our natural resources, pollution and food production in a rather ingenious way. A number of scenarios were explored and the S-curves almost all ended in overshoot collapses:

natural resources are depleted, industrial growth is slowed down, and population numbers drop sharply so that billions of people starve to death. I analyzed this with my research group and their model had the mechanism of overshoot collapse ingrained: whatever action you take, you almost always end up worse off than when you started. We put in different perspectives, linked to a number of uncertainties. Put simply: an optimistic, a pessimistic and a realistic perspective. This gave you different outcomes for each set of assumptions, including positive outcomes of successful transitions.

Pre-development Phase

In the pre-development phase, the phase of structural developments in the undercurrent (as we have seen with the development lens), much happens under the radar. There is plenty of experimentation with new ideas, but apparently not much appears to change. It all takes place in the undercurrent, and nobody sees or hears it. This long run-up is necessary to create sufficient diversity as a breeding ground for the new order. The main thing is to sow the seeds of change.

For example, I started working on an integral climate model in 1985, at a time when there was hardly any focus on the climate problem or the energy transition. I myself was also unaware of the pre-development phase we were in. It was not until the end of the 1980s and the beginning of the 1990s that the climate problem was put on the map and some awareness was created. The phase of intense polarization and resistance that we are now in is completely different: the climate problem is now much more tangible and concrete for people. Sustainable energy is a hot topic, but when people say that the energy transition has started now, that is not true. We have been at it for 50 years, and all that preparatory work in the pre-development phase was necessary to get to where we are now. Before a development – in the case of the energy transition to sustainable energy – scales up, experiments are conducted on a small scale: with solar panels, wind energy, heat pumps and insulation. In the pre-development phase, the structural developments of the undercurrent, a lot also happens in terms of awareness. First, you have to become aware that we need to use energy more sustainably, then you start looking differently, then you feel differently and only then do you start acting accordingly. That is why paradigm shifts happen so slowly.

A good example of the global change in consciousness is how we deal with nature. For a long time, we have exploited it on the basis of a feeling of superiority, with all the ecological consequences that this entails. But we are increasingly becoming aware that there is a kind of co-evolution between man and nature. That we are not superior to nature, but that it is perhaps the other way around. When I started doing climate research, we were very afraid that the Earth would not survive. Now we think differently. Rest assured: the Earth will survive. The big question is whether we humans will still be there. The realization dawns that we are exterminating ourselves. From the fear of Mother Earth to the fear of our own survival is a significant difference in consciousness from 35 years ago.

After a while, the undercurrent – the structural developments in the pre-development phase – hits the upper stream, a faster dynamic emerges, and developments reinforce each other. Or they don't. In that case, the system remains stuck.

In the In-between-period

A complex system – humankind, a company, society, the economy – continually strives to achieve balance but is thrown out of balance by changes in the environment. Then chaos, turbulence and unrest arise. The moment the invisible becomes visible from the undercurrent in the pre-development phase, the chaos phase begins. People then say: 'What is this?' and 'Where did that come from?'. In complexity theory, such a period of chaos is the phase between two periods of dynamic equilibrium. Such a phase of chaos is characterized by resistance, opposition, protests and a lack of insight and overview. It can seemingly go either way. We are now in that tipping phase.

Danielle Braun and Jitske Kramer, the authors of the inspiring book *The Corporate Tribe*, which draws organizational lessons from anthropology, call this tilting phase the in-between-period. The in-between-period is the time between 'it is' and 'it will be' and is about the power of 'in between'. In this phase, the old system is being broken down and the new one is being built up, but the existing system is usually broken down more slowly than the new one is built up. Although there are many new companies (start-ups and scale-ups) that form a new ecosystem and no longer need the old system to grow rapidly, the existing institutions and organizations still dominate. We, therefore, need an institutional hoover, a kind of ministry of demolition. The demolishers of the old system are just as important as the builders of the new because everything that disappears makes room for something new. We also need connectors, to connect the old with the new.

The transition research institute DRIFT, which I founded, has developed an X-curve as a variant of the S-curve, which shows both the construction and the breakdown of a system.

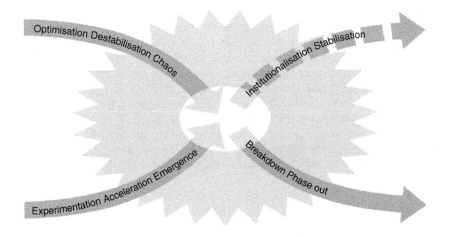

In the in-between-period, therefore, something new is glowing on the horizon, and that gives us hope: new connections, new values, new communities, new business, emerging new technologies, increasing awareness.

Zooming Out Prevents Cynicism

To see that chaos is a symbol of hope, you have to zoom out. Firstly, because people who want to change things are in the middle of it: things are moving slowly and don't seem to be making any progress. When you're in the middle of it, you see all the barriers, resistance, obstructions, opposition and power struggles. This is difficult and annoying, but you have to learn to accept this slowness. A transition simply takes at least two generations. If you zoom out and look at it from a distance, you can see all the changes that have been made and set in motion in the past 10 years. If you zoom in, you get stuck on events. Only when you zoom out do you see what is under the iceberg. Look, for example, at the 6 million young people who protested against climate change in 2019. That was unthinkable 20 years ago.

Secondly, it helps if you can see which phase of a transition you are in. That determines the degree of control required. In the pre-development phase, you have to initiate radical innovation and to experiment. In the in-between-period, in the chaos phase, you have to make crucial decisions for the future. When the old system is crumbling and the new one is emerging but still fragile, a smart and targeted intervention can have a big effect. So, if you want to exert influence, you need this in-between-period of chaos. It is precisely in this period when the chaos is at its greatest and the direction we are heading is uncertain that you have to make decisions for the coming decades. That requires courage and leadership because it requires a lot of investment and costs a lot of money. It also delivers a lot, but that comes later. This is dilemma management because it can also involve decisions with a high risk of failure, given the uncertainty. Take green hydrogen, for example; it can be compressed into a liquid and transported by ship, or it can be transported in gaseous form by pipeline. You have to bet on both options because you don't know yet what the dominant infrastructure will be. It was the same in the 1960s with mixed cargo and container transhipment: for 10 years, both transition paths were followed and at a certain point container transhipment made its breakthrough. In order to be prepared for this, you have to invest in several transition paths while you are almost certain that one or two will die out. These dropouts are options, measures and investments which you will almost certainly regret. Once it has become clear which path will become dominant, the transition will accelerate, heading for a stable phase with a new balance.

Thirdly, people often think: we are not even halfway there. But you don't need 50% of the population to create a change. You need about 25% to reach a tipping point.[1] The social dynamics of transitions show that for a long time nothing seems to happen, and then suddenly there is a steep increase. When you reach that acceleration phase, it is relatively easy to get the rest of the population (75%) on board, because then there is no way back and the transition becomes irreversible. More and more people will see it, and that will attract and strengthen those who do.

People often ask me how I have managed to keep going for 35 years, while so little has changed.

My Answer: Zoom Out!

When I zoom out and look back 35 years, I see that quite a lot has changed in terms of awareness, attitude and behaviour. The word 'transition' alone was not used by anyone when I started; now everyone uses it. Thirty-five years ago, anyone who talked about system change was looked at in a strange way; now system change is the order of the day. We used to talk about the CO_2 problem, then the greenhouse problem and only later about climate change. Thirty-five years ago, only a few people were actively involved in this; nowadays there are masses of people. It is now one of the most important election themes in Europe, which was hard to imagine at the time. So, a lot has changed in terms of awareness and behaviour, and we are now in the process of changing behaviour. That is the most difficult phase. In short, zooming out helps and prevents you from becoming cynical.

The in-between-period is relatively short because it consumes energy, but it can last 10–15 years. In this short period of chaos and instability, a system seeks a new balance. It looks for a new direction, reorganizes itself and creates a new structure. The system reinvents itself, as it were. If it fails to do so, it dies – something that also happens regularly.

For a system, chaos is a relief, because it offers opportunities to survive or develop. Without chaos, a system freezes. In essence, therefore, it is a positive phenomenon, but because its deeper meaning – chaos opens the windows and doors for essential change – is often not seen, it is not properly understood. Chaos is also order, namely disorder, an order that you do not yet know. One without a clear structure and orientation that can go in any direction. This upsets people. It creates panic, anger, resistance, protests, lawsuits, conflicts and polarization, exactly what is happening now.

Populists Only Feed Fear

A striking example of this statement from my own country is that I, together with a number of Dutch politicians, was depicted on the front page of a big

(Continued)

(*Continued*)

newspaper as 'the green dragon'. On the pages that followed, we were criticized and portrayed as 'green scaremongers'. I find it bizarre, but I also enjoy the resistance: if you don't get any resistance, you are not making an impact. For 20 years, I received little or no resistance. The fact that this is happening now is a good sign for me.

The power of populists is also overestimated. Look at Donald Trump and the energy transition. People think that he has stopped everything but, because so much has already been set in motion over the past few decades, the energy transition has become an autonomous process. No one can stop it now; at most they can slow it down. Whereas Trump's policy seems disastrous in the short term, it actually creates and strengthens a counter-movement. He has only made the green undercurrent bigger and stronger. During his time in power, there has never been so much investment in solar energy, wind energy and hydrogen. That is because a number of states in the United States accelerated the transition in response to Trump. At the same time, we cannot go back to old sources like coal – there is no money in them anymore. In the extraction of shale oil and shale gas, too, the vast majority of investors have already withdrawn, because it is too volatile and cannot be made profitable.

It is important to realize that polarization is always temporary. It is part of the chaos. But in the end, everyone realizes that what has been set in motion is irreversible. If you come to a higher level of consciousness, you will never go back to a lower level. You start seeing things that you didn't see before, and it's hard to filter that out. You realize that, when you go back, you also take a step back in time. We will never go back to coal mining again, nor, in 20 years, will we be using gas and oil.

A successful transition cannot take place without chaos. The greater the chaos, the deeper we get to the core of a transition. We must, therefore, realize that chaos will in fact take us further and that we can then continue in a different way. But that requires an enormous change in ourselves. People don't like this phase, in which the pain becomes palpable. The pain of saying goodbye to the old and familiar and the fear of the unknown and new. We want to avoid this transition pain at all costs, but we need it in order to move forward in our growth and development. There is a great lesson in pain. Learning to see that chaos is not only a problem but also an opportunity to do things differently is part of our personal transition. Looking for that pain, going to the dark places in yourself, gives you the chance to find happiness and positivity again.

The German philosopher Peter Sloterdijk makes it convincingly clear in his book *You Must Change Your Life* that you must constantly practise to change yourself. Search, learn and experiment. He argues that paradigm shifts always start with the elite, something that British-Venezuelan innovation thinker Carlota Perez also states. Because 'elite' has a negative connotation, I prefer to speak of 'pioneers'. Connectors then widen the group and the 'tilters' say, for example, 'We are going to tackle the smoking industry'. Then the transition enters the acceleration phase.

It Slowly Creeps In

The transition from smoking to non-smoking was mainly a cultural change that started with an elite (I will come back to this later). A cultural change also plays an important role in the food transition. Slowly but surely, eating meat is seen as something that no longer fits in with a healthy and sustainable way of life. This, too, started with a vanguard that is gradually expanding. It is therefore possible that in the future an unhealthy fast-food hamburger will become as bad a symbol as a cigarette is today. If you smoke and eat fast food now, you are actually a loser, because you are deliberately damaging your health. If you extend that to 20 years from now, you're a loser if you still use gas for central heating or have no solar panels on your roof. This is something that creeps in very slowly, and while many people think that the transition is determined by the hardware – technology, money and policy – the software is at least as important. Social norms are changing insidiously, deep within ourselves. In terms of mobility, for example, we are not there yet, but we have already started to look at cars differently, and the diesel car could become the 'smoker' of traffic in the future.

Transitions take a long time because you cannot force people to think and act differently. It's a process of internalization, and that also applies at the system level. But, once the undercurrent becomes manifest, there is no way back. Once you start looking and feeling differently, it is irreversible. Then a breakthrough can take place. Therefore, learn to see the beauty of chaos. Learn to love chaos. Accept that it is not a problem, but that it beautifully shows the phase we are in. At this point in time – which is why I call it a tipping point – the transition is irreversible, and you break through. So, it can still go either way, but we can't go back.

Scale Lens

In the scaling lens, we distinguish between three scale levels: macro, meso and micro.

Scale lens

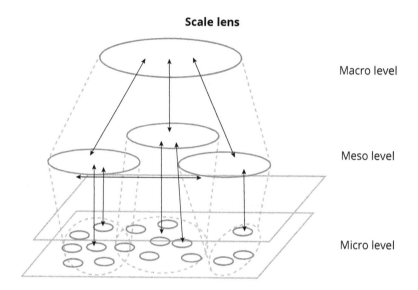

Macro level

Meso level

Micro level

At every scale level, we see that there are trends and developments which influence the transition and accelerate (+) or slow it down (1).

If we look at the energy transition, we see at the macro level that continents, but also individual countries, want to become energy independent. Climate change and geopolitical tensions are increasing the urgency: you don't want to be dependent on oil and gas for too long. On the other hand, and this is a downside in the scales, there is still an abundance of fossil fuels. There is, for example, oil in the ground for at least another hundred years.

Scale Lens: The Energy Transition

Macro Level

+ Energy autonomy
− An excess of fossil fuels
+ Geopolitical tensions
+ Climate change

Meso Level

+ The Paris Climate Agreement
+ Fit for 55 European policy
− TTIP trade agreement
− Legislation

Micro Level

+ Solar and wind energy
+ Decentralized energy production
+ Energy entrepreneurs
+ Local energy cooperatives

At the micro level, you have an abundance of breakthrough technologies and ideas. For example, solar and wind energy are ubiquitous. These technologies enable a bottom-up movement, and you see citizens uniting in local energy cooperatives. There are now about 650 of these in the Netherlands. Almost every municipality now has one or more local energy cooperatives. As a result, energy entrepreneurs also see business opportunities and start-ups around sustainable energy are established, leading to decentralization of energy production.

The meso level forms the buffer between the slow dynamics of the macro level and the fast dynamics of the micro level and it usually causes inertia and resistance. It's the existing order that, to a large extent, maintains the established regime – the dominant structure, culture and ways of working – through financing, legislation and trade agreements. Laws and regulations are always behind the times and are almost always designed to be protective of the current regime. Right now, that regime is still the fossil energy regime. Shell, for instance, has helped determine energy policy in the Netherlands for years. The Paris Climate Agreement in 2015 and the EU's 'Fit for 55' plan represent a positive breakthrough for energy transition at the meso level.

The niches at the micro level want to develop power and take over the existing regime. Once they have become the regime and renewable energy is dominant, new niches will emerge at the micro level to oppose the regime. Then the current sustainable energy initiatives at the micro level, which by that time belong to the established order and have become multinationals, will oppose the then-emerging circular initiatives, which say that solar panels are not sustainable at all because they contain too much silicon and that we have to demolish windmills because they contain too much neodymium. This is the evolutionary development of a transition. It's a power struggle, where the emerging power becomes the established power at some point and then resists the new emerging power. So, it's too simplistic to speak of *The Good Guys and the Bad Guys*.

The scales indicate that if developments at different scales reinforce each other in the same direction, a transition will accelerate. The trick is to recognize the underlying patterns, such as bottom-up or top-down patterns, or a mixture of these. Playing with scale levels and underlying patterns is still fascinating to me, even after more than 35 years.

Steering Lens

Transitions are capricious, complex and accompanied by a great deal of uncertainty. That makes people restless: people want to get a grip on things in order to exert influence and control a situation. Just think of the covid crisis. But you don't have that control with transitions: a transition cannot be managed. Even if you do nothing, a complex system develops. So doing nothing also leads to dynamics because a complex system develops together with other systems. We call this self-organization: the ability of a complex system to constantly adapt to new circumstances under its own steam. Even without external influence, spontaneous structures emerge, and, in this way, a complex system creates order itself. For example, if you try to tackle the problem of traffic jams by imposing measures, people will still try to avoid them: they will take the exit at a petrol station in order to avoid a bit of traffic jam. Because a transition is complex and uncertain, with too many determining factors, you cannot steer a transition in the traditional sense. However, you can steer a transition by influencing its speed and direction with a planned change from above, a spontaneous and decentralized change from below or a mixture of the two: sometimes planned, sometimes occurring suddenly. This mixed form is the most appropriate form of control for transitions.

I once introduced the term transition management and, together with René Kemp, developed the underlying concept of evolutionary steering: searching-learning-experimenting. Later, my former PhD student Derk Loorbach elaborated this in the form of a steering cycle for transitions. Today, we use transition governance: not managing but smart navigation, more adjusting than steering and anticipating, not a project but a process, and not a purposeful but a goal-seeking process. Managing complex systems is only possible if you can acquire a deeper insight into their dynamics. You have to know the causes of transitions (which, as we have seen with the development lens, lie in the undercurrent) and you have to know which direct – and especially which indirect – effects interventions can have.

Steering lens

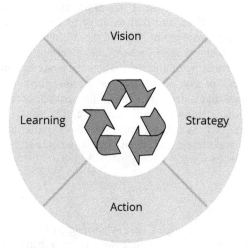

Adjustments are made on the basis of a vision and an influencing strategy. This consists of a repertoire of interventions to influence the direction and speed of a transition. A transition agenda lists the actions, projects and experiments you can learn from. You use what you have learned to adjust your vision and strategy. It is therefore a cyclical process, or rather an upward spiral.

The more subtle the way you try to influence, the better, and the greater the chance of success. That is why it is better to start small and not from a broad base. Start with real frontrunners and start experimenting. Afterwards, try to select and scale up to achieve a breakthrough. This allows for regular adjustments based on new insights and experiences. This also requires a number of starting points: steering at the system level is crucial, the goals must be flexible and adaptable, and the timing of the intervention must be right. In transition governance, complex systems theory is translated into practical tools for governing social transitions. Here are three core concepts from complex systems theory:

(1) Co-evolution. The interaction between different systems that have an irreversible impact on the dynamics.
(2) Emergence. The emergence of new, robust structures in complex systems.
(3) Self-organization. The ability of a complex system to constantly adapt to new circumstances under its own steam.

The idea of transition governance is based on these three concepts. Meanwhile, this form of steering is being applied in dozens of countries and hundreds of regional and local cases. There is a wealth of transition knowledge available on what has been learnt over the past 20 years.

Chapter 2

Crisis as Opportunity

The feeling of our time is that we are living in a kind of permanent crisis, and in a way that's true. One crisis follows another, and they are also related. When I analyze this through my transition lenses, I see a society that is in multiple systemic crises. I speak of a system crisis when a crisis is deeply rooted in our vital systems, such as trade, food, energy, mobility, care, education and democracy.

I see a coherent set of systemic crises: we have a financial-economic crisis, an ecological crisis, a moral crisis and a democratic crisis, which all interact and reinforce each other. This multiple system crisis affects us deeply and confronts us with persistent problems in our vital social systems. These systems are nearing their end and no longer meet the demands that we, as humans, place on them. Yet we have built them ourselves, and they have served us well for a long time, but now they are turning against us. That is the eternal duality between man and system, a love-hate relationship. The systems must now reinvent themselves, but we humans must reinvent ourselves too. That is the essence of system change.

Complexity Theory

In the previous chapter, I briefly touched on complexity theory, an inter disciplinary field of science that involves studying the nature of complex systems in society and in the economy. Complexity theory, also known as complex systems theory, is my field and, as a mathematician, I have greatly enjoyed it. Now I don't want to bore you with complicated theories, but if you realize and understand that chaos, instability and therefore unrest are inherent to the development of complex systems such as our society, economy and our people themselves, then this can already give you a lot of reassurance.

How do complex systems work? Every complex system constantly adapts to its environment, behaves erratically and is only partly predictable. A complex system is usually in a dynamic balance: there are many mutations, but the structure and order are relatively stable. The system develops in the direction of a certain attractor, a situation 'desired' by the system. Over time, things change within the system and new structures arise through emergence. But change also occurs in the environment of the system. This can be a shock or a slow development. As a

Embracing Chaos, 27–45
Copyright © 2023 Jan Rotmans and Co-Writer Mischa Verheijden
Published under exclusive licence by Emerald Publishing Limited. Translation by Michael Gould.
The moral rights of the translator have been asserted. Copyright © 2021 Jan Rotmans en Mischa
Verheijden. Original title Omarm de Chaos. First published in 2021 by De Geus, Amsterdam
doi:10.1108/978-1-83753-634-420231004

result, the system slowly 'alienates' itself from its surroundings, until it reaches a critical point, at the interface between two attractors. This leads to a crisis, a relatively short period of instability and chaos. For a system, a crisis is not a problem but an opportunity to really change. A system can then reorganize itself and create a new structure. The system then develops in the direction of a new attractor, on its way to a new dynamic equilibrium, with a higher degree of complexity. However, there is also another possibility, namely that the system cannot adapt and renew itself in time. In that case, the system eventually dies.

What can we learn from this? First, that a crisis is not a problem for a system, but an opportunity. Without a crisis, a system cannot really change. Secondly, that a system either adapts in time and therefore flourishes, or it dies. Thirdly, that long periods of equilibrium alternate with short periods of chaos, and finally that actors can contribute to system change by interventions that change the basic structure. This effect is greatest in times of chaos.

Take the energy transition. The global energy system was fixated on fossil-fuel energy and is now heading in a new direction, namely that of sustainable energy. With lawsuits, protests, conflicts, legislative changes, bankruptcies, uncertainty and fierce resistance, the energy transition is now in a chaotic phase that is full of turbulence. In fact, this is a good sign, because it signals that we are at the tipping point and have reached the point of irreversibility. And the greater the resistance, the closer we are to the heart of the transition. This means that sustainable energy will win, and that the fossil-fuel system will be dismantled. The direction is clear, the only question is how long it will take to build up and break down.

The demolition of the fossil-fuel system is in full swing. This can be seen in the phasing out of coal-fired power plants around the world, large fossil-fuel companies getting into trouble, investments in fossil fuels increasingly being seen as a financial risk, and almost two thousand climate lawsuits against governments and companies. There is no turning back; the only question is how long will it take? One generation? Or two? Just like other sectors that have died out, such as the textile industry, shipbuilding, the car industry and coal mining, steel, oil and agriculture will suffer the same fate if they do not transform and adapt to the new era.

If there is anything I want to achieve with the book you are reading now, it is to make you realize that the world is at a crossroads. The coming climate crisis and the nature crisis that follows will create much more chaos. Yet I believe that this is what is needed to really bring us to our senses. I am and will remain positive and hopeful because we can still avert the impending doom, but time is running out and we will have to pull out all the stops. One thing is certain: 'If we don't change direction, the chances are we will arrive where we are going'. That is a Chinese proverb. And, as I wrote on the first pages of this book, this lack of direction is the cause of our unrest. That is why I want to indicate a possible direction so that we can realize the breakthrough to a society and economy that are more in balance.

Because of this lack of direction, we are also constantly in a hurry and do not sufficiently settle down. Those who are always in a hurry are tossed back and forth in time and never have a chance to finish anything. On top of that, advancing digitalization has changed the way we use time. We are constantly multitasking and doing several things at once. We divide our time into small bits, as it were, that are constantly running into each other. As a result, what we do has no clear beginning and end: we don't really finish anything, because we are constantly interrupted by new impulses that demand our attention. In this way, we receive a lot of stimuli that we cannot process adequately. This can lead to insomnia, burn-out or depression. In other words: breakdown. The solution to this lies within ourselves. We have to learn to embrace chaos and regain direction in our lives and in the way we spend our time. Taking time for relaxation. Not so much chrono-time (linear clock time), but Kairos time, time for reflection and deepening. For a restless mind, that is a serious task, but it is at the heart of the matter because the systemic crises lie deep within ourselves. It is precisely because people, like other living ecosystems, are so sensitive to chaos that I am hopeful of a breakthrough towards a society and economy that are more in balance. After all, complexity theory also teaches that fluctuations in the behaviour of a few people can change the behaviour of the group as a whole. In a period of chaos, systems become vulnerable and unstable and are susceptible to interventions. Smart interventions at the right moment can have a major impact. Precisely in this vulnerable, chaotic period, a smart group of change-minded people can create a breakthrough.

Changing Values

The covid crisis mercilessly exposed the flaws in our social systems. We steer these systems on the basis of economic values such as return on investment, efficiency and effectiveness. Everything is lean and mean, standardized and optimized, which means that we do everything just in time and on the edge. But any shock or disruption will immediately cause problems. You can see this now in healthcare. The decades of cutbacks – in the past 10 years alone, 10,000 hospital beds have disappeared in the Netherlands – and the underpayment and under-appreciation of healthcare workers are taking their revenge during the covid crisis. Major problems arose and even face masks and medical equipment had to be imported from abroad. Despite the heroic work of the care workers, the care sector turned out not to be resilient.

The covid crisis also showed how vulnerable our food system is to disruptions. Lockdowns and closed borders create problems in every link of the global food chain: from production and distribution to marketing and consumption. This can lead to serious disruption of the global food market, resulting in sharp price fluctuations. Food can become expensive and unaffordable for part of the population because of the loss of income due to the covid crisis. In addition, the food system is often dependent on seasonal migrants, and because they are now absent, harvests fail, resulting in large-scale famine, especially in Africa. The root cause is the economization of the food system, which is all about growth, volume and productivity. The whole system is built on the illusion of cheap food. Food prices are low because the damage caused by our food production is not included in the price. This damage is considerable: reduction in biodiversity, disrupted nutrient cycles, climate change, ever-emerging animal diseases, pesticides, pests and food waste.

This damage has become so great that the limit of this sick food system has been reached.

In the in-between-period, characterized by shocks and crises, we must reinvent our systems and make them more resilient. In this respect, we can learn a lot from nature, which does not just develop along the lines of efficiency and profitability. Nature is diverse, has a buffer capacity and is naturally crisis-resistant. Diversity and buffer capacity offer protection against extreme situations and shocks. For us, this means a change to other values, because the current ones are cold and bleak: return, efficiency, effectiveness, cost/benefit. They reflect a rock-hard society in which many people no longer feel at home, but rather are trapped between the coldness of the market and the bureaucracy of the government. People yearn for warmth and intimacy, for time and attention, for trust and freedom of choice. Resistance to this spreadsheet society is therefore growing by the day, and the underlying change in values marks the end of neoliberalism, which is clearly on the wane.

In itself, there is not so much wrong with market forces, but there is with excessive market thinking. Not everything revolves around profit, competition and yields. We are also social beings who want to cooperate (homo sociologicus). Why does a hospital have to make a profit and compete with other hospitals? Who came up with that? Healthcare companies are not there to make as much money as possible but to provide the best possible care. And people are not 'clients' or 'patients': if you call a person a client, you reduce him or her to an economic production factor. It may seem like a detail, but language is important and part of a discourse. We, therefore, need another language, more human and warmer than the cold system language. We must make the move from a focus on profit to attention to people and their needs.

Education is not a market either, but a public good and schools should not compete with each other, but rather cooperate and operate on their own merits. Colleges and universities are engaged in fierce competition, but why? Who came up with that? Universities and colleges are not factories of education but havens of higher education. Nor do they simply process consumers of education; they should offer students the opportunity to develop themselves. Studying is more than just passing your exams and earning your diploma efficiently. Studying is also about developing yourself, exploring your boundaries and discovering life. We must therefore challenge students much more to get the best out of their situation.

This change in values goes hand in hand with a change in thinking. Linear thinking (the future will be similar to the past) has led to an excessive focus on the short term. This suggests that we are in control, but nothing could be further from the truth: it is only a sham. We think and look no further than today – at most tomorrow, but not the day after. This attitude has led us into multiple systemic crises. There is a financial-economic crisis, an ecological crisis and a moral crisis, all of which are inextricably linked.

The Financial and Economic Crisis

The stock market crash of 2007 led to the deep economic recession of 2008, which is still being felt today. For more than a decade, the world economy has muddled along, teetering on the brink of recession. This graph from the UN makes no bones about it:

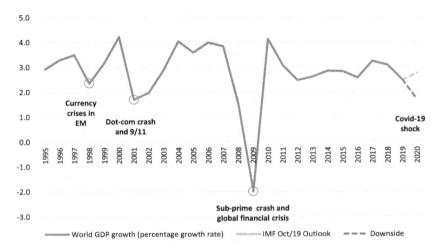

Growth of Global GDP (growth in %). *Source:* UNCTAD calculations based on IMF, WEO, October 2019.

GLOBAL DEBT REACHES RECORD HEIGHTS

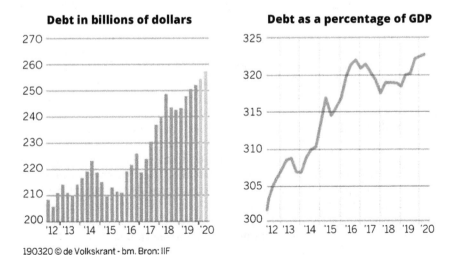

190320 © de Volkskrant - bm. Bron: IIF

Global Debt Reaches Record Heights

Naturally, measures were taken after the systemic crisis of 2008. Legislation and regulations have imposed restrictions on banks, and as a result, with large buffers, they are in a much better position now than they were then. But the debts are still piling up. Since the financial and economic crisis of 2008, not only the national debt but also the debt mountain of households and companies has only increased. And since 2019 it has been going downhill fast.

An important difference to 2008, when risky loans – junk mortgages – to individuals were a major cause of the crisis, especially in the USA, is that now Asia is also participating fully in the accumulation of debt and the granting of risky loans to companies. The impact of the next financial and economic crisis will therefore be many times greater. Because the same flaws are still in the financial system, experts stated long before the appearance of covid that the not if, but when a new economic crisis will occur. And they were not thinking of the covid crisis.

The first flaw in the financial and economic system is that there is still no brake on the size of the financial sector. In terms of gross national product, the financial sector is now four times larger than the real economy. In 1980, these were still about the same size. Between 1970 and 2020, more than 150 national banking crises occurred, according to the International Monetary Fund (IMF). So, these crises in the financial system are the rule rather than the exception. The derivatives trade grew from a few million dollars in 1970 to 100 million in 1980, 100 billion in 1990, 100 trillion in 2000 and its current value is estimated at 1,000 trillion dollars. That is about 20 times the size of the world economy. So, this is completely out of control, and you do not need a crystal ball to see that, as long as no brakes are put on it, the financial sector will dominate rather than support the real economy, so that the chances of it going wrong eventually are extremely high.

The second flaw in the financial and economic system is related to money creation and financial instability. When the economy is going well, commercial banks create too much money and provide too many loans too easily. When times are bad, they do too little. This urge for more money creation and more credit supply has characterized the financial system since 1980. After all, more and higher credits provide more (interest) income. This has led to an explosion in the money supply and an increase in debt. It is a ticking time bomb; the risk of another crisis is immense. Of course, the banking and credit crisis of 2008–2009 was followed by more control and supervision, but when you look at the global debt mountain of governments, companies and households alike, you will be struck by the fact that the instability of the system can easily lead to another crisis.

The third flaw is the allocation of money. As much as 95% of newly created money goes into the virtual economy and is used to create even more money. This creates bubbles in the financial and housing markets, which eventually cause the system to blow up. For example, since 2008 an insane amount of money has been pumped into banks and financial institutions. As a result, stock market prices have climbed to record heights, but the growth figures of the real economy have not followed. This also applies to existing money. Only a small proportion goes to useful social projects to improve education and care and to green the economy with zero-energy houses or renewable energy sources. Most of it, however, goes to derivatives trading or fossil energy projects, which yield very short-term financial returns. Fortunately, this is now changing, as the return on fossil-fuel investments is coming under increasing pressure and in fact, poses a risk on the financial markets.

There are also promising niche developments, such as microcredit and microinsurance. But for many people, it is still exceedingly difficult to get credit because they cannot bring in their own money or collateral and are therefore not creditworthy. People with money and property, on the other hand, can borrow quite easily. This is and remains unfair, and every systemic crisis widens the gap between rich and poor, as the covid crisis is proving.

The conclusion is that in our current financial-economic system, financial values are more important than social and ecological values. In the long run, this is untenable, and the financial-economic system will blow itself up because it is seriously ill and is permanently on a drip-feed. This consists of interest rates, which are kept artificially low and have been close to zero in Europe for 10 years, and of constantly printing money so that banks and financial institutions have new money at their disposal, which incidentally only reaches companies to a limited extent. These measures have not helped much and are more likely to reinforce rather than resolve the flaws. That is why the bubble had to burst again and, in this case, covid was the trigger. The cause lies much deeper, however, in the persistent systemic errors.

Fossil-fuel investments represent a completely different and ever-increasing systemic risk in our financial and economic system. Oil prices fluctuate enormously and are part of a geopolitical power game. For example, during the last oil crisis 6 years ago, the price of oil fell from USD 130 per barrel to USD 30 per barrel in a few months, because Saudi Arabia did not want to reduce its oil production and the United States increased its production of shale oil. At the beginning of 2020, the threat of covid and a dispute between Russia and the Organization of Petroleum Exporting Countries (OPEC) on limiting oil production caused the price of oil to plummet in a few hours. It is a sign of the vulnerability of the oil sector, which is facing a sharp drop in demand for oil not only due to the covid crisis but also structurally due to the rise of electric transport.

Although the constant fluctuations of oil prices are, according to experts, the prelude to a structural decline of the oil industry, the world will continue to lean on oil as the main raw material for decades to come. But the rise of renewable energy, electrification, climate policy and social resistance will eventually lead to the demise of the oil industry – and the fossil-fuel system as a whole. Years ago, I invited everyone to the approaching 'funeral of the fossil-fuel industry'. At the time, this was met with a good laugh, but now the funeral is in preparation. The question is no longer whether it will happen, but how long it will take before it does. The fact that large pension funds are already no longer investing in oil because of the major financial risks involved, is a clear sign that things are moving towards a phase of 'dying off'.

We have been growing for hundreds of years at the expense of the Earth. We borrow raw materials from the Earth but do not pay anything back. Anyone who borrows but does not pay back builds up debt and eventually goes bankrupt. We have now built up an ecological debt which, expressed in money, amounts to about 35% of what we all earn together. Compare that to a normal financial deficit of 3% on average and you realize that this is unsustainable. Thus, the ecological crisis is driven by the economic crisis and, vice versa, the ecological crisis is costing the economy more and more money. But not intervening costs us even more money.

The Ecological Crisis

We are living in the Anthropocene, the geological age of man. This is the era in which humankind fundamentally influences the Earth, with far-reaching consequences for both the Earth and humankind. This influence is becoming increasingly visible. Three examples are the 'plastic soup', the loss of biodiversity, and climate change.

The 'plastic soup' is a relatively new phenomenon, which has only recently become known to the general public and featured on the political agenda. It refers to the large collection of plastic that is accumulating in the waters of the world and which now covers an area in the Pacific that is about 34 times that of the Netherlands, a terrifying figure that you can scarcely imagine. All this plastic kills a million seabirds every year.

We produce 250,000,000 tonnes of plastic a year and use a million plastic bags every minute, half of which are only used once. Every day, 12 million pounds of plastic ends up in the ocean. Twenty countries cause 85% of the plastic pollution, and China is the absolute front runner with 2.5 million tonnes of plastic ending up in the sea every year. This is followed by Indonesia, the Philippines, Thailand and India. The first Western country, the United States, ranks 20th. On the other hand, it is Western companies that are the biggest plastic polluters: Coca-Cola, PepsiCo, Nestlé and Unilever. So, we live on a plastic planet with all its harmful consequences.

Yet plastic is not a persistent problem, because it is not intertwined with our lifestyle. There are alternatives available. We can stop the 'plastic soup' from growing relatively easily by taking effective measures to reduce the use of plastic. For example, a legal ban on plastic litter in California proved particularly effective. Companies were given six months to comply. If not, a sky-high fine awaited. The Netherlands introduced a ban on free plastic bags in 2016 and since then the use of plastic bags has decreased by 80%. In England, we also see that a ban on plastic is highly effective.

In 2019, a United Nations biodiversity panel made up of authoritative scientists found that humans are destroying nature on Earth on a large scale. The main causes are the expansion of agricultural land by 300% since 1970 and the doubling of urbanization since 1990. As a result, 1 million species are threatened with extinction and 75% of the planet and 66% of the oceans are severely impacted by humans.

When I started my career 35 years ago, the adage was that the Earth would not survive because of human expansionism. That has since changed: the Earth will survive, but whether we will survive is very much in question. If we destroy nature, we ruin the lifeline for our food and drink and ultimately destroy ourselves. That's literally what my colleague Professor Bob Watson said when presenting his infamous report. Unlike the 'plastics soup', the loss of biodiversity is a persistent problem because it is at the heart of our lifestyle and our economy. As long as we do not put a price on the destruction of nature, and the eco-services that nature provides us, we will continue to do so. So, this affects us both directly and indirectly. There are no simple solutions to this.

Perhaps the most intriguing problem is that of climate change. It has become an important part of my professional life. Thirty-five years ago, I started doing research into climate change, which at the time was still called the CO_2 problem. I developed the computer simulation model Integrated Model to Assess the Greenhouse Effect (IMAGE), the first integrated climate model in the world in which the causes, the physical/biological/chemical mechanism and the socio-economic effects of climate change were calculated. It contained money and molecules, of course, surrounded by many uncertainties, which I, as a mathematician, therefore paid due attention to. When I obtained my doctorate on the model at Maastricht University in 1990, I did not receive a *cum laude* for my dissertation: the assessment committee was very positive, but also considered it to be controversial research. One committee member described it as a 'fascinating study of a problem that may turn out not to exist in the future'. Twenty years later I collected the bottle of whisky from the bet I took on it at the time.

In retrospect, my projections have turned out to be too optimistic. Global temperature increase and sea-level rise are going twice as fast as I calculated at the time. At the time, I was advised not to continue with the IMAGE model because it was too uncertain but, being stubborn, I continued to develop it, including a European model version, before handing it over to others after 10 years. Today, 35 years later, the model is still being developed at the Netherlands Environmental Assessment Agency (PBL) and hundreds of people have worked on it. The IMAGE model has also been used extensively in international climate negotiations and national policy submissions. I am proud of the fact that I continued to work on the climate model against all advice. It has become a kind of life motto: if I have a new idea and others advise me against it, then I'll go ahead with it. Conversely, if others advise me to go ahead with it, I start to have my doubts because it's probably not radical enough.

We are now several decades down the road, and a lot of time has been lost. Still, no drastic measures have been taken to reduce CO_2. What is being done is not what is needed, but what is possible. If we had intervened earlier, however, we would already be much further ahead with the energy transition. In terms of sustainable energy, the Netherlands is now in third to last place (25th out of 27 EU countries) in Europe. When I started my career we were in the top 10, and now we've become the laughing stock of Europe when it comes to the energy transition. At the same time, a lot has changed and been set in motion. In the beginning, I walked around The Hague almost every day, with civil servants asking me: 'Jan, how can we get the citizens and businesses on board?' Nowadays I spend far less time in The Hague, but I do visit municipalities and citizens who ask me: 'Jan, how can we get The Hague onboard?'

This is a sign of the enormous change that has taken place: a great deal of policy has been developed. When I started, there was no climate policy or climate agreement. Climate policy is now no longer in the hands of the government, but of very many people. The policy has been decentralized and has moved from The Hague to the regions and municipalities, a logical and positive development. And who could ever have thought that the climate would be one of the three most important election themes in Europe? Worldwide, it is also seen as one of the most important tasks we face as human beings. The biggest change, therefore, took place in our awareness and attitude. The last phase, drastically changing our behaviour, is the most difficult hurdle to take. We can only do this if we fully experience and feel the urgency of the climate problem. After all, a large part of the problem lies within ourselves. Part of us is selfish and greedy and always wants more, better and faster. We grow because we think we need to, and it makes us happier. Practice, however, proves otherwise: over the past 50 years, our material prosperity has tripled, while our happiness level has remained constant.

Planet of the Humans

More economic growth means more production and consumption, and that costs energy, resources, materials, water and space. It places an ever-greater burden on nature. That point is also made in the environmental documentary *Planet of the Humans* by the well-known documentary maker Michael Moore, directed by Jeff Gibbs. Rarely has an environmental documentary caused as much uproar as this one, in which the filmmakers examine the assumptions and solutions of the environmental movement and argue that they are wrong. In doing so, they throw a stone into the environmental pond.

Tens of millions of people have now seen the film (if you haven't seen it yet, you can watch it at www.planetofthehumans.com) and, unsurprisingly, the reactions are divided into two camps: right-wing populists and climate sceptics cheer, and the environmental movement expresses scathing criticism. There is indeed much to criticize in the documentary: the first hour is full of outdated images, outdated numbers, factual inaccuracies and misleading frames. With the Chevy Volt (one of the first electric cars), outdated solar panels, and old small wind turbines with broken blades, the film presents a technological picture of what it was like 10 years ago. That is no longer the reality, and thanks to the strong increase in the production of renewable energy, CO_2 emissions have been slowed down and part of the climate damage avoided. Otherwise, we would have been much worse off.

And yet Michael Moore has a point. In the last half hour of the documentary, he painfully exposes the fact that unlimited growth on a finite planet is not possible. And that finiteness is not so much determined by the climate, but by raw materials, nature, biodiversity and space. Replacing fossil-fuel-based energy with sustainable energy is necessary but does not solve the problem of finiteness. Take the discussion of biomass: it is coarse-grained and one-sided in the film, but it does make sense and touches on a sensitive issue. Science is divided and the environmental movement does not have an unambiguous position either. The fact is that in recent years we have begun to think differently about biomass. Ten years ago, biofuels were seen as a panacea; now biomass is in the doldrums. But that is not entirely true: there are many kinds of biomass, such as corn, sugar cane, rapeseed, palm oil, wood chips, algae, residual waste, biodegradable waste and sewage sludge. These can be used as biofuel to generate energy or as a raw material to make bioproducts. Certainly, as a building block of the biobased economy, biomass can be of great value for high-value bioproducts such as polymers, building materials, food, feed, cosmetics and pharmaceuticals. But large-scale burning of biomass to generate energy is not a sustainable alternative to fossil-fuel-based energy because it does not produce sufficient CO_2 reductions, as scientific research has established. Similarly, the large-scale clearing of rainforest for the production of palm oil, as shown in the film, is devastating and scandalous. Just like the large-scale co-firing of biomass in coal-fired power plants is very harmful because it leads to large amounts of particulate matter and NO_x, while it hardly produces less CO_2. Investing billions in biomass power stations and technologies to remove CO_2 from the air to meet the 2-degree climate goal of the Paris Climate Agreement is insane because we are thereby simply perpetuating the old economic system. That's why the climate problem and the energy transition require more than playing games with technologies. It is impossible to separate them from our own behaviour and the underlying growth paradigm. By decarbonizing every unit of economic production, we may have started to produce in a cleaner way in recent decades, but we are still growing at the expense of nature.

Moreover, Michael Moore has a point when he argues that we as humans do not ask ourselves enough questions about whether we are on the right track. We push that question away and think that it is enough to implement sustainable technology, but that's ultimately a dead end. We can't solve this problem technologically or economically alone. Solving the climate problem in a hyper-capitalist way is a trap that leads to even more growth and destruction. Deep down, the problem is not in the technology or the economic system, but in ourselves, and until we recognize that, we will not solve these problems. So here Moore is right: our view is in fact too narrow, limited to the climate issue and the energy transition that we want to solve technologically. But this is no game: if we simply replace fossil-fuel technology with sustainable technology, then we create an even bigger monster. Looking too narrowly and sticking too tightly to climate goals leads to the perpetuation of the capitalist economic system which is based on neoliberal values. This fundamental debate, which has been dormant in science for decades, is something we avoid publicly and politically. Also, as Michael Moore exposes, there is too little attention paid to it within the environmental movement. Why are we still using gross national product (GNP) as a starting point, when we know that we are deliberately damaging nature and therefore the economy? Why don't we recalibrate the concept of growth? This could mean 'no growth', 'green growth', or 'growth that focuses on sustainable progression and not on income growth or material growth'. 'Agrowth', as economist Jeroen van den Bergh calls it.

I am glad that we have already replaced as much fossil-fuel-based energy as possible with sustainable energy. Otherwise, we would be much worse off. But now the real work begins: we must focus on the core of the problem, and that is deeply anchored in the capitalist system that we ourselves have created. We are now mainly cleaning the outside, but the inside is still dirty. As long as we don't see that, we won't solve our problems. If it's embedded in the current economy, which is based on unsustainable growth, the transition is doomed to fail. A successful energy transition and solution to the climate problem require a value change based on a different economic paradigm. We are still pointing too much at the systems and we're still placing the problem outside of ourselves. But we are the system. The systems have become so deeply entrenched in us that we ourselves have become the greatest limiting factor and stand in the way of a real solution. This brings us to the moral crisis.

The Moral Crisis

We have become slaves to the system and that's logical because there is an eternal duality, a love-hate relationship between people and systems. We have created these systems ourselves and they have also allowed us to function well for a long time. However, we also tend to over-organize, and then the systems gradually take over from us. Then there comes a time when they get in our way because everything becomes too complex and too bureaucratic. At a certain point, we no longer see through the complexity, as we experienced during the financial crisis of 2008. At that point, systems are no longer just in our way, they even turn against us.

Look at healthcare, education, employment and pension schemes. We set all of these up in the nineteenth century and developed them in the twentieth century. They functioned well for a very long time, but the underlying principles are and remain neo-centric, namely collectivist and egalitarian. In other words: every human being is equal, while we now know that every human being is unequal. Today's starting point would be: every person has equal opportunities. So, I came to a school where there is a beautiful motto: 'We treat every student unequally'. That sounds crude and strange, but if you treat every student the same, you end up with inequality. So, we are moving towards personalized systems such as customized care and education, and a personalized pension system that you manage yourself.

But there is a fear of tackling this. Many people point at the system and say: 'We do want to change, but the system makes it impossible for us'. But we are the system; we invented and set it up ourselves. So, we also have the ability to take it back and change it. If you really want to change, you look for the change in yourself.

The covid crisis also lies deep within ourselves. There are more and more of us on Earth and our globalized trade, our explosively increased travel behaviour, our eating habits and our contact with (wild) animals have ensured that covid has been able to spread around the world. Diseases that would have remained local in the past now travel around the world at lightning speed. Wuhan, for example, became the breeding ground for Covid-19 and caused a pandemic that plunged the world economy into a deep recession. Covid is not only the result of our modern lifestyle, but it is also inextricably intertwined with our way of life. From the dominant world view of the money-driven free market and the dominant human view of homo economicus, we direct our social systems primarily on the basis of economic values. Everything is aimed at competition and the individual, and this is how we have gone too far in nearly all our vital social systems. To such an extent that we have lost trust not only in each other but also in social systems, CEOs, large companies and the government.

It is also evident from the annual confidence barometer which the American PR and communication agency Edelman has been compiling for 20 years and which it presents during the World Economic Forum in Davos. Worldwide, confidence in democracy, politics and CEOs declined further in 2021, a downward trend that has been in evidence since the last economic crisis in 2008. The crisis and global unrest are the main causes of the decline in trust, and that is not even counting the coronas crisis. The Edelman report of 2021 also makes no bones about the fact: it speaks of an epidemic of misinformation, causing distrust in social institutions and leaders worldwide. Because the business world, the government, NGOs and the media appear unable to turn the tide, the confidence barometer even speaks of an information bankruptcy.

The covid crisis has made this all the clearer: there is declining confidence in our democracy. In the current structure of democracy and parliament, citizens are at a great disadvantage. Many people do not feel recognized and seen. This position makes people susceptible to extreme ideas about all kinds of social issues and to the polarization of standpoints. It is also a breeding ground for rising populism. As Hannah Arendt a century ago already aptly put it: 'The demise of democracy begins with people for whom the distinction between fact and fiction no longer exists'. These times call for new forms of democracy, based on a renewed balance between top-down and bottom-up. The government sets frameworks within which citizens are given direct influence and control. Modern digital technology enables the direct participation of millions of people. Experiments are needed with new forms of democracy, such as citizens' panels. Compared to countries such as Switzerland, France, Belgium and Scotland, the Netherlands is lagging behind.

As a result, we now have an extremely efficient but chilly society, in which many people do not feel at home and are longing for warmth and bonding on the basis of human values. After all, human beings are also homo sociologicus, social beings who function in groups, belong to other people and are influenced by others. The covid crisis has made this clear once again. A human being is also a homo ecologicus, who lives in balance with nature and is part of the world as an ecosphere. Even though the relationship is different for each person, we are all a mixture of these types. However, the human image of the homo economicus, who is selfish and strives to maximize his utility, supported by the dominant neo-liberalism, has left a heavy mark on our society. Greed is a major driving force behind unbridled growth. As soon as it gets too close, we tend to put it outside ourselves and point at others: at the system, at capitalism, at the world.

But, if you blame the world or the system, you put it outside yourself and you avoid your responsibility. If you really want to change, you have to find the change within yourself. I noticed recently during an online lecture on the covid crisis that not everyone is aware of this yet. A few students dryly stated that covid was an external factor, bad luck actually and that they did not see the connection with our lifestyle. That is in line with many economists, who say the same thing and are only concerned about the resulting recession. I always point out the systemic nature of the coronas crisis, that it affects our vital systems (food, health care, education, transport, energy), that it mercilessly exposes the systemic errors in terms of short-term profitability, which is why we are not crisis-proof, and that the indirect long-term effects are often greater than the direct effects. For example, intensive livestock farming in the Netherlands, with its mega-stables with 100,000 chickens in one shed, in which deadly mutations of the bird flu virus can occur, is the breeding ground for the next pandemic.

Triple Imbalance

Every crisis is a symptom of imbalance, of a system that is out of balance. This leads to tension between the system and its environment. Today's period of chaos is such a period of imbalance.

I see a triple imbalance in our society and economy: the imbalance between man and nature, between people and between the short and long term.

(1) *Imbalance between man and nature.* Man believes he is superior to nature and also to animals. This moral superiority leads to the destruction of nature and to the extinction of animal species. How we treat nature and animals is a major cause of the covid pandemic. It could just as easily have occurred in the Netherlands, the most cattle-rich country in the world. In addition to 17 million people, there are 115 million pigs, cattle, chickens and goats in the Netherlands. Every year, 15 million pigs, 2 million cattle, 1.5 million calves and 600 million broilers are slaughtered. By no means do all of these come from the Netherlands: half of the calves slaughtered in the Netherlands come from abroad and, after being slaughtered, are re-exported mainly to Germany, France and Italy.

This constant movement of animals and meat between countries represents a major systemic risk. Wherever so many people and animals live in close proximity to each other, there is a great risk of zoonoses, as we have already seen with the outbreaks of Q fever, BSE (mad cow disease) and bird flu. That is why I argue that the next pandemic could also occur in the Netherlands. Nature will strike back hard. And this is only the beginning because a climate crisis now seems inevitable. The consequences of that would be even more drastic, not to mention the wave that would follow: the biodiversity crisis.

This calls for a renewed balance between man and nature, where we see ourselves as part of nature and are prepared to learn from nature's vitality, resilience, agility and diversity. Nature has been designing, producing and innovating for billions of years without depletion, pollution or de-generation. Nature feeds the life that feeds on it. If it does not work or no longer works, it disappears. 'What is of no value, what adds nothing, dies',' says the Belgian innovation biologist Leen Gorissen. Do you remember when I said that when I started out as a scientist, we were mainly very afraid that the Earth would not survive? Today, we see things differently: we can wipe ourselves out.

(2) *Disparity between people.* The social and economic inequality between people is increasing and is a source of social unrest. With each new crisis, this inequality seems to increase: the vulnerable become more vulnerable and the strong a little stronger. The covid crisis was not a social equaliser either; on the contrary, the poorest and most vulnerable people are hit hardest. Think of people in slums and refugees in primitive relief camps. But also in rich countries, people with low incomes are more at risk. Frontline workers, such as nurses, bus drivers, police officers, elderly caregivers, hospital staff, shopkeepers and shelf stackers, are poorly paid and face a higher risk of being infected because they are exposed to the virus more often. The self-employed and small and medium-sized companies often have no financial cushion and are disproportionately affected by this crisis. The myth that covid affects everyone equally, regardless of origin, skin colour or place of residence, has thus been dispelled.

In 2019, the growing socio-economic inequality was a hotbed for protests against inequality that engulfed the world, with young people as the driving force behind these protests. This too calls for a new balance between people. A new foundation is needed, consisting of an inclusive economy, in which everyone can actively participate, including vulnerable groups of people who are in danger of falling by the wayside due to the crisis, and an inclusive society where everyone is given equal opportunities: in education, in the labour market, in the housing market and in the area of social security.

(3) *Imbalance between certainty and uncertainty.* We find it difficult to deal with uncertainty. From the tendency to control and master the world around us, we prefer to focus on certainty, which is often false security. And because everything is so interwoven in our modern world, the complexity threatens to grow over our heads, causing us to lose control and become unmanageable. The German sociologist Ulrich Beck stated that we live in a risk society, where we neglect the big risks and try to monitor and control the small ones. We focus on small-impact events that occur more frequently, while we overlook those events that occur infrequently but have a large impact because they are out of our sight. We can see this in the figure below, the Rumsfeld Matrix, which shows different types of uncertainties. Three of them are important for transitions. I will therefore highlight these.

Unknown-Knowns
(Hidden facts)
 	
• These are untapped
  knowledge.
• You don't know about it,
  but someone else with
  the community knows.
	Unknown-Unknowns
	(Unknown risks)
	
	• You don't know about
	  it.
	• Also, someone else
	  within the community
	  or sphere of influence
	  does not know about it.

Known-Knowns
(Facts and requirements)
 	
• Not risks!
• These are managed
  as part of project
  scope.
	Known-Unknowns
	(Known risks)
	
	• Classic risks. More
	  predominant.
	• You have the knowledge
	  of probability and impact
	  values of such risks.

Figure.   The Rumsfeldt Matrix.

(1) *The known unknowns: we know what we do not know.* The 'known unknowns' are blank spots in our knowledge, things we do know, but about which we do not have all the information. For example, how does a financial and economic crisis arise and how can it best be combatted? We have the ingredients: tax breaks and tax cuts, stimulus packages and austerity measures. But we do not know the recipe.

(2) *The unknown knowns: we do not know what we know.* The 'unknown knowns' are the blind spots in our knowledge, things we don't realize we actually know. It is unconscious knowledge that you prefer to suppress so that you do not have to take care of it. So, we know that our economy is wasteful, polluting and unjust. But until we are confronted with the facts, we suppress them. For example, many people think that more than half of the energy in the Netherlands is generated sustainably while, in reality, it is only 14%. Covid, which caused a global recession in 2020, was a blind spot: something that was known that could happen, but of which people were unaware. It was known information that people preferred to suppress.

(3) *The unknown unknowns: we do not know what we do not know.* These 'unknowns' are the so-called 'black swans', things we do not know that we do not know, and of which we are also not aware that we do not know.

Literally and figuratively. The black swan was known in Australia, but not in Europe. That is until the Dutch explorer Willem de Vlamingh discovered the black swan in Western Australia at the end of the seventeenth century. The question is, in retrospect, whether it could have been known in the rest of the world. Well-known figurative black swans are 9/11 (the attack on the Twin Towers in New York in 2001), the collapse of the stock exchange as a result of the banking crisis in 2008 and the nuclear disaster in Fukushima. All three are highly improbable events that cannot be (properly) predicted, have a major impact and that people try to explain afterwards.

There's a fine line between the 'unknown knowns' – the blind spots – and the 'unknown unknowns' – the black swans. After all, if you take a good, long look at the undercurrent of structural change, you can already see the seeds of the black swans. Then it turns out that the unknowns – the black swans – are often white. The banking crisis and 9/11 are examples of black swans that are actually white: highly improbable events that, in retrospect, are less improbable than previously thought. The shape and the moment cannot be predicted, but we could have seen them coming because they are embedded in the undercurrent. For those who look closely and long into the undercurrent, these events are merely manifestations of deeply rooted structural developments, and it is logical that they happen.

Black Swans and Blind Spots

9/11

The attacks on 9/11 were rooted in an undercurrent of hatred against the West and especially against the decadent, immoral American lifestyle. Against American imperialism and moral superiority, reinforced by American support for Israel and dictators in the Middle East, and by sanctions against Iraq. So, the deeper causes are political, strategic, cultural and religious. This mobilized increasingly radicalized youths for a jihad against the West. Security experts saw this ticking time bomb and warned of terrorist attacks well before 9/11, but no one listened, no one took them seriously.

The timing and the method were not foreseeable, but it was foreseeable that there would be a major terrorist attack in America. Yet the event was a complete surprise and shock for the whole world. The images of the hijacked planes crashing into the Twin Towers in New York are etched on our retinas and in our collective memories. Many Americans could not think of a single reason why their country was attacked like that. 9/11 triggered two American wars in the Middle East, in which many European countries were involved. But above all, the attack on the Twin Towers changed our sense of security: from a security perspective, the world was no longer the same after 9/11. Our view of conflicts and antagonisms in the world has changed fundamentally because since then they have been placed in a religious perspective.

(Continued)

(*Continued*)

The banking crisis of 2008

The accumulation of debt, bad mortgages and the reckless behaviour of banks and investors around derivatives created enormous financial bubbles, and thus sowed the seeds for the deep recession of 2008. 'The only surprise of the 2009 crisis was that it came as a surprise to many', wrote Nobel Prize winner in economics Joseph Stiglitz. American businessman and investor Steve Eisman, British Financial Times journalist Gillian Tett, American economist Nouriel Roubini and Dutch financial specialist Tonko Gast saw it coming and warned about it. All of them were ignored.

Corona

The covid pandemic came as a surprise to almost everyone, while experts had been warning for years about a worldwide pandemic with many victims. In the Netherlands, safety experts pointed out the danger of a pandemic in 2016, and it was even part of the National Safety Strategy. The risk of a pandemic was estimated as 'real', and the possible shortage of intensive care beds during such a pandemic crisis period was explicitly pointed out. But nothing was done with this information, so we were not prepared for the covid crisis. Even Bill Gates, in a 2015 TED lecture, warned 'that if anything is going to claim more than 10 million lives in the next few decades, it is more likely to be a highly contagious virus than a war. Not missiles, but microbes'. He also indicated that such a pandemic could bring the economy to a standstill and that we were not prepared for it.

After the outbreak of the SARS virus in 2003, researchers found other SARS-like viruses in bats in Southeast Asia. So, they knew that Southeast Asia was a hotbed of all kinds of viruses that could break out sooner or later. According to virologists, the new covid was, therefore, an 'accident waiting to happen'. But this was systematically ignored. All attention was focused on terrorist attacks, not on pandemics. Covid-19 is therefore not a black swan, but a blind spot: we knew about it, but we ignored that knowledge. It was uncomfortable information that we preferred to suppress. But structural insecurities cannot be trivialized or dismissed, or they will come back and hit us like a boomerang.

If we return to business-as-usual after the covid crisis and allow the systemic errors to fester, we will be waiting for the next systemic crisis. The climate crisis is already looming, but so is the social crisis, with growing discontent and permanent unrest as a result. However, repairing system errors costs a lot of money and time and is only accepted when the urgency is widely felt. That moment is now. So, we have a choice, and if we make the wrong one, we will move from one crisis to another.

Yet we will largely return to business-as-usual. It's an illusion to assume that the world will look radically different after the covid crisis. People are simply stubborn and by nature prefer not to change. If people learn and change at all, it is because of crises. But it is also naive to assume that nothing will change after this crisis. For example, the economic crisis in the 1930s had far-reaching consequences. This crisis was rooted in the 'roaring twenties' and formed a breeding ground for dictatorial movements such as communism, national socialism and fascism. But the crisis also had positive effects: Roosevelt came up with the New Deal to give the economy a boost, companies were forced to modernize, and the welfare state was created in many countries to offer citizens social security.

The social impact of a crisis, therefore, depends on the soil in which it is rooted. The current crisis is rooted in a time of global unrest. In recent years, the number of protests has increased around the world, and 2019 was the year of protests worldwide. Yellow vests, climate strikers, young people, the elderly, farmers, builders, care workers – the list seemed endless. The protests are rooted in massive discontent about increasing inequality (which now mainly affects the middle class), in dissatisfaction about the lack of adequate climate policy, and in the desire for democracy, as in Chile and Ecuador, or for autonomy, as in Hong Kong and Catalonia.

This is why it is quite conceivable that the covid crisis will reinforce this feeling of dissatisfaction with the current 'chilly efficiency' society, and economy. It will lead to the end of the market's excesses and deep-rooted neo-liberalism. It may also mean that we will invest in a society that is more humane, fairer and healthier, and in an economy that is more sustainable, resilient and stable. This will require courage, leadership and stamina to break down the current systems step by step and build new ones. It will be a fierce time, full of chaos, turbulence and instability, with uprisings worldwide. But it is necessary: a period of decades of construction and dismantling that will meet with fierce resistance.

Extremes, events with a small chance but a big risk of occurring, are increasingly becoming the norm. We must therefore learn to deal with structural uncertainty. A new paradigm is needed, one in which structural uncertainty is the starting point. A paradigm that takes account of shocks and fluctuations instead of gradual developments. A paradigm in which periods of imbalance between equilibria become the norm rather than the exception, as in the current paradigm. Such a new paradigm, in which high risks and extremes become the norm, also requires a new toolkit to deal with them. It means a shift from controlling and managing to anticipating and learning, and from reducing and eliminating uncertainties to accepting them and learning to deal with them. Not holding back but moving with the flow. Not steering for short-term values such as efficiency and returns on investment, but for long-term values such as resilience, agility and diversity. A shift from coercive steering to flexible adjustment. From a static blueprint to developing organically by searching, experimenting and learning. These shifts require a major culture change in governments, companies, organizations and people.

Chapter 3

Civil Servants Can Make the Difference

My father was a civil servant for 40 years at the Municipal Energy Company in Rotterdam. I could have had a job there too, but after 3 years of holiday work, I found it deadly boring. A civil servant was the last thing I wanted to be. But times have changed. Now I would love to be a civil servant. Who would have thought that I would ever say that? Certainly not my father. I can see the smile on his face.

In order to connect with the demands of modern society, the government has to relate differently to the fast, furious and fundamentally changing environment. The combined social, digital and spatial transition constitutes a great challenge, and it is forcing the government to fundamentally reconsider its role and way of working. Today, therefore, it is not 'fatally boring' to be a civil servant. On the contrary, it could not be more exciting than in the current period of chaos that marks the transition between two eras. Precisely in this in-between-period of chaos and turbulence, in which society is being rearranged and the economy is getting a new foundation, the government is being asked to have the courage and leadership to make hard choices and temporarily take back control.

The covid crisis was forcing the government into that other role. It had to solve the crisis, while large companies were knocking on its door *en masse* for support. We cannot go back to the old days, to the all-determining, dominant and bureaucratic government. However, in a large number of countries, the government is trying to abuse its new position of power by quickly pushing through legislation to further increase its power. In the Netherlands, we saw this with the Corona Act, which caused a storm of criticism in all sections of society. This shows that there are enough checks and balances to prevent the new, temporary power of the government from becoming permanent.

Looking beyond the crises, an agile government is needed, which can play different roles in different domains. Sometimes a strong steering role, sometimes a facilitating role and sometimes a protective role. This requires a transition of the government itself so that it works in an agile, smart, flexible and integrated way. As a civil servant, you can make a difference right now by influencing the course of these transitions.

Embracing Chaos, 47–55
Copyright © 2023 Jan Rotmans and Co-Writer Mischa Verheijden
Published under exclusive licence by Emerald Publishing Limited. Translation by Michael Gould.
The moral rights of the translator have been asserted. Copyright © 2021 Jan Rotmans en Mischa Verheijden. Original title Omarm de Chaos. First published in 2021 by De Geus, Amsterdam
doi:10.1108/978-1-83753-634-420231006

System Trends

From a larger system perspective, four trends can be seen that will determine the future role and method of working by the government. These trends force the government to reinvent itself and to think (culture), organize (structure) and work (practice) differently.

Emerging Citizenship

Citizens are increasingly adopting a different attitude: they no longer accept standard solutions, and they want customized solutions. A vanguard of citizens wants to actively think about this and participate. As a response to the bureaucracy of the government and the coldness of the market, they are driven by values such as trust, cooperativeness and the human dimension. Supported and strengthened by technology, they can organize themselves quickly and intelligently into communities and cooperatives. In this way, this group of citizens forms a micro-power that is capable of organizing its own living environment.

The covid crisis has led to an increase in citizen initiatives aimed at helping vulnerable people. This is in line with the general explosive increase in the number of civic initiatives in the last decade. For example, the Netherlands already has around 650 energy cooperatives, more than 400 healthcare cooperatives, hundreds of 'bread funds' (collectives that allow independent entrepreneurs to provide each other with temporary sick leave) and food cooperatives, involving around 1 million people. This is followed by the vanguard of the pack, with some 2 to 2.5 million people, then the pack itself and only then the laggards. This is not just a Dutch phenomenon: worldwide, there is talk of 'the commons', a bottom-up movement that involves hundreds of millions of people. There is therefore a growing group of citizens who are willing and able to actively participate in society through a wide range of initiatives. But there is also a large group of laggards who are not yet ready for this, and who still rather passively expect the government to organize things for them. The government must relate to these diverse groups of citizens and provide them with customized services where possible.

Decentralization

Active citizenship is part of a broader trend of decentralization at the meso level. More and more tasks, responsibilities and finances are being transferred from the national government to municipalities. This decentralization is partly motivated by savings and efficiency considerations, but there is also a philosophy behind placing administrative responsibility at the lowest level of scale. For example, in the social domain, the national government mainly has a supervisory role and implementation is entirely in the hands of the municipalities. Since the introduction of the Social Support Act, the Participation Act and the Youth Act in 2015, they have been responsible for youth and elderly care and employment. With the exception of calamities in youth care, especially in the larger municipalities, the transfer of tasks, responsibilities and finances has gone reasonably well. The municipalities assumed the governing role and put the administration in order, distributed the money as evenly as possible and arranged everything to provide everyone with care.

But that was precisely not the intention. Of course, in the transitional phase of a transition, a municipality is forced to play the role of director but that should be temporary at most. At the moment, however, municipalities mainly operate as care offices. They have a directing role, whereas they should have a facilitating role. This requires a change in basic assumptions from traditional assistance to modern support, from 'providing for' to 'providing that'. This means for the municipality not wanting to organize everything ourselves but enabling others to do so. This is desperately needed: at the district level, you see everything coming together, and it is becoming painfully clear that institutions are working in parallel. For example, numerous agencies deal with problem youths from the perspective of housing, debt assistance, youth care, medical assistance, education and financing. Of course, this cannot and should not be the intention, but it is the hard reality. That is why experiments are so needed to start thinking and working more holistically.

It is a misunderstanding to think that a facilitating role is boring. On the contrary, it means that the local government is proactive, stimulating and agenda-setting. Facilitating means that the local government gives direction and offers space to other players in the social domain: giving direction by setting clear frameworks and formulating clear rules, offering space by removing mental, legal, financial and organizational barriers and stimulating unexpected coalitions. This requires a different way of thinking, working and organizing from all those involved on a local scale. This cultural change has hardly gotten off the ground yet and is biggest challenge for municipalities in the years to come. At the moment, we are still largely doing the same things and making the same mistakes in the social domain, only with less money and on a smaller scale. Eventually, municipalities will have that facilitating role, but a cultural change requires time and patience and cannot be planned or organized. Such a change in organizational culture, which can take up to 10 years, takes place in phases. It is an evolutionary process with a radically different outcome. You cannot force people to think and work differently; at the very most you can create the preconditions for them to do so based on intrinsic motivation. That is why it is wise to start with people who are open to it, and thus to create a larger support base step by step. I call this organic support development.

It is hopeful that all municipalities are experimenting in the social domain at the district level. It is precisely these experiments that differ from the norm: they put the person in his or her social environment – and not the organization – at the centre of everything. The experiments are also intended to create more harmony and coherence and to work integrally. The integration of the social and medical domain is particularly important here because a person cannot be divided into a medical and a social part, as is currently the case. This integration is not exactly easy, because it involves ingrained entrenched patterns and because there is a dominant impermeable layer of institutions ('clay layer') that are used to interfering.

Some of the experiments succeed, but not all. It is just as well that the necessary experiments fail because more can be learned from the failures than from the experiments that succeed. In this way, municipalities make progress step by step. Unfortunately, not enough time is taken to scale up the experiments and make them part of the structure. Because experiments are quickly followed up by new experiments, they are not given enough time to sink in, so the structure and culture of the organization cannot change substantially. Taking the time to scale up the experiments and have them become part of the organization and culture is therefore just as important as the experimenting itself.

It is also striking that little is learned from other municipalities, and therefore no scaling up takes place between municipalities. When I started doing transition research nearly 30 years ago, I was rather naive about scaling up experiments. My thought was that once people see the good examples they will apply them in their own context. However, in practice, this is not always the case. Of course, the context of every municipality is different, and you cannot just roll out experiments everywhere one by one, but often the 'not invented here' syndrome prevails and every municipality wants to do things in its own way. That really is a missed opportunity.

There is a treasure chest of learning experiences. That is why I advise council members and civil servants to take a tour of successful and less successful experiments, to learn from them and to apply those learning experiences in their own context. For this, you need connectors and translators. Connectors connect different contexts, and translators can translate insights from one context to another. People with these skills are worth their weight in gold! This, in turn, is my own learning experience from practice, which I then translate into theory. In this way, the transition theory is nurtured and shaped by practical experience.

Digitalization

The new economy is data-driven, and it revolves around digital platforms. Tech giants from Silicon Valley (GAFAM: Google, Apple, Facebook, Amazon and Microsoft), but also increasingly from China (BAT: Baidu, Alibaba and Tencent) are monopolizing the data market and collecting more and more data from citizens. Like the robber barons in steel, oil, coal and railways during the Industrial Revolution in the nineteenth century, they are the robber barons in today's digital revolution, dominating the economic playing field with their data monopolies. The power of these tech companies and the monopolization of this platform economy is forcing the government to take legal measures to protect citizens from the negative consequences of digitization. Without government protection, citizens are defenceless against these giants of manipulating data. In view of smart cities, the tech giants are also increasingly using their power to determine urban development in cities such as Toronto and New York. In doing so, they are entering an area that previously belonged only to the government.

Data and digitization, therefore, deserve to be the top priority in government. The unprecedented 'harvesting' and commercial marketing of personal data of citizens is, after all, at odds with their individual freedom and they are becoming increasingly dependent on the data companies. Ultimately, this affects the identity of citizens and deeply undermines democracy itself. In the nineteenth century, the power of the industrial monopolists was tackled by breaking up these companies. Competition law was introduced, and social uplift took place, in which people were made more resilient through education, among other things, in order to climb higher on the social ladder. Now, too, the government must intervene to break the power of the data companies. These companies must be broken up, and new laws and regulations are needed to better protect citizens against abuse and manipulation of the data collected about them. The government can do this by increasing the awareness of citizens so that they are less naive and careless with their data, and do not give it away just like that. Government can also encourage initiatives in which data becomes and remains the property of citizens, through cooperatives that collect and manage data for groups of citizens. In addition, the government can develop platforms that support public values.

This has far-reaching consequences for the organization of the government. Digitalization cuts straight through the silos of the government, which is one more reason to abolish them. But while the digital revolution is quietly taking place, many municipalities do not even have a digital department yet. And the national government does not yet have a digital ministry either. Yet it is obvious that, as companies organize themselves as digital platforms and citizens increasingly communicate digitally, the government will also organize itself as a digital platform. A digital government platform is horizontal and integral, in which the government interacts with various communities of citizens, companies and social organizations. A municipality can then position itself as a platform provider with an open platform of public and private systems, in the service of the public interest. By linking data and information flows in different areas, the government can use complex and integral data analysis to implement a proactive policy that serves citizens in an integrated way. This is still in its infancy but will become an important theme in the near future. Think of the variety of data and information flows (medical, social, financial, housing, education, work) in the social domain, which can be optimally coordinated digitally. In the spatial domain, this is also made possible by digitally coordinating data about waste, energy, raw materials, pollution and traffic.

In this way, a municipality can develop its own platforms with its own data analysts for public services such as social security, green spaces, the environment and care. The interests and protection of citizens are central to this. The municipality can also take on a role as platform curator, making binding agreements with market parties about the conditions under which they are admitted to the digital municipal space. This limits the manipulation and abuse of data as much as possible. Of course, all this is complementary to what municipalities already do in the field of public services. On a European scale, a network of cities is needed to exchange experiences and jointly develop rules against globally operating monopolists. The City of Amsterdam has already taken the initiative to set up a European urban network of Chief Digital Officers.

Spatial Integration

Climate, water, drought, nature, environment and energy are inextricably linked. Together they form an integrated spatial task such as we have never seen before. Climate change and the related rise in sea level necessitate a review of the Netherlands' water defence policy. With an expected sea level rise of half a metre to one metre this century, and further land subsidence in the coastal areas of half a metre to one metre, parts of the Netherlands will be situated 7–9 metres below sea level. This raises the question as to what extent these extremely low-lying polder areas can still be kept dry by pumping and draining. There will come a time when this is no longer justifiable, not only from a safety point of view but also from a cost-benefit point of view, and when polder areas have to be flooded.

There are also increasing droughts worldwide. This requires a mitigation strategy from governments. In the short term, it is particularly important to use water more sparingly, to retain it for longer in retention areas with reservoirs and to distribute water more intelligently. In the longer term, the natural water balance needs to be restored, by means of smarter land-use planning.

Nature in the Netherlands is in a bad state, especially on farmland and in moorlands. Biodiversity is declining. For example, animal species have declined by an average of 50% since 1990. Agricultural grasslands and fields are still green, but where they were once rich in butterflies, insects and herbs (around 1900), these have now almost completely disappeared. With targeted management, heathland can remain purple with heather, but there too used to be a lot more herbs and many more insects and birds. The main causes of this enormous loss of biodiversity are nitrogen fertilizer, pesticides and desiccation. Agriculture, industry and traffic are mainly responsible, and every day almost eight hectares of open space are sacrificed for houses, roads or industrial estates. That is 16 football fields every day, without any clear overarching idea behind it. Surely that is not possible. Yet it happens, day in and day out.

It is probably clear to you that we are therefore struggling with a major imbalance in terms of water and nature, which is also being aggravated by climate change and the energy transition. The energy transition has far-reaching spatial consequences due to the integration of solar and wind energy into the landscape, but also due to biomass cultivation, geothermal energy, heat networks and energy storage lakes. Never before has the Netherlands faced such an integrated, and therefore complex, water-space-nature-energy-climate challenge, and the current laws and regulations are seriously inadequate for what lies ahead. The new Environment Act, which will most likely come into force in 2023, can help address the integral spatial task. In this Act at least 26 laws in the field of the physical environment will be merged into one integrated law. This will make it the biggest legislative amendment since the introduction of the Constitution. The Act is necessary because of the inadequacy of existing legislation, which is a patchwork of laws and regulations that are mainly focused on partial aspects and partial interests. The present time demands an integrated approach and a weighing up of the various partial interests in relation to each other, at the local and the regional level. The Environment Act thus marks the transition from sectoral to integrated policy and forces municipalities to think and work in an integrated way. The Environment Act places the initiative not so much with the government, but with the environment. This also requires a proactive attitude from the actors in the living environment: citizens, businesses and social organizations. Even though there are no prescriptions as to how they should do this, local and regional governments are obliged to set up a participation process with all these actors. However, many people still need to acquire these skills. We naturally think in compartments, as that is also how we were trained and educated.

The Environment Act, therefore, requires a different role and method of working from the government. The role of the local and regional government shifts from director to a facilitator: 'serving' instead of 'managing', and that requires letting go of one's own ideas and plans and putting oneself in the shoes of others. Civil servants and administrators will no longer just make plans themselves, but also facilitate the plans of others. And no longer evaluate plans but stimulate initiatives. As is the case in the social domain, the cultural change required for this is the greatest challenge.

Distance Between the Municipality and Citizens

Commissioned by the city of Rotterdam, I conducted research in neighbourhoods into citizens' initiatives and how the city can best help these initiatives. Together with a couple of mischievous civil servants – we called ourselves significantly 'the Partisans' – I talked to citizens, companies, district managers, civil servants and administrators. Here I share with you some impressions as a rough sketch. First of all, there are many civil servants within the municipality of Rotterdam who work with heart and soul for and with the city, to make the city more beautiful, better and more fun. Nevertheless, the distance between the citizens and the municipality is even greater than I had thought beforehand. This shocked me, and I tried to understand it.

Even though there are big differences between the districts, there are quite a few district initiatives across the board. There are examples of successful initiatives. Thanks to the municipality, but also in spite of it. If I look at the generic factors that play a role in all the districts, I see that every district struggles with the municipality, and vice versa. The distance between the system world and the district world is huge, even greater than I had thought beforehand. The impermeable layer within the municipality is tough and impenetrable, and the Real Estate and Work & Income departments in particular have a notorious reputation. There are barriers within municipalities in the structure (partitions and clusters), in the culture (spreadsheet - and accountability culture) and in the method of working (bureaucratic and distant).

Looking at the district-specific factors, the DNA of a district also appears to determine the level of participation. In some districts, it is in the blood, and

(Continued)

(*Continued*)

history is steeped in citizens who act. In other districts, it is much less so. Of vital importance for participation are proactive leaders and connectors in a neighbourhood and committed social entrepreneurs. Cooperatives are often successful and a connecting factor. The district manager and the civil servants who get involved in the district can also be decisive.

Success factors for district initiatives are the stimulating role of the municipality through funding, the facilitating role through district managers and the participation of people in the district. Organizations that commit themselves to initiatives, such as a bank or supermarket, are also important driving forces. Especially important are the 'boundary spanners' in neighbourhoods, creative residents who know how to find their way in the unruly system world. Together, they form an ecosystem of proactive stakeholders. The strength and solidity of such an ecosystem is decisive for the success of district initiatives. A factor that could lead to failure is the tough, coagulated local council, as a result of which many initiatives fail. The budget system is also crippling for district initiatives. Residents are approached unnecessarily often by the municipality, and because many officials hardly ever visit the districts, they have no affinity with the initiatives there.

Agile Government

The conclusion is clear: the government must reinvent itself. The playing field is changing, the rules of the game are changing and so must the players. The rapid and substantial changes in the environment compel the government to reconsider its own role and approach. Not moving along with them is not an option, because then the government will lose support in society, and its identity and legitimacy will be called into question. The government should not see this as a threat but as an opportunity to recalibrate itself. Responding proactively to these far-reaching changes is sensible, and to some extent, it is happening, although there are large differences between municipalities, provinces, ministries and water boards. The government will have to look for new roles and ways of working that meet the demands of modern society. The role of the government may differ per domain and per transition and may vary from facilitating to directing, from protecting to activating.

In the social domain, the government mainly plays a facilitating role. However, more guidance is needed from the national government to adequately combat excesses within youth care in particular. In the spatial domain, the government plays different roles: currently, it still has a strong guiding and activating role, but in the future, under the influence of the new Environment Act, it will mainly be facilitating and stimulating. Frameworks (rules of play) are needed to prevent municipalities from ending up in a vacuum between the theory and practice of the law. And in the digital domain, the government's main role is to protect the citizen from data abuse and manipulation by data giants, through legislation and regulations. In the energy transition, on the other hand, the government has a strong directing role, both from the national government and at the provincial and municipal levels. Seen from a larger system perspective, a government is needed which can play different roles in different domains. This requires a transition within the organization, on the way to a government that is agile and works in an integrated way.

How wonderful would it be if the government were to take the lead in the major transitions that we are all part of? I can see my father's smiling face: 'One day you will understand why being a civil servant is a fine, honourable profession', he said. But the situation is not as he could have foreseen: not the civil servant as a guardian of the status quo, but as a driver of change.

Chapter 4

How Can You, as a Business, Survive the Next Crisis?

We are experiencing the greatest economic transition in a hundred and fifty years. The new economy is digital, sustainable and circular but, step by step, new forms are emerging, such as a maker economy, robotics and the sharing economy. Sometimes I think: just imagine being a company director in these turbulent times, in the middle of a deep crisis that comes on top of an already weak economy. It's not easy for a company to survive.

Disruption

The word of our time is 'disruption': of the economy, a sector, company or business model. This disruption of the economy and companies is caused by disruptive technologies and innovations, such as blockchain, digital platforms, Internet of things, 3D printers, artificial intelligence, quantum computing and nano -, neuro - and biotechnology. These are all developments that put pressure on the normal course of business and have far-reaching consequences for the business models of existing companies. Apart from blockchain and digital platforms, I will not go into detail about all these individual technologies and innovations here. All of them – there are and will be many more – disrupt the linear chain with many links between supply and demand.

In many sectors, from logistics and construction to food, there are still linear chains. There are dozens of parties between a container transport from Shanghai to Rotterdam: loaders, unloaders, drivers, port authorities, customs officers, banks, etc. And the construction chain is one long spaghetti string of parties who all want to add something to the chain: clients, architects, contractors, subcontractors, contractors and only then the client. There are far too many parties between supply and demand, between client and customer. That is really still the nineteenth century. Nowadays, things can be done much smarter, simpler, faster and cheaper thanks to disruptive technologies such as blockchain and digital platforms.

Blockchain is a digital ledger in which all transactions are stored. Not by a central organization as gatekeeper, but via the computers of all participants in the

Embracing Chaos, 57–80
Copyright © 2023 Jan Rotmans and Co-Writer Mischa Verheijden
Published under exclusive licence by Emerald Publishing Limited. Translation by Michael Gould.
The moral rights of the translator have been asserted. Copyright © 2021 Jan Rotmans en Mischa Verheijden. Original title Omarm de Chaos. First published in 2021 by De Geus, Amsterdam
doi:10.1108/978-1-83753-634-420231008

blockchain network. The blockchain is an open, safe and reliable data environment in which all parties involved share information with each other. This requires an open attitude and trust on the part of the parties involved, who are currently often still protecting their information because they believe it can give them a competitive edge. With blockchain, you give all parties involved access to your data and information. You give them the data key, as it were. Although many parties still find it scary, more and more companies are experimenting with it, such as for example container transport. At present, container transport between Shanghai and Rotterdam easily takes 40 days, of which the containers lie idle somewhere for an average of 14 days, waiting for the next link in the linear chain. Communication between the various parties involved still often takes place by telephone or e-mail. Sometimes, people do not even know where the containers are for days on end. In this way, valuable time is lost, and transport is unnecessarily expensive. Every hour that a ship is at the quay longer than necessary can easily cost an extra 50,000 euro to 100,000 euro, and thousands of ships enter the port of Rotterdam every year. Imagine your profit if you can speed this up. With blockchain, this is possible.

Companies like Uber and Airbnb are very disruptive because they do something revolutionary via digital platforms – that may sound grand, but it can just be an app on your mobile phone – they connect digital supply and demand directly with each other. All intermediate links fall out of the chain. Uber connects drivers to passengers, nothing more and nothing less. It couldn't be simpler, faster or cheaper, and that is how Uber has become the largest taxi company in the world. But what doesn't Uber have? Taxis! But then you don't need a big organization for that. The same goes for Airbnb, the world's largest real estate company, but what doesn't Airbnb have? Real estate. So, these disruptive companies mark the transition from possession to use.

I hear you sigh: is this a good development? What do these kinds of companies add? Isn't it unfair competition? These are all valid questions. Uber and Airbnb are hyper-capitalistic companies that are out to make as much profit as possible at the expense of nature and people. The way Uber treats its drivers is reprehensible, but protesting against Uber actually means turning your back on the future. The resistance is understandable and justified because in certain countries Uber breaks the law and abuses drivers. That calls for new laws and regulations and Uber must be punished. But if Uber continues to misbehave, it will soon be overtaken by disruptors who do behave morally, or public pressure will force them to behave properly. But, even if you force the Ubers and Airbnb's of this world to become decent companies, the business model remains the same and will endlessly multiply.

The digital direct interconnection of supply and demand will also have a disruptive effect in other sectors because all the superfluous links in the chain will disappear. You can already see them in the energy world: companies such as VandeBron (now taken over by Essent) link a farmer with a wind turbine directly to a customer, and in this way connect supply and demand directly with each other in a digital way. Direct and digital matching of supply and demand will thus become the starting point for companies in all sectors, and new services and business models will emerge. It's just a matter of time before there will be an Uber for construction. And an Uber for healthcare. And an Uber for education. And whether you like it or not, as a company you will have to relate to disruption. Otherwise, you will be overtaken left and right by all the Ubers of this world.

Transformative Companies

In daily practice, many companies struggle with this. Most of them only look at today, some at tomorrow, and only a few at the day after tomorrow. The delusion of the day reigns and the focus is on the ultra-short-term. The dominant behaviour is risk-averse and there is a basic fear of change. This is a battle of survival, and so many have survived the previous crisis by making drastic cuts and working more efficiently, but now they are faced with another crisis. As a rule, companies fall back into crisis management: cutting costs and reorganizing.

Since the covid crisis, I have been in contact with many companies, from small to large. Company managers were panicking and the chaos around them was enormous. The standard response: 'Jan, we have to survive. We are going to conduct a major reorganization and only then will we be able to make any real changes'. So, they paused to restore the old and postpone the new until later. I understand that and I am not condemning it. I am simply pointing out that this strategy does not lead to a structural improvement, because it is precisely the old that is a cause of the crisis and the new that can offer a way out. When the storm hits, you have to create space to really change. It takes courage, guts and leadership to move forward into the future and seize the opportunity of the crisis to accelerate change. Research shows that only 5%–10% of medium-sized and large companies are transformative, 15%–20% are proactive and the remaining 70%–80% are active or reactive. A transformative company is one that notices external signals and quickly translates them into new concepts and business models.[1]

Proactive companies are also outward-looking but have difficulty in translating external signals into new concepts and business models. The largest group, consisting of (re)active companies, mainly waits, tries something new every now and then or does nothing new at all. This group of waiting companies will not survive the transition. A transition is an evolutionary revolution, it is a Darwinian process of death or survival. In the tipping phase of the current transition, many of the wait-and-see companies are dying. It is therefore not the biggest and brightest, but the most agile and resilient companies that survive.

Manoeuvrability

The manoeuvrability of companies makes them likely to survive a transition. When are you agile as a company? When you are simply organized without much

---

[1] Loorbach, D., Rotmans, J., & Lijnis-Huffenreuter, R. (2014). Entrepreneurship in transition: business transitions as an innovative model for sustainable business.

overhead and bureaucracy. If you are a learning organization that systematically records what is learned and actively transfers that to people and projects. If you bring different disciplines together in a multidisciplinary project environment. If you work on the basis of trust, give employees responsibility and offer them room to develop. And if you understand your clients.

In my experience, many companies meet at most a few of these agility criteria, and it appears that top management often has a rosier image of this than the people on the work floor. In business sessions, I regularly experienced that management scored high on the agility criteria (3 or 4 out of 5), while the employees scored much lower (1 or 2 out of 5). Especially the aspects 'trust', 'learning organization' and 'understanding customers' received low scores in similar sessions. Especially the latter, understanding customers, sounds simpler than it is. It is not about market or consumer research; that is too coarse-grained and not meaningful, but about understanding the latent needs of customers. Steve Jobs never asked customers if they wanted to use an iPhone. Market research would probably show that there was no market for an iPhone because customers would say that they did not need one. In 1998, documentary maker Frans Bromet made a famous film in which he asked people whether they had or would use a mobile phone.

The answer was no. People had no need for a mobile phone and did not see any point in using one: 'I don't need it at all. I don't like the idea of being reachable at all times', a woman replied. A mother with a child on the back of a bicycle said, 'Suppose you're out cycling and then you get a call'. A man who is tinkering with his car said, 'If I get stranded somewhere, there will be a phone box or a farm with a farmer with a phone'. And a young man said, 'If they want to reach me, they can do that by post'.

Twenty-one years later, these people were asked again. They all have a mobile phone, and they all say they can't live without it. It's fascinating that more than 20 years ago they had ignored their own latent needs.

If a company wants to investigate the latent needs of its customers, it helps to employ social psychologists: people who understand people. At the car company Daimler, I once came into contact with social psychologists. I asked them what they did in a company that revolved around automotive engineering. They said they were doing research into the pros and cons of customers, from the past, present and future. I was surprised, but it was actually quite logical, and when I subsequently went to a large Dutch construction company and asked how many social psychologists they employed, the answer was: none. No need for one, they said, because they did regular market and consumer research to understand their customers.

Resilience

Being agile is necessary to survive a transition, but more is needed to survive a crisis. A company must be resilient in order to absorb the shocks of a crisis. When is a company resilient? If it works in a future-oriented way and is continually concerned with the future, among other things by exploring possible future paths through scenarios. This is how you also learn to deal with structural uncertainties, which cannot be reduced by more knowledge or technology, but which we must constantly consider.

The blind spots and black swans explained in the chapter crisis as opportunity are particularly interesting. These are the events with a small chance but a large impact. Covid-19 is such an event: we knew that there would be an outbreak of a pandemic, just not when or how, but we ignored and suppressed that knowledge. However, this can be crippling for companies because they are caught off guard every time. For example, Shell was confronted with negative oil prices, something that until recently was considered to be science fiction. Resilience is not about how big the chance is that it will happen, but whether you are prepared for it when it does. Due to increasing complexity and interconnectedness, companies have to prepare for more and more of these types of events that can lead to a crisis. By developing risk strategies based on structural uncertainty analyses, resilient companies try to anticipate crises. They dare to take risks. To be resilient and thus future-proof, it is also important that companies build up buffer capacity and do not just operate along the lines of efficiency. Nature doesn't do that either: it has the buffer capacity and diversity to absorb shocks. Only a few companies are resilient, because, as mentioned, the vast majority of companies focus on today and not tomorrow, let alone the day after tomorrow.

Even more exceptional are companies that are agile and resilient, and therefore survive several crises. These are companies that are consciously working on the future and are investing in business models that will only be profitable in 5 or 10 years' time. They see continuity and change not as a contradiction but as complementary to each other. On the one hand, they continue to do what they have always done and what they are good at. That is what I call the first or primary line, which is how you make money and add value. At the same time, from a future-oriented orientation, they invest in a second line or shadow line, in which they work on new earning models with new services and products for new customers. It is therefore emphatically an 'and and' story. In the initial phase, most of the budget goes to the existing line, and a relatively small group works on the new line with a modest budget. After all, you are investing in something with an uncertain outcome and with a lower return than usual. You cannot expect the same return from experiments with new products and services from the shadow line as from products and services from the primary line. Step by step, the budget, personnel and time shift from the primary line to the shadow line, and over a period of 10–20 years there can be a shift to new profit models. Because this shift costs money in the first place and does not produce an immediate return, it requires a great deal of courage, guts and leadership to resist the pressure from shareholders, for example, and to believe in your own vision.

Jeff Bezos, the founder and CEO of web shop Amazon, is a prime example of such a leader. In a famous letter to his shareholders in 1997 (!), he explains his vision and key business principles. The word 'customer' appears 25 times in the letter. In Bezos' eyes, everything revolved around the customer. 'Even if they don't realize it themselves yet, customers want something better, and your desire to satisfy them drives you to innovate in the interests of your customer', Bezos said. He saw the latent need of customers to buy products and goods over the internet. It saves them money and valuable time. But the Internet was still in its infancy at the time. He started a web shop that was user-friendly, open 365 days a year and 24 hours a day. In 1997, you could buy gift vouchers with a single click, and reviews, content, recommendations and drastically lower prices showed how important this customer focus was. It started with books, but soon expanded to a very wide range, from cheap cameras to children's toys.

It now contains more than 1 billion products. Bezos saw the internet as a tidal wave and was convinced that Amazon could become very big. He was very clear with his shareholders: If you expect quarterly business performance, don't invest. If you expect long-term business performance, then get involved. With Bezos, it is all about the long term and quick decision-making, and from that perspective, he has made different decisions and trade-offs than the competition. This is how Jeff Bezos built Amazon into an online shopping giant of unprecedented proportions, with a stock market value of around US$1,500 billion. The company profited enormously from the coronas crisis: consumers bought much more online, as a result of which sales exceeded US$100 billion, and profits rose to more than $8 billion. Important factors behind this success are the ultra-focus on the customer, extremely fast decision-making, a sceptical view of processes, the rapid embrace of external trends and always trying to set the bar as high as possible. If you think that Jeff Bezos is the big guru here, he was already very clear about that in 1997: 'The success of the past year [1997] is the product of a talented, smart, hard-working group, and I am immensely proud to be a part of this team'.

Yet in recent years, criticism of Amazon has been mounting. The internal work culture is said to be rock-hard, the working conditions poor and the salaries of employees low. Former employees even speak of exploitation. 'They care more about their robots than about their employees', said one of them. Under high pressure, Bezos did raise the minimum wage for his employees a few years ago. The company is also under fire for tax evasion. For example, Amazon's European branch would not have paid a single cent in corporate tax in Europe by 2020. This example shows that it is certainly not easy, is it? It is no coincidence that so many companies struggle to stay sharp, alert and focused. The easiest way is to keep doing what you are good at, but that's a dead end. They will survive, but the question is for how long. Their survival is more like a death struggle. The hardest road is the most challenging road. Fortunately, there are still examples of companies that are good at this. A multinational such as DSM is such an example and has already made several transitions. First the step from a petrochemical to a fine chemical company and later to a biochemical company, where, for example, high-quality products such as medicines are now made from biomass. This is always done strategically, in order to stay one step ahead of the global competition and even gain a lead, just like Amazon. Then the competition follows, and another step is needed. It is a fascinating and repetitive game. I count myself lucky. I am fortunate to have been directly and indirectly involved with companies that are or were in the eye of the hurricane. I will give you a number of examples of companies with which I have been directly or indirectly involved.

IKEA: From Sustainable to Circular

IKEA is a great example of an innovative company. It is an ironclad brand with a green image, even if that is not entirely justified: for example, they are not in the global Top 100 Sustainable Businesses. Because I was invited to give a lecture to the International Top 200 employees at IKEA, I delved into the company's background. From my preliminary research, I learned that they are doing quite well. In recent years, for example, they have consciously invested a great deal (around 1 billion euro) in sustainability. The furniture giant now has its own wind farms, there are solar panels on the roofs of all branches, local renewable energy is stored in batteries, half of the wood used comes from sustainable forestry, the shops are equipped with LED lighting and the restaurants serve sustainable food. All positive developments for the company, the environment and the world.

Why I still say that they are only doing 'nicely' is because they are mainly picking the relatively low-hanging fruit. The most difficult part of the transition is yet to come. If you look at the underlying structural developments in the world, IKEA is struggling with two fundamental problems. The first is the disposable culture: IKEA has an image of making simple and cheap furniture with a relatively short lifespan. This is at odds with the structural development in the undercurrent towards a circular economy, in which things last as long as possible. The second fundamental problem lies in the use of materials and raw materials. IKEA consumes around 16 million m³ of wood annually, 1% of annual global wood production. This does not even include the raw materials for paper and packaging. It is also striking that a relatively large amount of material, such as chipboard, plastic, metals and packaging material, cannot be reused or recycled. Barely 25% of the plastic used by IKEA is recycled.

The real transition challenge for IKEA is therefore not in the energy transition, but in the raw materials transition, i.e., how the company deals with raw materials. So, the challenge is not to become sustainable, but to become circular. The turnaround that this requires actually makes IKEA a different company with a different orientation and philosophy, with different products and a different business model. It is the transformation of a company that makes cheap disposable products in a smart, innovative way into a company that makes sustainable products that last a lifetime. Products will no longer be chairs, tables or cupboards, but a collection of reusable raw materials. IKEA thus becomes a raw material processor and raw material supplier, remains the owner of the raw materials as a producer and is therefore also responsible for their management.

In this way, the company is evolving into a circular business model: a customer borrows or rents a collection of raw materials in the form of a chair, table or cabinet and returns it after a period of time. In this way, what was previously regarded as waste becomes the raw material for new furniture.

The first steps in the transition described above have now been taken. The transition approach is based on the vision that IKEA wants to be fully circular in its use of wood, paper and plastic within 10 years. For example, the company has started renting or leasing furniture. These are pilot projects for specific target groups, such as students who can rent furniture for 2 years for 25 euro a month.

These trial projects – part of the shadow line – can be scaled up step by step to eventually become IKEA's primary line by 2030. This transition from selling to renting furniture is rooted in a broad societal shift that has been going on for some time: the shift from owning to using. Use is the future: renting, leasing, sharing or borrowing things is becoming the social norm. Ownership is also increasingly seen as ballast, with disadvantages such as maintenance. In the automotive world, use has been commonplace for some time: you don't need to own a car, you just want to use its functionality. We are now also seeing this emerging in other sectors. You don't have to own furniture; you just want to sit or lie down comfortably. And you can take it further: why should you buy lamps if you can also lease or rent them? After all, you don't want to own a lamp, you just want to make use of the function of lighting. In this way, almost everything can be offered as a service. Even maintenance, repairs, insurance and even project management can be provided as a service.

Rabobank: Forward to the Past?

The world in which banks operate is changing rapidly and violently due to systemic crises, long-term low-interest rates, digitalization, the rise of disruptive financial start-ups (fintech), crypto-currencies, changing customer requirements and sustainability. Back in 2016, I sketched this picture of a world in transition, which banks must relate to, for the CEOs of the four major Dutch banks: ABN AMRO, ING, Rabobank and SNS Bank. 'Are you prepared for this?' I asked the CEOs, adding somewhat provocatively that two of the four banks would no longer exist in 10 years' time. They uncomfortably turned on their chairs. All four said that they were working hard to anticipate these changes, that they were streamlining the organization, working together with fintech and that they were getting a better view of their customers. But none of them had a really clear answer to my question about how they were preparing for these disruptive changes. All four were convinced that they would not be among the two banks that did not survive.

It is clear that the survival of traditional banks is threatened if they do not adapt to their rapidly changing environment. In the in-between-period, it is adapt or die. Because banks are by nature cumbersome, bureaucratic, top-down organized and far from agile, let alone transformative, I am not so optimistic about the survival of traditional banks. Their distinctive character is simply insufficient. The primary functions of a bank are money creation, payments, lending and risk management, but these days these functions do not necessarily have to be performed by a bank. Moreover, digital platforms will soon be able to do this faster, more flexibly and more cheaply because they have far fewer overheads and do not own expensive buildings. There are already digital platforms where people can take out loans directly from investors, without the need for a bank.

The current generation of over-40s still has a certain trust in traditional banks, but with the rise of a new generation of young people, this will soon change. They are growing up with digital platforms and no longer have any ties to a bank as a brand. This is putting the identity of banks under severe pressure. For young people, they are something from an earlier era. Banking has evolved faster than banks themselves in recent years. The modern bank branch is a mobile phone. Whereas 10 years ago you still paid monthly with giro credit slips, you can now conduct financial transactions every minute of the day using your mobile phone. You don't need a bank anymore for financial transactions. The new generation of customers wants to be facilitated more and more. Convenience and personal contact are paramount, but that is precisely what banks are not good at or are no longer good at. Contrary to the trend in other sectors, where you see more and more intermediaries disappear due to the rise of digital platforms, there are increasing numbers of intermediaries active between the bank and the customer who process the information and data for banks so that they can advise their customers better. But that is an outdated model. It is increasingly about direct contact with customers, with as few intermediaries as possible.

Just think of the disruptive effect of the Ubers and Airbnb's I wrote about at the beginning of this chapter. This disruption is also occurring in the banking world. Instead of plunging into digital products as well, banks would be better off focusing on the full range of services around digital products. As a result, banks become open platforms where customers can do business with providers of financial products and with each other. The distinctive character of banks is then determined by the value they add for customers: convenience, service and experience. To do that well, however, banks must get to know their customers better. And although the four CEOs claim that they are getting a better view of their customers, I know from my own experience that this is not the case at all.

I received an e-mail from Rabobank that said: 'Dear Sir/Madam, we regularly organize meetings about the transition to a sustainable economy. You might find it interesting ...'. I have been doing that for more than 30 years! People at the bank really have no idea who I am and what I do. Shortly afterwards, I received another e-mail, which said: 'In order to better organize our services and to serve you even better, we have decided to close our office in your neighbourhood. We are considering a pop-up branch to serve you even better'. But that local Rabobank office around the corner was important to me for the personal contact with the bank. It illustrates how far Rabobank has drifted from its core, from the customers for whom they work. And it was precisely Rabobank that was founded as a cooperative in the nineteenth century that was remarkably close to its clients. In essence, there was a relationship of trust and confidence between the bank and the client. The bank lent money (that alone sounds different from 'loans provided') to farmers and entrepreneurs, who were often personally guided to spend the borrowed money as wisely as possible.

How painful it is that Rabobank has cut its cooperative roots. Partly because of those roots, I myself am an account holder and customer at Rabobank. I see that in Rotterdam they are still involved in many community initiatives, and I think that is a good thing. After all, there are not that many banks that are active at the district and neighbourhood level. And Rabobank invests relatively quite a lot in sustainability, although there is still room for improvement there. Overall, that part of the picture is positive. At the same time, I see Rabobank struggling with its identity. I have regularly shared my transition knowledge with staff. They recognize that a transition within the bank is necessary and, although they believe that steps are being taken in that direction, they indicate that a culture change has yet to really get off the ground. And as ex-CEO Wiebe Draijer explained, they are streamlining the organization, aiming for greater efficiency and have opted for a regional organizational model. Local banks, which often operated as independent franchises, have largely disappeared. More than 400 local branches have closed in the past decade and more than 15,000 jobs have been cut.

So, they have not really started thinking and working differently. The prevailing culture, with fairly dominant leaders at the top, is still closed, risk-averse, subservient to superiors and the bank. The organizational structure is still complex, hierarchical, formalized and legalized, and the way of working is procedural and strongly focused on short-term profit maximization. Rabobank wants to become an ordinary commercial bank, with a focus on agriculture and small and medium-sized enterprises. The big question is whether the considerably slimmed-down and more centrally managed Rabobank will be able to restore contact and loyalty with local farmers and entrepreneurs. 'Forward to the past'* would be a good motto for the bank: going back to the essence in a modern and innovative way, putting the customer first. That requires a change in culture and a different kind of organization, in which the customer really is the focal point. In order to get to know and understand that customer better, social-psychological knowledge is particularly important, but hardly any social psychologists work at Rabobank. So, there is still a long way to go, also for the other three major Dutch banks. For the time being, all four still exist. But for how long?

ABP: Sustainable Leadership in Demand

Pension funds are struggling in these uncertain times. They have been struggling with their funding levels since the 2008 financial crisis. To give pension funds room to improve their financial situation, the minimum required coverage ratio has been temporarily lowered to 90%. In the near future, this bar will be raised to 100% again. Now that pension funds have again lost tens of billions of euros as a result of the covid crisis, the coverage ratio has fallen to between 82% and 88%, which means that they will have to cut pension benefits. This precarious financial situation is partly due to the artificially low-interest rate, but mainly to the investment choices made by pension funds, even though they have to meet increased investment requirements. For example, Dutch pension funds are legally obliged to take three non-financial factors into account in their investment decisions. They must consider the possible consequences of their investment decisions for people, the environment and the surroundings. They are not allowed to invest in the tobacco industry, are not allowed to invest in companies that do not respect human rights and are not allowed to invest in companies that do not respect human rights and not in companies that damage the environment. Research shows that pension funds are struggling with these obligations. Only one in four pension funds has investment principles for responsible investment, and less than half discuss them with their participants. The impact of the investment portfolio is also still not sufficiently measured: yes in terms of increasing amounts of CO_2 emissions, but hardly for the impact on people and the immediate environment.

---

*'Forward to the past' is a quote from farmer Paul Bos.

You also notice from the language used that pension funds still have a long way to go. They still talk about 'socially responsible investing', a term from the last century. Nowadays, impact, and especially positive impact, is a common concept: as a company or investment fund, you have to be able to show what your positive impact is on people, on the environment and on the surroundings.

Positive Impact

In the new economy, companies will increasingly be judged on whether they have a positive impact: on their employees, on their surroundings and on the environment. By definition, a company extracts value from its surroundings, such as raw materials, energy and knowledge. A company in balance also adds value to its environment and provides energy, raw materials and knowledge in return. But it goes further than that. Companies are increasingly being asked to contribute to the great social challenges that we face.

More and more companies are therefore creating a positive impact. This is a completely different starting point than corporate social responsibility or sustainable business, where compensation is given for damage that was caused in the first place. This idea of compensation is now outdated, and direct positive impact is now the goal. For example, Tesla does not so much want to electrify the car industry, but to make a positive contribution to solving the global energy problem.

That is why Tesla is investing in integrated solutions with solar roofs, home batteries and electric cars that together can form a whole. Of course, there is still a lot to be said about Tesla and it is still far from being a fully sustainable company. However, the philosophy is clear: they act consistently – even in difficult times – and they have created a breakthrough in the automobile industry with their pioneering technology. In this way, Tesla is setting the tone for other companies that also want to become 'the Tesla' of their sector. For the time being, these are still exceptions and there is still a long way to go, especially for multinationals (large companies), which are increasingly coming under fire.

Impact has different dimensions. I distinguish ecological impact (environment, climate), social impact (welfare, health), economic impact (prosperity, employment) and business impact (care for employees). Unfortunately, it has not yet been clearly defined what exactly this positive impact is and how it can be measured. The advantage is that companies can adopt a broad approach, the disadvantage is that greenwashing is lurking, and companies can keep up appearances, but in the meantime do not really work in an impact-oriented way.

More and more companies are taking the United Nations Sustainable Development Goals as their starting point. These are 17 goals that range in the broadest sense from poverty and equality to climate and water. These goals are abstract and vague, not unambiguous and not quantitative. Nor are they binding. I, therefore, consider these sustainable goals to be primarily a moral compass on which a company can base its course. But in order to make the sustainable objectives as hard and concrete as possible, they must be translated into the specific context of a company. A number of companies are actively working on this. Examples of multinationals with a positive impact are DSM, Philips, Unilever and IKEA.

Social pressure on pension funds is noticeably increasing. Public awareness is growing, and participants and shareholders are increasingly vocal. While students protest against fossil investments, scientists intervene in public opinion to speed up the switch to sustainable investments. This is reinforced by the banks, which point out the financial risks of fossil investments. Klaas Knot, president of the Netherland's Central Bank, already warned in 2016 in a report entitled *Time for Transition* of a 'carbon bubble', the depreciation of investments in fossil-fuel companies under the pressure of stricter climate policies.

That warning applies particularly to pension funds because, with an average of 12.5% of their assets, of which about 5.4% is invested directly in fossil energy and the rest indirectly in chemicals and greenhouse horticulture, they face the greatest risk. Banks invest around 10% in fossil fuels and insurers around 4.5%. The social and political pressure on investment funds will increase enormously in the years ahead; there is no escaping this. But the pension funds do not seem to have any idea of what is in store for them. In recent years, I have been invited several times by pension funds such as ABP, PGGM and PFZW to give a talk. They all ask the same question: what should we invest in? A good question that is not so easy to answer. I point out the importance of investing in ecological, social and economic sustainability. Research also shows that investing in sustainability pays off. It is true that the return advantage of less than 0.5% is still small, but this advantage is expected to increase. Those who invest in sustainability are therefore more resilient to disruption.

A Myth Dispelled

An NN IP survey among 15,000 listed companies shows that 3,000 companies have a positive impact. The main focus was on reducing CO_2 emissions, the circular economy and caring for employees. The companies with a positive impact have been shown to generate higher turnover, grow faster, have lower capital costs and have a higher return on investment. This dispels the myth that social return comes at the expense of financial targets.

Can Shell Reinvent Itself?

Shell is in a difficult position. It is under increasing social, political and economic pressure to become more sustainable. The social pressure is enormous if only reflected by the dozens of lawsuits from citizens, civil society organizations and governments against Shell. The pressure has now been maximized by the ruling of the Dutch court in the climate case against Shell. The judge obliges Shell to reduce its CO_2 emissions by 45% by 2030 compared to 2019. There is also great political pressure on Shell to comply with the climate agreement and take bigger steps to reduce CO_2 emissions more quickly. Shell was one of the most popular employers among young students for a long time but, because of its negative image, many young people no longer want to work there. In the past, you could proudly say at a party that you worked for Shell, but nowadays you have some explaining to do.

And with volatile oil markets and diminishing returns, even shareholders are increasingly grumbling. The activist green shareholders of *Follow This*, under the inspiring leadership of Mark van Baal, are gaining influence and trying to force Shell to adopt a greener strategy that complies with the climate agreement concluded in Paris in 2015. At the last shareholders meeting, almost a third of the shareholders supported *Follow This*'s climate resolution.

Shell has made numerous mistakes and misjudgements in recent decades. A series of scandals have been linked to the company, including paying too little tax, pollution in Nigeria, oil drilling at the North Pole and earthquakes in Groningen as a result of gas extraction. Apart from these scandals, perhaps the most important mistake made by Shell was the decision in 2009 to stop investing in solar and wind power because of disappointing returns. This was done, not unimportantly, at the intercession of the then president of Shell International, Jeroen van de Veer, who once spoke the historic words: 'The Stone Age did not come to an end because there were too few stones, but because better alternatives emerged'. The decision to stop investing in solar and wind power is hard to understand because it was taken at a time when experts were predicting a golden future for renewable energy.

It is also hard to understand because Shell in particular was once particularly good at developing scenarios and projections for the future. Approximately 30 years ago, I was approached by Shell to help develop information material about climate change for use in secondary schools. This resulted in a clear brochure about the causes of and solutions to the climate problem. I thought it was courageous of Shell to objectify the complex discussion about climate change at a time when it was not yet really on the scientific and political agenda. When I was working for the UN climate panel (the Intergovernmental Panel on Climate Change) a few years later, I worked on climate scenarios with Shell's scenario department under the leadership of Ged Davis. I was impressed by the quality of the young people and the imaginative scenarios they developed: real transition scenarios aimed at radical change, with tipping points and discontinuities, in which sustainable energy was given a primary role in the future. This was highly unusual at the time, but Shell was ahead of its time in terms of scenario thinking.

Then, things went wrong because Shell adopted a more conservative course and became less innovative. I strongly criticized this and, to their great annoyance, also started campaigning against the unsustainable course they were following. Shell even started a Twitter account, where everything I claimed as a scientist was questioned. After fierce protest from Twitter followers, that account was closed down again. I was also unpleasantly surprised when Rein Willems, who was the president of Shell Netherlands from 2003 to 2007, became involved in the energy transition project that I supervised and that was commissioned by the Ministry of Economic Affairs and the Ministry of Housing, Spatial Planning and the Environment. His appointment as chair of the Energy Transition Task Force also delivered the death blow to the project. He literally said to me: 'Jan, you mustn't go too fast, because that's not in the interest of Shell nor in the interest of the Netherlands'. A few years later, at the start of a new government in October 2010, Bernard Wientjes, chair of the largest employers' organization,

VNO-NCW, advised the government to stop the energy transition project because, in their view, it was going too fast and was too threatening to the business community, especially to multinationals. And so it happened, and within a few weeks the successful project, in which a considerable amount of money had been invested and which had already produced a number of transition paths and hundreds of experiments involving thousands of people, was finished.

In that same year, I predicted that Shell would no longer have a right to exist if it did not pursue a sustainable course. There was a lot of laughter about this at the time, but the laughter has since died down. The oil giant was hit hard by the covid crisis and the ensuing oil crisis, in which the company was confronted with what was thought to be an impossible situation: a negative oil price. Yes, really: you got money if you acquired oil. Thus, during the covid crisis, 60% of the company's market value evaporated and a Shell share fell below 10 euro and – for the first time since the Second World War – the company reduced its dividend. Investors are increasingly critical of Shell. 'Just imagine having inherited a real estate portfolio from your grandfather that includes, say, Shell, ING and Unibail-Rodamco. That gives you sleepless nights', says a stock market expert. In addition, the company is conducting a major reorganization, called Reshape, in which 9,000 of its 83,000 employees worldwide will lose their jobs.

Shell itself now admits that it has made errors in judgement and is turning the tide. It is aware of the finite nature of the fossil fuel revenue model. According to the oil giant, oil will never be what it was, and 2019 was the year in which Shell's oil production reached its peak. Slowly but surely, the company is saying goodbye to oil and is divesting eight of its fourteen oil refineries (unfortunately not the ones in Rotterdam and Moerdijk). Shell now invests 10% of net profits in sustainable energy and plans to invest 25% of the US$20 billion in sustainable energy each year until 2025. This means that until 2025, US$5 billion a year will be spent on solar and wind energy, green hydrogen and biofuels. But of course, the market for renewable energy has not stood still since 2009, and competition is fierce. For the time being, therefore, 90% of the investments are still in oil and gas.

Because of all the mistakes and misjudgements made in the past, Shell is now in trouble. The company is forced to react too late instead of anticipating. But it is not only about a different portfolio in a technical sense; it also requires a change of culture and a different type of organization that is agile and resilient. If Shell wants to be fossil-fuel-free in 25 years' time, that means investing roughly 50% in renewable energy by 2030, 80% by 2040 and 100% by 2045. And, at the same time, it needs to reduce its investments in oil and gas: from 50% in 2030 to 20% in 2040 and 0% in 2045. This transition path is not impossible, but it will take a lot of time, and the question is whether this time is available. In fact, Shell has to reinvent itself, which is difficult for a company that is not used to that. It requires Shell to break down the old DNA of oil and gas and build up a new DNA of sun, wind, biofuels and green hydrogen in one generation, about 25 years. This is not only a huge technological challenge but also an organizational and mental one. It is an impressive leap of scale. It requires an agile and resilient organization (less hierarchy, less bureaucracy and less introspection) and a culture focused on change, taking and accepting risks and developing leadership. This also requires people with other competencies. Not just engineers and managers, but also people such as social psychologists, philosophers, designers, artists and other creative people with the power of imagination. More attention should be paid to social rather than technological innovation, and to the personal transition of employees in order to develop learning skills and stimulate proactive action.

Two years ago, Marjan van Loon, ex-president of Shell Nederland, asked me to help think about Shell's future. She wanted to open the windows and doors to fresh thinkers and lateral thinkers. She agreed to my proposal to start a transition process with a number of frontrunners within the company. There was some nervousness within Shell about this unfamiliar path with an activist professor who had been so critical of them. I also felt this nervousness: could I justify doing something with the company that was the big enemy in the eyes of my supporters? But this is the time when the big players have to move. A hundred of the world's most polluting companies produce 71% of CO_2 emissions. Twenty of them are responsible for 33% of those emissions, and Shell is in the top 10: after Saudi Aramco, Chevron, Gazprom, ExxonMobil, National Iranian Oil and BP, Shell occupies the seventh position. We must put maximum pressure on all these large companies directly and indirectly, through our consumption patterns, with lawsuits and by putting political and social pressure on them. But we must also help them turnaround from within.

That is why, against the advice of some people around me, I started it anyway (my life motto, remember?). I asked Yolanda Eijgenstein to help me. Together we put together a small team to guide a transition process with 25 leaders within Shell Netherlands. A varied group of men and women, seniors and juniors from different parts of the company. After intensive intake interviews with the participants, a kick-off session was held in Rotterdam for the directors, management and invited guests. In six intensive sessions, we went through the transition steering cycle: from problem analysis to transition assignment and from transition experiments to transition agenda. This process stirred up a lot of emotions, and in the sessions (which often lasted 6 hours) emotions often ran high. Each session started with a stimulating and penetrating story from me, followed by interactive sessions in small groups, which we concluded in plenary. This touched the participants, also because I stimulated and challenged them. But it also touched me because I felt increasingly connected with these people. Fine people, who fought with heart and soul within Shell for a more sustainable company, and who also tried to live up to this. I was impressed.

Afterwards, the participants indicated that they had started thinking differently about the transition task and its urgency. They came up with a range of innovative ideas and solutions in the areas of technology, organization and culture. This resulted in a transition agenda for the coming years. However, the exciting and beautiful journey was rudely interrupted by corona, which put Shell in a crisis. The company is now in the middle of a deep reorganization that for the time being is taking up all of its time and energy. Hopefully, there will be a continuation of the process we started, because it has changed a lot for me too, together with this group of people. I have noticed that the people who work there are not really motivated and stimulated to 'bash' Shell. They have become almost immune to it, hardened after years of scorn and ridicule. Although I can assure you that it still affects them personally, more than they would sometimes like to admit.

What does motivate and stimulate these people is to show understanding, to have an eye for beautiful innovative things that happen and that offer a perspective for the future. I feel connected to these courageous people who are fighting for a more sustainable Shell and a better world and try to live accordingly. Although they still face all kinds of barriers and resistances, this group of frontrunners, the ambassadors of innovation within Shell, are relentlessly pursuing their missionary work, as demonstrated by the *Future Energy Lions*. And with success: the group that really wants things to be different is growing fast, and only a few are still in denial. I am therefore convinced that, if there is one oil giant that can make the transition to a sustainable energy company, it is Shell. It is still possible. Time is running out, but the company can still bring the almost impossible task it faces to a successful conclusion if it pulls out all the stops and dares to opt for radical change. This now seems to have been set in motion. The knowledge, the expertise, the network, the lobbying power and the financial capacity are there, but the hardest part is still to come: the cultural change. The key question then is: is there enough guts, courage and leadership within Shell?

Rising Resentment

The mood among the general public has changed in the last decade. There has been a growing distaste for large companies and the market mentality that has gone too far. Large companies seem to have become detached from society, are plagued by tax scandals (dividend tax, profit tax, energy tax) and do not contribute sufficiently to solving major social issues such as inequality, energy transition, climate change and the destruction of nature. The relationship between politicians and multinationals is chilled, but also between the general public and multinationals.

This resentment was reinforced by the covid crisis. The government had to solve this crisis and large companies were knocking on its door *en masse* for support. In good times, however, the big companies themselves want as little government intervention as possible and only distribute the profits among shareholders. In short, they privatize profits and socialize losses. This is to the great annoyance of more and more people who see that when it really comes down to it, the big companies do not solve their problems but rather choose to maximize profits. This touches on the dark side of globalization and neoliberalism. Citizens feel the coldness of the market, and that is not a pleasant feeling. At the same time, they feel the bureaucracy of the government, which is not a pleasant feeling either. Citizens are, as it were, caught between the coldness of the market and the bureaucracy of the government. They experience the worst of both worlds. This pleads for a new balance between citizens, market and government. We cannot go back to the old days, to the all-determining government, nor can we do without the market, but both must reinvent themselves.

This may mark the end of neoliberalism with its exclusive focus on growth, profit, efficiency and effectiveness. These are all cold, masculine values. New, feminine values are needed, such as trust, cooperation, self-reliance, coordination, quality and freedom of choice. These are also universal values that will become important in the new society and economy.

KLM: Will the Pride of the Netherlands Survive?

The covid crisis has inflicted deep wounds on tourism and has also hit aviation hard. The minuscule virus even grounded all the mighty KLM planes for a while, something that was never thought possible. It has saddled KLM with a gigantic debt. Thanks to 5 billion euro in government support, the company is still able to survive, but this support cannot be unconditional. Multinationals that want to qualify for this support will have to meet a number of requirements. Companies must contribute to a sustainable economy, demonstrate social justice and contribute their fair share when it comes to paying taxes.

There is still some sympathy, which I share, for a Dutch flagship such as KLM, which is part of our national DNA. The company is in our blood, we were always proud of it. I don't know how it is for you, but when I see the KLM flight attendants walking around in their blue suits, it makes me happy. It takes me back to the hangars in Amsterdam where Anthony Fokker built aircraft and Albert Plesman founded KLM in 1919. But, once the pride of the Netherlands, today the company is increasingly a symbol of the old economy, and I sometimes wonder aloud whether KLM – and airlines in general – still has a future. I wonder whether we should keep a symbol of the old economy going. And yet I have become such a strategist that I say: 'Let's try to save KLM!' You can get angry and walk away, or file another lawsuit, but if you want to have a chance, you have to help them transform from the inside out. Now if it were a bank, I would say 'let it go'. We already bailed out the banks in 2008, and they didn't learn much from it. We won't do that a second time. But for KLM, it is the first time they have asked for state support on this scale, and I think it is legitimate to offer them that support under certain conditions.

The covid crisis had already far-reaching consequences for our mobility behaviour and might influence our flight behaviour permanently. Where it used to be *bon ton* to fly back and forth to New York for a weekend, that seems to be a thing of the past. We now look at it with a certain embarrassment. It is not for nothing that the word 'flight shame' has become a new word in our vocabulary. Our thinking about mobility will change. We will travel increasingly online, for example by climbing a mountain via Virtual Reality or visiting a museum online, and we will travel less for the sake of travelling. Business trips will also be (largely) replaced by online meetings. KLM must relate to this, and I have had discussions about this with their transformation manager, among others.

However, the transition path that I proposed did not have sufficient support at the top of KLM. In the coming years, their focus will be on reorganization, with thousands of people being given notice. As much as possible through natural wastage, but partly through forced dismissal. Perfectly understandable, this is causing a great deal of unrest and anxiety among employees about their future. And yet now is the time to act and not only to reorganize but also to transform into an agile, resilient and future-proof company. In its current form, KLM is not agile and resilient, and therefore it's not future-proof. The adage is to get as many people as possible from A to B in as small a space as possible at the lowest possible price. That is a kind of bio-industry because, in fact, you are transporting people like cattle. When I fly, I can't move my legs, I hardly get anything to eat, and I don't have a choice in what I want to eat. Then, at the end of the flight, a flight attendant says that she hopes I had a pleasant flight. If you want to keep that up, then you don't have a right to exist anymore. And if you don't have a plan B, you're not going to make it.

Like with Shell, these times call for KLM to reinvent itself with a different orientation and philosophy, with different services and a different earnings model. Understanding that reorganization and transformation can go hand in hand is a characteristic of leadership. That leadership is lacking, and the longer KLM waits to transform, the harder it will be to survive. And it will be clear to you from reading this book that the covid crisis will not be the last. Ever longer production chains, in which efficiency is paramount and insufficient buffer capacity has been built up, have made our economic system extremely vulnerable to shocks. When the next crisis comes, the companies that have not transformed themselves by becoming agile, resilient and future-proof will again be on the drip. The future of KLM is therefore extremely uncertain.

Transition Compass for Organizations

By now it must have become clear to you that the current government and many companies and organizations are not future-proof, because they lack agility and resilience. They are too cumbersome, too bureaucratic, too hierarchical, engage in too little learning, too much based on distrust, and they are insufficiently concerned with the future in order to respond to the demands of modern society and economy. As a result, they also lack the resilience to cope with crises. Governments and companies, therefore, have to reinvent themselves. This means that they have to think (culture), organize (structure) and implement (practice, method) differently. Thinking differently is about changing values and ideas that are dominant and often fixed. Organizing differently is about changing attitudes and behaviour. It is about ingrained patterns and routines. Doing things differently is about changing procedures and rules.

Of these three, changing the culture is the most difficult. After all, you cannot force people to think differently. In fact, the more you try to force them, the greater the resistance. But you can give people insights, on the basis of which they can start thinking differently themselves, from the inside. Suppose you want to change something essential in your organization, where do you start and how? The latter is probably the question I get asked most often, and I don't have the answer. There is no recipe or blueprint for a transition within an organization. It's a quest, and the process will be different in every organization. What I do have are insights from the transition field that can serve as a kind of compass for that quest.

Learn From Each Other

Before you start on a transition within an organization, it is wise to first learn from others. This sounds logical, but unfortunately, it happens far too little. There is a tendency within organizations to reinvent the wheel. For example, municipalities are struggling with the transition in the social and spatial domain. As I indicated earlier, this transition has far-reaching consequences for the organization. It is therefore sensible to start with radical experiments and then to scale them up. The Netherlands is now teeming with interesting experiments, and there are a few to be found in every municipality.

That is why I keep advising council members and officials to take a tour of successful and less successful experiments. I even offer to come along and make a road map of instructive experiments. Not a single municipality has accepted this offer. It seems as if every municipality wants to reinvent the wheel itself, while there is a lot to be learnt from experiments, and most of all from the experiments that fail. Whoever does that has already won half of the transition process. You can learn so much from other people's experiments and use those learning experiences in your own context. That is why you should also take along translators and connectors on your tour: people who can translate learning experiences into their own context and people who can connect contexts with each other.

This also applies to the world of business. There too, there is a wealth of knowledge available about internal transitions within the organization. When I follow such a course with a company, I bring in guest speakers from other companies with similar experiences. And then it strikes me time and again how little is known about the transition experiences of other companies, and how little is done with that knowledge. This is despite the fact that knowledge is shared between companies in other fields, for example when it comes to making the production process more sustainable, building management, the vehicle fleet, etc. This is then about content. Knowledge about change is also content, but it is often not seen in that way.

Don't Take Everyone Along at the Same Pace

I often attend when the management of a company announces a change of course and they go 'in transition'. Then there are hundreds of people in the room who react enthusiastically and openly support the change as a matter of course. The management thinks that there is broad support, but nothing is further from the truth. People are cognitively dissonant and say that they want to change and will participate, but in reality, there is an awful lot of resistance, and they don't do it. It is therefore important, first of all, to realize that as soon as an organization really wants to transform, a lot of people will become restless and afraid. Many people associate big changes with threats. They fear going backwards: loss of work, income, status, etc. because the change is a threat to the organization. This in itself is not so strange, because from an evolutionary point of view we naturally strive for peace and stability. At the same time, there is always a small group of people who long for real change, who see opportunities and feel that it can be better for the organization and for themselves.

In a transformation process, you have to deal with fear and unrest on the one hand, and with desire and hope on the other. Both fear and hope are important and deserve attention. You can roughly divide the organization into four groups:

(1) A small group, at most 10%, who can and really want to change.
(2) A group of, say, 25% who want to change but cannot.
(3) A group of also about 25% who can but do not want to change.
(4) And a large group, about 40%, who neither want to nor can change.

These figures are rough estimates and can vary greatly from one organization to another, but the essence is that the vast majority of people within a company do not want to change and/or are unable to change*. Only a small group has the guts and the capacity to really change. A large group does not but merely pretend to want to change. I call these people 'change pretenders'. They pretend to be enthusiastic, but in reality, they are dragging their heels. Most enthusiastic people clap enthusiastically for a transition programme, but then come home and think: 'I'm not taking part. I now have a nice job or run a nice department, and it will probably be at the expense of my job or department'. This is a very natural reaction of a large group of people, namely from cognitive dissonance to say 'yes', but to act 'no'. It makes no sense to take the most reluctant directly into a transition process. That is when maximum resistance arises. It makes more sense to start with the small group who are open to it.

Because an organization in transition breaks down into different parts, it makes little sense to bring everyone into the transition process at the same pace and in the same way. This insight from transition science leads to an unusual approach: do not start with a broad base of support, but with a narrow and deep base of support. This is counterintuitive and goes against the Dutch polder culture, which is geared towards a broad consensus. But if you do that, you bring all the resistance to the table and the process gets bogged down. In the beginning, it seems to go fast, but as soon as it becomes difficult and difficult choices have to be made, it often bleeds to death. In a radical change process, therefore, choose an evolutionary approach and do some organic support development, making it broader within the organization step by step.

Start with a small transition team, a group of 10 to 15 frontrunners and connectors. Give these people time and space and develop with them a shared perspective on the future. Start with them the first experiments in working on a cultural change. Then involve a larger group of people who are open to change, but do not yet know how to change. In this way, broaden the transition team and increase the number of experiments step by step. Only at the end – when there is no way back – involve the group of people who are not open to change. Incidentally, this group is shrinking and chooses eggs for its money or leaves.

It can also be effective to involve supporters from outside your organization. People who look at the organization with fresh eyes and who can exert pressure. After all, successful organizational transitions are often the result of pressure from within and from outside. I myself am regularly asked to put pressure on organizations, for example, to become more sustainable more quickly. Keep

---

*Loorbach, D., Rotmans, J., & Lijnis-Huffenreuter, R. (2014). Entrepreneurship in transition: business transitions as an innovative model for sustainable entrepreneurship.

informing and updating everyone in the organization about the process and the approach, so that no unnecessary unrest is caused. This will prevent distrust or secrecy from emerging, which will only increase resistance. Transparency is important in a transition because it creates a certain peace in the midst of the turmoil.

Ratio Is Just as Important as Intuition

People often follow their feelings, and that is necessary, but not sufficient for a transition. It also comes down to playing chess on different chessboards. Strategy is just as important as feelings. When it comes to strategic decisions, our feelings often fail us, according to research by Daniel Kahneman and others. He shows that we have two thinking systems: an intuitive system for fast thinking, and a conscious system for slow and logical thinking. The intuitive system is dominant and dominates the logical system, even in complex issues, which can mislead us and lead to wrong decisions. Thinking through complex issues thoroughly and at length is a prerequisite for reaching the right decisions. Implementing a substantial change within an organization is like playing chess on three chessboards simultaneously: the chessboard of your environment, that of your organization and that of yourself. Thinking and acting from the outside in and from the inside out. But reason alone is not enough. Feeling is also important. That is why I call it intuitive chess.

It works as follows. Suppose you want to change something substantially on the basis of a certain goal, on the basis of your mission. Then you start an intervention to set the change in motion. Try to estimate in advance what kind of resistance you will evoke and where it will come from. It is also important to organize your own backing. If something goes wrong, you will be covered by someone in the organization, preferably a manager. It is important not to do it alone, but to look for allies, people with complementary qualities. Then analyze the potential effect of the next intervention and create the time and space for it. Start with the next intervention and analyze what it does to the environment. What changes, what moves, what dynamics arise, where is the support and where is the resistance? Then reflect on your own feelings. If it no longer feels right, for example, because you have had to make concessions or because it releases too much tension within yourself, do not hesitate to take a step back. Standstill also creates movement.

It can help to zoom out and look at yourself and your surroundings from a broader perspective. If it does feel right and the intervention has succeeded, take time to celebrate. Many changemakers wants to do things too quickly and do not give enough thought to their successes, however small. Learn from the interventions for the next steps and try to increase the support a little at a time. Find supporters from outside and inside and share the results with others. Then think carefully about the next intervention and start it, and so on. In short, this is chess by feel, a form of organic steering. Two steps forward, standing still or a step back, then another step forward, constantly looking outwards and inwards. That is what I try to do every day.

Take Your Time and Don't Be Rushed

A transition is an evolutionary revolution, a step-by-step change with a radical outcome in the end. A cultural change is an enormous challenge for an organization and requires courage and leadership. It means thinking big, acting small, starting from a vision and taking targeted action with a strategy of smart interventions. Take your time and create space. Creating peace, time and space amidst the turmoil of the organization is a continuous process, which you have to fight for constantly. Because, before you know it, the time and space will be clogged up again by the issues of the day.

Don't be afraid to say no. Change agents in particular need this. Change accompanists tend to get bogged down in their mission and do not say no easily. They would rather say yes and do everything in their power to achieve their goal. This is often counterproductive. Be aware that change can also come about from a standstill. A truly fundamental process of change is in any case a long-term process. Wanting too much too soon only increases resistance. All in all, you need about 10 years for an evolutionary change process. That sounds longer than it is because we are talking about a cultural and organizational change, a radical and intense process in which the trick is to maintain a certain calm in an already restless and chaotic time.

Create Mental and Organizational Space

Within organizations, there is often little room for radical experimentation, because performance requirements are invariably assessed within the planning and control cycle. That is at odds with the freedom that radical experimentation needs. It is not about working more efficiently, more cheaply or smarter, but about working and thinking in a fundamentally different way. This entails the risk that experiments may also fail. If people do not feel free, they cannot think and act differently. This means that you shouldn't judge people immediately if something fails or goes wrong. What's more, it's even a good thing if some of the experiments fail, because that's how we learn the most. And that is exactly what these experiments are for: searching and learning.

Organizational space is also needed so that experiments can withdraw from the compulsion of control and management and people are not forced into a straitjacket of deadlines and performance requirements. Radical experiments thrive best in relative seclusion, as part of a shadow track that runs parallel to the primary track. They do not damage the primary process, the first line, and provide a certain peace and visibility. They bring the future closer and provide insight into what is to come without immediately posing a threat. A much-heard objection is that the primary track requires continuous production and does not lend itself to experimentation, but one does not have to come at the expense of the other. It is an 'and and' story. The trick is to put something alongside the primary line where you can experiment to your heart's content. Step by step, you try to scale up successful experiments and transfer them to the primary line. In this way, more and more people participate in the change. This is the organic development of support.

All too often, one experiment after another is piled up, but experimentation is not a goal in itself. That is emphatically not the intention, because it does not create systemic change. An experiment is part of a shadow line that must eventually become part of the primary line. So, make sure that successful experiments can be scaled up and transferred to the primary production or policy track so that they form a path towards the vision of the future to be realized. Little by little, the primary track will change radically. In 5 to 10 years' time, the experiments of the shadow line will form the core of the future culture and the backbone of the future organization.

Not a Marching Path But a Quest

There is a tendency to turn a transition trajectory into a rigid project with goals and deadlines, a kind of roadmap with markers. Kerb this tendency; it has a suffocating effect and kills the creativity and openness that is so desperately needed. There is also a tendency to problematize a transition trajectory and make it heavy as lead: change, well, that won't be easy. Next, meetings are held, and structures are devised, preferably with steering committees, sounding board groups and steering groups. This is typically Dutch. Don't do it; it's a recipe for failure! Ten years ago, I myself decided not to take part in any more steering committees, advisory boards or sounding boards. These kinds of bodies only slow down the necessary renewal and revert to what we want to get away from: control and management. It only takes up the space that is needed to do new, exciting things. Of course, a change strategy is needed, but not a rigid one, rather an organic one. While you are planning, things can change. This requires a strategy with flexible goals based on a long-term vision and room for surprises, intuition and creativity. This makes it an exciting voyage of discovery, with the aim of moving together towards a place that is more attractive, more beautiful, more fun and more exciting. Think of it as a joint quest for the unknown, in which the participants sometimes get lost and learn while stumbling, but nevertheless make progress together. The idea is that participants get lost because that is what they learn the most from. My advice is to travel as light as possible, with as little baggage as possible. In fact, 'travel light in times of transition' is my motto.

The vision serves as an inspiring panorama that gives direction. In order to give substance to that vision, scope is given to projects and experiments. Objectives are adjusted on the basis of lessons learned from these experiments. The trick is to link vision, strategy and action organically. Vision without action is meaningless, but action without vision is directionless. If this connection is missing, the intended transition will eventually stagnate. My best experience was with a combination of top-down and bottom-up, giving direction and offering space at the same time. Only bottom-up gives so much space that people can drown in it and then become rudderless. That is why today there is a great need for connectors who can bridge both worlds.

Give the Transition a Face

Transitions are often started with a detached and technocratic approach. However, an organizational transition is not a cold, technical process with goals and deadlines, but a warm, human, emotional process with fears, feelings and desires. Making an organizational change personal is therefore particularly important. This gives the transition a human face. After all, an organizational transition requires above all a personal transition. Outline a future for the employees involved and try to make them see that their job or position can also become more enjoyable as a result of the transition. The motivation for this can only come from within when people overcome their deep-rooted fears and start following their inner compass. This requires connecting leadership and means creating time and space for employees to actively work on their personal transition.

Celebrate Your Successes, However Small They May Be

Many changemakers wants to move too fast and don't give enough thought to their successes, however small they may be. They tend to look at what is not going well and get stuck in their desire for change. That is why zooming in and out is so important. Those in the middle of the change process mainly experience how slow and sticky things are. Those who zoom out see that some things have changed. This gives positive energy, which you desperately need in a process that takes a long time and consumes a lot of energy.

Chapter 5

Palette of Transitions: Challenges and Solutions

You may be frightened by the enormity of the task ahead of us. I understand that. The total integral task of these transitions is so complex that it regularly makes my head spin. But it is reassuring to know that we all have the collective intelligence to tackle this formidable task. And since there really is no time to wait, I hope that the overall picture I want to sketch here will help you to see the complex connections and that it will also create a sense of urgency in you. That is why I paint a picture of 10 transitions in this chapter.

Four of the biggest problems we face as humanity form the starting point: climate change, water availability, loss of biodiversity and social and economic inequality. Solutions to these extraordinarily complex tasks require system transitions, ranging from 'hardware transitions' such as the energy, raw materials, circular and financial transitions, to 'software transitions' such as the social, health, educational and democratic transitions. Transitions are about stubborn, almost unsolvable problems that are deeply rooted in our attitudes, behaviour, systems and institutions. That is why there are no ready-made, simple solutions. There are no vaccines for transitions. But there are transition accelerators, key factors which can speed up a transition. It is striking that we have formulated so few concrete goals for the four biggest problems. Only for climate change there are concrete and hard goals, but for water, biodiversity and inequality there are no such goals at all, except indirectly in the form of the United Nations' Sustainable Development Goals. These, however, are not nearly as concrete as the climate goals laid down in the 2015 Paris Climate Agreement. At that time, the upper limit for global warming was set at 2°C and the goal at one and a half degrees. If you think that half a degree more or less makes little difference, let me put it to you: if the earth warms up by one and a half degrees, there will still be ice on the North Pole, but if the temperature rises by two degrees, that ice will have disappeared completely. With a one and a half degree warming, about 25% of the coral still survives, but with a two-degree rise, all the coral dies. That half degree of warming is more or less the difference between a 20 and 30 cm rise in the sea level, causing low-lying islands to disappear. This half-degree makes the

Embracing Chaos, 81–134
Copyright © 2023 Jan Rotmans and Co-Writer Mischa Verheijden
Published under exclusive licence by Emerald Publishing Limited. Translation by Michael Gould.
The moral rights of the translator have been asserted. Copyright © 2021 Jan Rotmans en Mischa Verheijden. Original title Omarm de Chaos. First published in 2021 by De Geus, Amsterdam
doi:10.1108/978-1-83753-634-420231010

difference between heat waves lasting four or eight weeks and determines whether hundreds of millions of people end up or remain in poverty because of extreme weather conditions. In short, half a degree more or less of warming makes a world of difference. So together we must fight for every tenth of a degree because it can save human lives, natural species and ecosystems.

In order to meet the objective of not exceeding one and a half degrees of warming, we must reduce global emissions of greenhouse gases, especially carbon dioxide (CO_2), methane (CH_4) and nitrous oxide (N_2O), by 55% by 2030 and by 100% by 2050. That means net zero greenhouse gas emissions in 2050, or in other words: we must switch to a carbon-free economy in one generation! That is almost impossible to imagine. In practical terms, this means that we have to phase out coal-fired power stations worldwide within 10 years and oil and gas within 30 years. It also means large-scale reforestation with a total area the size of India, more than 80 times the Netherlands. This requires an annual investment of about US$800 billion in clean energy. For Europe alone, that is about 260 billion euro annually. For Europe, it means a CO_2-free steel industry by 2030 and a 90% CO_2 reduction in the transport sector by 2050. These are staggering figures for a world that still runs 95% on fossil energy, which we will have to phase out within a generation.

To achieve the objective of no more than 2 degrees of warming, we must reduce global greenhouse gas emissions by 25% by 2030 and by 80% by 2050. That too is a formidable task, as global CO_2 emissions are currently still rising. There was a temporary covid dip of 6% in 2020, but in 2021, CO_2 emissions are already on the rise again and are even expected to increase by about 5%. If you then consider that in 2020 a large part of the world was in lockdown for a long time and that this situation resulted in a net reduction of CO_2 emissions of 6%, you can imagine what a 50% reduction would mean.

What path are we on now? The gap between actual CO_2 emissions and what we should achieve in order to meet the Paris climate targets is getting bigger every year. Two-thirds of those emissions come from China, India and other emerging economies. If we stay on the current path, we are heading for a 3-to-4°C temperature increase. If you are now beginning to wonder how realistic it is that we will achieve the 'ideal' scenario of one and a half degrees of warming, I have to tell you in all honesty that I think there is no chance.

If we pull out all the stops, there is still a small chance that we will achieve the objective of a maximum 2 degrees of warming, but the signals I see do not yet point in that direction. Virtually all countries are lagging behind on their self-imposed climate targets, and the covid crisis has not been seized as an opportunity to accelerate sustainability. A green recovery could have given an enormous boost to achieving the climate targets, but unfortunately, that did not happen. The IEA (International Energy Agency) has calculated that only 2% of the money that governments worldwide spent on economic recovery was used for clean energy. As a result of all the economic recovery plans, global CO_2 emissions are expected to reach record levels by 2023 and increase even further in the following years.

Energy, raw materials and the climate have us in a deadly embrace. The extraction of raw materials is in the hands of the fossil industry and costs more and more energy. The switch to sustainable energy depends on the availability of scarce raw materials, such as earth metals, and large-scale extraction of raw materials and energy is the main contributor to climate change. Therefore, we have to reckon with a period of crises concerning raw materials, energy and climate, which will have repercussions on the economy. Paradoxically, the systemic crises are also our hope for a more sustainable future. That is why I have translated this colossal task into 10 system transitions:

(1) Energy transition
(2) Raw materials transition
(3) Circular transition
(4) Agricultural/food transition
(5) Spatial transition
(6) Financial transition
(7) Educational transition
(8) Health care transition
(9) Social transition
(10) Democratic transition

The Energy Transition

The energy transition is a complex transition because it involves a threefold change:

(1) *From fossil fuels to sustainable energy.* This transition involves, on the one hand, the demolition of the old energy infrastructure of oil platforms, oil refineries, coal-fired power stations and gas pipelines and, on the other hand, the construction of a completely new energy infrastructure with pipelines, tubes, grids, wind turbines and solar panels.
(2) *From a centralized to a decentralized energy system.* This requires a different way of thinking: from centralized to decentralized production and distribution. You currently associate a car with a petrol pump, but soon you will associate it with a power outlet. Although a great deal will be decentralized in the future, we will still be generating energy on a large scale. Think of wind at sea, in combination with green hydrogen.
(3) *From top-down to bottom-up organizing and acting.* Not so long ago, all the signposts – laws and regulations – pointed towards the fossil economy. Those laws and regulations must be abolished, and new ones introduced.

If you let this sink in, you realize how complex and extensive the energy transition is, but also how beautiful and challenging. Who wouldn't want to be part of this revolution? As always, the biggest barrier is in our minds. We can hardly imagine a completely different energy supply, with an exchange of electricity and heat in a cascade of energy levels. At street level, it means an exchange of electricity between an electric car, a smart charging station and a house, and at the neighbourhood and district level, a general exchange of electricity and heat. And likewise, within the region, between regions and between countries. This is a beautiful and beckoning perspective, and whoever sees it realizes where the resistance comes from and what gigantic investments are required.

The idea that the energy transition can be budget-neutral is a misconception. In Europe alone, it will require investments of up to 1,000 billion euros by 2030, and around 260 billion euros per year thereafter. For the Netherlands, the required investments until 2050 are estimated at around 100 billion euros. In time, energy will be free, but for the time being, you will see energy bills rise. By 2030, they could be about twice as high as they are now. The citizens will help pay for the large investments in the new energy infrastructure. After that, energy will gradually become cheaper and cheaper. However, we deliberately speak of investments rather than costs, because in the long term the energy transition will create a lot of jobs, innovation, health and a new, clean energy economy.

Worldwide, the energy transition has therefore become 'big business', a game of power and poker in which thousands of billions of euros are involved and hundreds of billions of euros are invested every year. A power shift is taking place towards China. Today, the country still relies largely on coal, oil and gas, and produces twice as much CO_2 as the US, and in 10 years' time, this will be three times as much. At the same time, China is the absolute front runner in the field of renewable energy. The country has a clear vision in this respect: it wants to provide the current generation with fossil-fuel energy, but future generations with sustainable energy. It focuses on solar, wind, nuclear and hydrogen energy and already invests around 100 billion euros a year in solar and wind energy. This makes it by far the largest producer of solar and wind energy in the world. So, China has a black and a green side and – together with India and other emerging economies – has now surpassed the US in achieving the Paris climate goals. However, perhaps contrary to expectations, the USA has invested more than ever in renewable energy since Trump took office: more than 40 billion dollars in solar energy and more in wind energy than shale gas. Little has come of Trump's notorious shale oil and shale gas revolution.

As you can read in Chapter 4 about Shell, this market is too volatile to be of interest to large investors because of the constantly fluctuating oil prices. The fact that the USA is nevertheless making great strides is mainly due to the fact that states and cities can act autonomously, and therefore go much faster than at the federal level. The 'Trump effect' on the energy transition is therefore not as great as was feared beforehand. This is because the energy transition has been going on for decades, and so much has happened since then that it has become an autonomous process that cannot simply be changed. The energy transition is unavoidable and irreversible and cannot be stopped by anyone. At most, it can be slowed down. That in itself is good news, but the reverse is also true: you can't just accelerate the transition.

Europe is limping along behind China and the USA, but with the 'Green Deal' it does have considerable ambitions to make the continent climate-neutral by 2050. The concrete result is the ambitious climate plan 'Fit for 55', presented by the EU in July 2021. A huge package of 12 legislative proposals, for, among other things, sustainable energy, forestry, land use and energy taxes. These should ensure that emissions in the EU decrease by at least 55% compared to 1990, with the intention of keeping the global temperature increase well below 2 degrees. The package has been described as 'the European Union's new industrial revolution'. The core of the plan is that companies and individuals will pay substantially more for their CO_2 emissions. However, there will be a social fund to help citizens and companies, so that the transition will be as fair as possible. A side note to this revolutionary plan is that all legislative proposals still have to be approved by the European Parliament, which will be difficult enough and could easily take another two years.

In Europe, Germany and Denmark are the absolute frontrunners. Unfortunately, the Netherlands and Belgium are lagging behind. In the Netherlands, this is mainly due to our famous polder model, which leads to compromises and a lack of political leadership, as a result of which no radical and clear choices are made. All of this with the idea that this will ease the pain of the transition. Well, on the contrary. In Belgium, the complicated structure of the state, with governments at the national level and at the regional level in Flanders and Wallonia, is the main obstacle. The framing in Europe is different. We are talking about the new economy that is developing rapidly, potentially already involving 25 million Europeans. In 2020, the new economy already accounts for about 7% of the workforce, and it is estimated that it will account for 30% in 2030. Every euro that we invest in the new economy generates three euros in terms of employment, innovation and structural improvement. In contrast, every euro we invest in the old economy costs us two euros in harmful side effects, according to calculations by the Dutch Planning Bureau for the Living Environment.

In any case, the global energy transition is at a turning point. This in-between-period, the most interesting phase of a transition, is characterized by chaos, unrest and turbulence. There is a lack of insight and overview so that things can seem to go in any direction. For many people, it is surprising what happens, but for those who look deep and long into the undercurrent, it is logical. There you can see the seeds for the big changes that will follow later. From these seeds, the patterns emerge that determine the future. For a long time, the energy system seemed stable, and changes took place mainly under the surface. Now that the under-current is touching the overcurrent and the tipping point is being reached, events and processes are interacting and reinforcing each other in the same direction. This accelerates small changes and turns them into big changes.

There are plenty of indications that we are at this point in the energy transition. The current energy crisis triggered by the war in Ukraine is a wake-up call for the world and in particular for Europe, which has become far too dependent on Russia and naively relied on Russia as a reliable gas supplier. In the search for alternatives to Russian gas, Europe and the world are mainly relying on liquefied gas and keeping coal-fired power stations open for longer. That means a fossil reset for the coming years, which will lead to additional CO_2 emissions, further pushing the climate targets out of sight. At the same time, the good news is that there is an accelerated focus on sustainable energy: wind, sun and green hydrogen. In addition to sustainability and security of supply, the pillars of the energy transition are now also geopolitical and affordability: how do we keep it affordable for everyone. This marks the tipping phase in which the energy transition is, everyone feels the transition pain in their wallet and there is no turning back.

What we see is an energy battlefield that marks the chaos. Fossil fuel companies that go bankrupt, large investors and pension funds no longer invest in oil because of the financial risk. Solar and wind energy are growing at a rapid pace, are becoming cheaper and cheaper and can already compete with fossil energy in more than 30 countries and regions without subsidies. Also, laws and regulations that favour fossil energy are gradually being abolished in favour of laws and regulations that promote renewable energy. Another good indication that we are at a tipping point is the rapidly increasing number of protests, conflicts and court cases concerning climate and energy. A striking example of lawsuits is Urgenda's climate case against the Dutch state, which was followed worldwide. In Belgium, the climate case started in March 2021. At the moment, there are almost 2000 climate lawsuits pending worldwide, instituted by citizens, social organizations and cities against countries and fossil companies, although by no means all comparable with the Urgenda climate lawsuit.

About 20 years ago, I stated that Shell would not survive if they continued on the fossil-fuel path with oil and gas. There was a good laugh about that. Shell was a rock, the uncrowned king of dividends. A world without Shell was considered unthinkable. And now look at this: Shell has run into trouble, was confronted with negative oil prices, is under enormous social and political pressure and had to cut back and reorganize heavily. Recently, ex-CEO Ben van Beurden announced a radical change of course: Shell is really going on the sustainable route, with a portfolio of wind, sun, hydrogen and biofuels. The climate lawsuit against Shell, won by Friends of the Earth, Netherlands, is forcing the company to become more sustainable more quickly.

I also proclaimed that the port of Rotterdam, which still largely runs on fossil fuel, and in particular the Botlek area and the first Maasvlakte, with its chain of oil refineries, power stations and petrochemicals, would end up as a fossil mausoleum. This led to indignant reactions from many port representatives, who jumped to protect their pride. Until my image of a fossil mausoleum surfaced last year in the Dutch Financial Newspaper, with the subtitle that this was a real prospect for the port of Rotterdam. Meanwhile, the energy transition has become the port of Rotterdam's most important project and it is making great strides, although there is still a long way to go. And, last but not least: everyone thought we had no chance when we took the Dutch state to court with Urgenda until the contrary was proven. Let that be an inspiration for the energy transition. We can make the impossible possible.

However, the fact that we are in the tipping phase does not mean that the energy transition is a done deal and will go smoothly. If we want to meet the climate target of no more than 2 degrees of warming, we will have to leave two-thirds of the fossil reserves underground. These stranded assets, or lost revenues, comprise an order of magnitude of US$100 trillion. Looking beyond the tipping point, we see a fierce battle with many clashing interests between world powers and continents, with many conflicts and even wars. It is 'eat or be eaten' and resistance will be maximum, but the outcome is inevitable: renewable energy will win from fossil-fuel-based energy. The only question is how long fossil-fuel energy will continue to dominate. Another 10 years? Another 20? Another 30? That outcome will also determine our future.

The Energy Transition Challenge

In order to make the not-to-be-underestimated challenge of the energy transition concrete, I have listed everything that needs to be done to achieve the climate targets set in Paris in 2030 and 2050. I take the Netherlands as an example and limit myself here to solar and wind energy and the built environment. I will not discuss agriculture, industry or traffic, because it is less easy to make them tangible and to express them in numbers. In the field of wind energy, much has already been set in motion. In the past 25 years, some 2,500 wind turbines have been installed on land and at sea. In order to meet the climate targets, another 15,000 wind turbines are needed, two-thirds of them at sea and one-third on land. In the next 30 years, we will therefore have to erect six times as many wind turbines as we have done in the past 25 years. These estimates do not yet include the need for green hydrogen. For that, thousands more windmills are needed. There is no such space in the North Sea, where it is estimated that there is room for some 10,000 wind turbines, potentially good for about 80 gigawatts.

As for the generation of solar energy, we have made great strides in recent years. In the last 20 years, 7 gigawatts of solar energy have been installed. That is about 10 million solar panels, or 10,000 football pitches. However, what is still needed to achieve the climate goals is gigantic: 70 gigawatts, or another 100,000 football fields. In the next 30 years, we must therefore install 10 times as many solar panels as have been installed in the last 20 years. There is now a threat of proliferation of solar fields on agricultural land, with foreign investors, in particular, coveting this cheap land purely for financial gain and profiting richly from large-scale subsidies. It is the old capitalist economy at its best. But besides polluting the landscape, these solar fields are also bad for nature, the farmers and the region, while only 10% of Dutch roofs have solar panels. Fortunately, there are more and more examples where part of the proceeds are chanelled back to the local population. But the rule is and remains first the roofs, then the facades and other hard surfaces, such as industrial estates, ports, noise barriers along motorways and railway lines. There is still a total of 2.5 billion m² of usable surface area for generating solar energy that is not yet being used.

All homes must be freed from natural gas. In the Netherlands, 7.5 million homes are connected to natural gas (95%), and we are still going to build 100,000 new homes with a natural gas connection. All these homes are responsible for about 20% of the CO_2 emissions in the Netherlands. Count your profit when we disconnect these homes from natural gas. There are numerous ways of doing this: from large heat networks based on fossil-fuel residual heat to small heat networks on geothermal or aquathermal energy, from green gas to green hydrogen and from all-electric to zero-to-the-metre homes. If we were to switch away from natural gas in 20 years, that would be about 2,000 homes a day. If we do it in 30 years, it will be 1,500 homes a day. In the past two years, we have removed about 2,000 existing homes from natural gas. So, in order to be rid of natural gas by 2042, what we have done in the past two years must be done every day for the next 20 years! Or, if we take 2050 as our final goal, what we have done in the last one and a half two years will have to be done every day for the next 30 years. That is almost inconceivable, and then I have not mentioned circular buildings yet. Only a very small part, say 25 of the one million buildings in the Netherlands, is circular. Nor have I mentioned biobased houses: building a million houses from wood and other biomass instead of concrete and cement saves 20 megatons of CO_2. And just replacing the existing fleet of petrol and diesel cars, buses and trucks with electric cars will take at least 20 years. All this – wind energy, solar energy and taking our homes and buildings off gas – forms an important part of the gigantic energy transition challenge facing the Netherlands. It will have to be done many times faster and smarter than we are doing now in order to meet the climate targets. Because we have failed to act sooner, we have 'lost' about 25 years and now we have to go through the energy transition at an accelerated pace. The haste we are now in has led us to make mistakes and go down the wrong path. Don't get me wrong: making mistakes is part of the process, it's searching, experimenting and learning. But we must have the courage to acknowledge our mistakes and revise our wrong choices. As the saying goes: better to stop halfway than to fail completely.

That also applies to myself. I used to think differently about biomass and fossil heat networks. The discussion about biomass has taken a remarkable turn. Whereas 10 years ago biofuels were still seen as the solution, biomass is now in the doldrums. This is partly correct, but partly not. There are many kinds of biomass: maize, sugar cane, rapeseed, palm oil, wood chips, algae, residual waste, biodegradable waste and sewage sludge. These can be used to generate energy, but also to make feed, food and building materials. Certainly, as a building block of the biobased economy, biomass can be of great value for high-quality bio-products such as polymers for cosmetic and pharmaceutical products. But scientific research by the European Academy of Sciences (EASAC) shows that large-scale burning of (woody) biomass to generate energy is not a sustainable alternative to fossil-fuel energy. It hardly produces less CO_2, but it does produce many emissions of fine particulates, NO_x, soot and PAHs. And certainly, if those trees come from North and South America, causing the disappearance of large quantities of forest and also causing them to travel long distances, this is at odds with the intention of the transition. To put it bluntly: setting fire to trees to generate energy is a very bad idea and harmful to people and the environment.

That is a progressive insight. Many billions in subsidies have been pumped into this and we have to go back on that. The climate targets are urgent and imperative, but we should not make the mistake of achieving them in an unsustainable way. In the Netherlands, for instance, we have erected hundreds of biomass power plants at breakneck speed. There are now 230, and about 150 more are planned. Often close to where people live, and the fact that they get sick and die from this is unacceptable. Reserving billions to subsidize the co-firing of biomass in coal-fired power stations is also a waste of money. Only the big energy companies benefit from this. The energy transition is not about playing with technologies where we replace one technology with another. By doing so, we keep the old economic system alive, and we continue to pollute and waste.

The fact is that without biomass we will not achieve our climate goals in the short term. Currently, more energy is generated from biomass (60%) than from wind (24%) and sun (12%). Today, about 14% of the energy is generated sustainably, while that was targeted for 2020. So, we have not achieved this climate objective. But we have never achieved a climate objective and we will probably not do so in the future either. But the worst thing we can do is to achieve the climate targets in an unsustainable way. That will keep the old economy going and we will not make any progress. We must therefore look for alternatives to biomass, such as green gas, geothermal energy and aquathermal energy. These are currently only applied on a very small scale and must be scaled up more quickly. The 11 billion euro of subsidy money for biomass can therefore be better spent on insulating homes, and on drilling for geothermal and aquathermal energy. As a temporary bridge, we will have to continue with natural gas for a while longer.

Heat networks are crucial as a replacement for natural gas. They are underground networks of pipes that transport hot water to homes or buildings. That hot water can come from various sources, from fossil-fuel residual heat to geothermal heat. From the user's point of view, it is important for heat networks to be open and hybrid, i.e., connected to different heat sources, so that the user can choose a heat source or disconnect from the heat network. From the government's point of view, it is important to speed up the development of heat networks. For this reason, fossil-fuel-based heat networks that run on the waste heat from industry are often chosen without much influence from residents, especially in large cities. For the network operators, this has the advantage of being fast and relatively inexpensive, but as a user, you are stuck with it for a long time. This is a dilemma: we want to make progress and fossil-fuel-based heat networks are indispensable for this, but the future belongs to small-scale, hybrid and open networks. More and more residents are resisting fossil-fuel-based heat networks, which they will be saddled with for the rest of their lives and are developing their own plans for sustainable heat networks. It is therefore becoming a mix of fossil-fuel-based and sustainable heat networks, with the focus shifting more and more towards sustainable, small-scale heat networks.

Solar energy is also a pillar of the future sustainable energy supply. After a very slow start, solar energy is finally picking up steam. However, only about 10% of Dutch roofs have solar panels installed. Because this is not fast enough, we are focusing on larger areas such as agricultural land. In recent years, solar fields (or solar parks) have sprung up like mushrooms, often near small municipalities in the east and north of the country. There is now even the threat of proliferation of solar fields on agricultural land. Farmers and dairy farmers are repeatedly called by investors with attractive offers. Farmers can get as much as 5,000 to 10,000 euro per hectare per year. Farmers who lease 25 hectares of agricultural land can thus easily receive around 200,000 euro per year. This is offset by relatively low costs. The majority of the investors in these solar fields come from Germany, England, Norway and China. In order to be profitable, these solar fields need subsidies. A minimum of 10 cents per kWh is needed to establish a profitable business case. With subsidies, which are paid out for 15 years, these fields are profitable, and the yield can be predicted fairly accurately.

It is a very predictable business with little risk and high returns of up to 15%. Meanwhile, about 75% of the largest solar parks in the Netherlands are in foreign hands. As a result, about 80% of the subsidy money disappears abroad. Project developers such as the Norwegian Statkraft and Unisun and the Chinese Chint Solar build large solar parks on agricultural land, which are then bought in droves by foreign investment funds. These companies are not interested in green power, but purely in the financial returns. They are not interested in how the landscape will look, they are not interested in resident participation, and they are certainly not interested in whether residents will benefit financially from the proceeds. If hot dogs gave a higher return, they would invest in them.

This is another example of the old economy in a new guise. Not only the millions of euros in subsidies, but also the profits that these solar parks make over a period of 20 years, flow abroad. All that money does not benefit the regions and local residents: only 4% of the production by solar parks is locally owned, while residents and local businesses should also benefit financially from a solar park. In the climate agreement, 50% local ownership is the goal, but this is not legally enforceable. The Netherlands has some 650 energy cooperatives, and they could play an important role in the local development of solar parks by becoming co-developers or co-owners of a solar field or park. The members then determine what happens with the proceeds, which are usually invested locally in sustainable projects, such as making schools or sports clubs more sustainable. Legislation must therefore be introduced immediately to make it easier for local energy cooperatives to develop solar parks. Otherwise, resistance among citizens will increase noticeably. As soon as people see that their neighbourhood is being built over with solar parks whose proceeds are disappearing abroad, they will start to object, and that will only lead to further delays in the energy transition. Fortunately, there are more and more examples of solar parks being built with local energy cooperatives, with part of the revenue going to the local community. However, this is still a small minority, so vigilance is still required.

My motto is that we should first use the approximately 2.5 billion m² of surface area that is potentially available for solar energy: roofs, facades, fallow land, industrial and business estates, dikes and noise barriers along railway lines and motorways. Only then should we start using agricultural land for solar fields. And if that happens, then only together with the local community.

All in all, we see a repeating pattern here. In the case of biomass, heat networks and solar panels, we need mass and volume in order to achieve our climate goals. That is why we quickly opt for large-scale solutions supported by billions of euros in subsidies. Big business is enthusiastic about this and profits the most from it, at the expense of citizens of course, which only increases the resistance. It is in fact the old economy: a fossil-fuel technology may be replaced by a sustainable one, but it is still dominated by the big companies, which only want to make money with these technologies and add little or no value.

Their solutions are not locally rooted. In the new economy, residents participate and invest together with companies in wind or solar energy, and part of the profit also flows back to them. In short, if the energy transition is not embedded in the new economy but continues to be purely about financial returns from the cut-throat competition, it will not help us at all. We will continue to exploit each other and nature, with all the harmful consequences this entails.

This Is How We Can Accelerate the Energy Transition

For 30 years, we have known what to do to accelerate the energy transition. We just didn't do it because we wanted to avoid the transition pain. It is too late for that now. We have to go through the pain now. The most effective way to accelerate the energy transition is to introduce a carbon tax for industry, which is responsible for almost a third of CO_2 emissions. Industry must pay a levy on this, according to the 'polluter pays' principle. This has proved to be an effective way of significantly reducing emissions because it provides an economic incentive for industry to become more sustainable. More and more countries are considering introducing such a CO_2 tax, and in Europe countries such as Sweden, Norway and France have already done so.

In the Netherlands, we want to introduce this step by step, increasing from 30 euro per tonne of CO_2 to 125 euro per tonne by 2030. However, this only applies to avoidable CO_2 emissions, while it is much more effective to tax all CO_2 emissions (a so-called 'flat tax'). Ideally, every tonne of CO_2 should have the same price, from whatever source, and preferably for every sector. If we make the uniform carbon price high enough (<50 euro per tonne of CO_2 has little effect anyway), we can achieve the UN's climate goals. However, this is not going to happen because of the great resistance from industry, which has been able to resist a CO_2 tax for a long time. Thanks to a powerful lobby, in the next few years industry will only have to pay if they exceed the average emissions of the best-performing industrial companies in Europe. That is not very effective. The urgency of the issue will force us to implement a more radical carbon tax.

The introduction of a CO_2 tax is inevitable not only for producers but also for consumers. Flying, driving a car and eating meat are climate-damaging and will therefore become more expensive. Clean products and activities, on the other hand, will become cheaper. This can be implemented in various ways, including in the form of a VAT tax. This will encourage both producers and consumers to become more sustainable more quickly. However, we must ensure that this is done in a socially just way and that the least well-off do not have to pay the price. This can be done, for example, by means of a social fund to compensate for the burden on lower incomes. In addition, energy saving is a highly effective means of reducing CO_2, both in companies and by consumers. After all, the most sustainable energy is the energy you don't use, but this area has been neglected for decades. There is a lot of profit to be made here. Saving energy in buildings and houses through good and smart insulation must be given top priority, as it is in industry. This can be done by redirecting the subsidy streams. If we stop the billions in subsidies for biomass, which are devastating, and start using them to make homes and buildings more sustainable, we will achieve a double profit. Using biomass to generate energy is not sustainable and hardly saves any CO_2, but better insulation of homes and buildings does save a lot of CO_2.

We can also accelerate the dismantling of fossil fuels. Stop immediately the four coal-fired power stations that are still open, reduce the subsidies for the fossil-fuel industry as soon as possible and offer fossil-fuel advertising. After phasing out coal, we will start phasing out oil, speeding up the removal of oil platforms in the North Sea, gradually replacing oil in industry with electrification and green hydrogen, and finally phasing out natural gas. This requires long-term investments in a new energy infrastructure. In the next 10 years, we will already be working on green hydrogen, which will require a lot of additional solar and wind energy, and a lot of subsidy money to get that hydrogen to compete with fossil alternatives on the market. At the same time, we must invest heavily in a new, decentralized, smart energy infrastructure, from local (street, district and neighbourhood) to regional (smart energy exchange between and within regions) and national level. The amounts involved are enormous, at both the centralized and decentralized level. Although estimates vary, they will amount to hundreds of billions of euros in the coming decades. These are not so much costs as investments in a clean future.

But more is needed. It is not only a technical transition but also a mental transition. A new, big story is needed. Not so much about energy, but about the economy. We are going to build a new, clean, circular economy, which will provide a lot of benefits: employment, innovation and a better competitive position. An economy that makes people healthier, that gives them more quality of life. A story that stimulates, motivates and inspires people. At the moment, we are problematizing it, by naming mainly the disadvantages and costs and increasing the resistance. While we could be much more positive so that people and companies are motivated to participate. The Netherlands has always been a purely commercial country. For a long time, we traded in everything that was dirty (peat, coal, oil, natural gas, waste). As soon as we realize that we can earn a lot of money from what is clean, sustainable and circular, things can move fast. It would be great if the Netherlands became a leader in the field of clean energy (solar, wind, green hydrogen, geothermal and aquathermal energy and bio-based building). And in its wake citizens, who enthusiastically participate. In the near future, it will be cool if you have an electric car or scooter, if you have a sustainable house, if you eat healthy food, if you wear sustainable clothing, if you produce little waste and do not fly unnecessarily. In fact, in 10 or 20 years, you will be a loser if you still live unsustainably.

The Hydrogen Hype

In recent years, a hype has developed around hydrogen. This is remarkable, because hydrogen, which is produced from natural gas and water, has been used in industry for decades. It is relatively cheap and can be produced quite easily and be moved over long distances in gaseous or liquid form. However, its production is energy-intensive. Hydrogen is therefore not an energy source but an energy carrier. A lot of energy is needed to make it, and about 30% of that energy is lost in its production. It also releases a lot of CO_2. What we need is green hydrogen, made from wind and solar energy. For a long time that seemed like a utopia, but with the rapid scaling up of solar and wind energy and the rapid phasing out of natural gas, green hydrogen suddenly seems within reach. However, there is no business case for green hydrogen yet. Because it is relatively expensive to produce, it is more advantageous to produce green electricity directly. Green hydrogen will only become profitable if gas prices remain high and electricity is cheap for a long time. It may be some time before we reach that point, and until then billions of euros in government subsidies are needed to get the production of green hydrogen going.

The route to green hydrogen is through blue hydrogen. Blue hydrogen is made from natural gas, where the released CO_2 is captured and stored under the seafloor or in empty natural gas fields. Because the necessary infrastructure for CO_2 storage still has to be built, is energy-intensive and also generates CO_2, blue hydrogen will not bring about much CO_2 reduction in the coming decade. But for the time being, blue hydrogen is still two to three times cheaper than green hydrogen and is needed to build up enough volume in the next 10 years. This means that hydrogen will only play a substantial role in the energy supply after 2030, will become a major pillar of the new, clean, CO_2-neutral economy and will be of great importance to Dutch industry. After all, if we want to achieve the UN's climate goals by 2050 – producing almost 100% less CO_2 than in 1990 – we will have to replace oil and gas in industry. This can be done with biomass, electrification and with hydrogen, where molecules are made greener with solar and wind energy. Hydrogen seems to be becoming more and more important as a fuel and raw material for green, CO_2-neutral industries. I do not immediately see large-scale applications of hydrogen in the building and transport sectors. However, it is useful to experiment with it on a small scale.

Another point is that we can only produce a limited amount of green hydrogen ourselves. On the scale of North-West Europe, we have to import more than 50%, and for the Netherlands, this may even rise to 75%. For the 25% of green hydrogen that the Netherlands produces, additional wind farms would need to be constructed in the North Sea, in addition to the wind farms that are already planned. The illusion that the Netherlands can become energy independent with hydrogen is therefore shattered. This also applies to Northwest Europe.

(Continued)

(*Continued*)

So, the Netherlands will become a country that imports green hydrogen, but where will we get it from? A hydrogen study by DRIFT shows that global trade routes are developing around hydrogen, partly following the oil trade routes. Potential major producers include Australia, the Middle East, North Africa, South America, Canada and Southern Europe. In particular countries and regions with a lot of space and sunshine are candidates for this, such as Libya, Algeria, Morocco, Patagonia, Qatar and the Middle East. These are geopolitically sensitive countries and regions, which could create new geopolitical relationships in the world. The Netherlands must make a strategic choice as to what position it wants to take in this new force field. Compared to the current situation, a switch to hydrogen would actually increase rather than decrease the energy dependence of the Netherlands.

The Raw Materials Transition

The energy transition is a huge task, but the raw materials transition is even more complicated. Our modern civilization and ongoing modernization is based on the availability of raw materials and is accompanied by a relentless and destructive hunt for them. Without coal and iron ore there would have been no industrial revolution and without oil and gas no global leap in prosperity. For the green and digital revolution, rare earths are crucial. In the current era, the hunt is on for critical metals such as cobalt, magnesium, graphite and lithium. They are critical metals because they carry a risk when it comes to supply. Within this group of critical metals, a group of 17 rare earths, including neodymium, scandium, dysprosium, gadolinium and lanthanum, deserve special attention. Although these earth metals are abundant in the earth's crust, they are very rare on the world market because their presence is disproportionately distributed in the world, and they are difficult to extract.

So, as you can see, only the type of raw material changes. The pattern repeats itself again and again. Today, too, the hunt for raw materials has neo-colonial traits. In colonial times, Western occupiers appropriated raw materials and products, such as cocoa, sugar, tobacco, rice and coffee, at the expense of the local population. This led to local dislocation and exploitation. In the post-colonial era, rich countries gained access to raw materials such as oil, iron, hardwood, gold and diamonds in exchange for money. Because the exploitation and processing were kept in their own hands, the former colonies hardly benefited and remained poor. Today, the attempts of developing countries to make more money from their own raw materials are blocked by rich Western countries, and the large-scale extraction of critical metals poses problems. Extraction is not only associated with great damage to the environment and nature, but also with corruption, conflict and violation of human rights. Think of the cobalt mining in Congo for our mobile phones. These are the neo-colonial features of modern resource extraction. Surely we are not going to make the same mistakes as in the past and become more sustainable on the back of poor people in developing countries?

But if we want to meet the climate targets, we need a lot of critical metals fast. At the moment, not enough critical metals are being produced to meet even a quarter of our climate ambitions. For the new sustainable economy, these metals, and especially the rare earths, are crucial for the production of wind turbines, solar panels, electric cars and smartphones. Before all cars are electric, many batteries will need to be produced. An incredible number of windmills and solar panels still must be installed before the switch to wind and solar power is complete. A lot of mines still need to be made operational and that can take anything from 10 to 20 years.

The expected global demand for rare earths will grow by more than 1,000% in the next 10 years. In 2030, the EU alone will need 18 times more lithium and five times more cobalt than today for electric car batteries and energy storage. And by 2050 it is estimated that 50 times more lithium and 10 times more cobalt will be needed. For some rare earths, in particular neodymium, terbium, indium, dysprosium and praseodymium, an increase in production by a factor of 10–15 is expected by 2050. Digitalization also requires many critical metals. The European demand for rare earths for digital equipment, electric cars and wind turbines is estimated to increase tenfold by 2050.

Perhaps the greatest problem in this respect is growing dependence on China, which possesses more than half of the proven reserves of scarce earth elements and currently produces 97% of them, and thus controls virtually the entire market for rare earth elements. We, therefore, risk exchanging the undesirable dependence on Russia for natural gas and the Middle East for oil for an even more risky dependence on China for critical metals. This is turning into a major geopolitical game, in which power is shifting from oil countries to countries with critical earths. China threatens to be the big winner because it holds all the trumps with a near-monopoly on earth metals. It is even considering keeping the production of rare earths entirely to itself. In the near future, this will lead to major tensions and conflicts between countries and regions of the world.

A striking example of this is the conflict between China and Japan over the uninhabited Senkaku Islands, where tensions rose to such an extent that China stopped the export of rare earths to Japan. Because these rare earths are indispensable to Japanese industry – without neodymium, for example, the pro-duction of the Toyota Prius would almost immediately stop – all alarm bells were immediately rung. Although the conflict was resolved and Japan regained access to these metals, the country was shaken up and set its sights on other countries, including those in Africa, in order to secure the supply of scarce earth elements. The United States, too, is well aware of the increasing raw material risks and is reopening large mines for the extraction of earth metals.

In Europe, however, alarm bells should be ringing because our continent has hardly any rare earths, but we are still taking a passive stance. Europe does not yet have a policy for rare earths. A few years ago, I received a call from the Ministry of Foreign Affairs asking whether there was a need for a raw materials policy. China has been doing this for 25 years, and Chinese foreign policy focuses on energy and raw materials. For example, 80% of the Dutch companies that use 10 of the 17 rare earths are already facing strong price fluctuations. Due to increasing demand and export restrictions by China, the price of neodymium has increased fivefold over the past 10 years, and that of dysprosium has even increased tenfold. The same companies do not yet have an active raw materials policy, nor are they supported in this by the government. How long will it take before Europe and the Netherlands wake up? The rapidly growing demand for these metals, the unequal distribution of raw materials across countries and companies, the increasing geopolitical power of emerging countries with large raw material reserves and the reduction of the harmful effects of raw material extraction mean that it is not a question of whether a raw materials crisis will occur, but when it will occur. I think it will not be long now.

This Is How We Can Accelerate the Raw Materials Transition

In a general sense, a change in mindset is needed. We have to learn to look differently and start to see each product as a collection of raw materials that we use temporarily and from which another product can be made after return. This must already be taken into account in the design, so that raw materials can be reused endlessly and we ultimately evolve towards a circular economy. This takes time and, above all, a mental leap in scale.

As far as critical earths are concerned, we need to focus much more on recycling. It is absurd that only 10% of our mobile phones are recycled. The rest is incinerated or dumped, while recycling is relatively easy and yields a lot. For example, a ton of mobile phones yields twenty times more gold than a ton of gold ore.

We must also focus on circular design so that, for example, wind turbines and solar panels are made in such a way that components and materials can easily be reused. For example, for the first time there are recyclable lightweight solar panels, which are being made in the Netherlands by Solarge. We can also look for other raw materials as a substitute in order to reduce the demand for critical earth metals. This is far from enough, but it will save us time.

We are forced to consider a revival of the European mining industry. Europe is almost entirely dependent on foreign imports of critical earth metals, but does have reserves in old, closed mine shafts. With new technological solutions, they can be reopened without too much risk.

And last but not least, we can develop a new kind of barter: commodity-for-knowledge-trading. Critical earth metals will be exchanged for access to our knowledge and expertise about, for example, food, digitization, water or sustainability.

I foresee a great future for this commodity-for-knowledge trade, especially for Europe and the Netherlands. But at the moment there is no sign of a strategic policy in that direction and we still have a long way to go for the raw materials transition. However, the urgency is great because the energy transition depends on the availability of raw materials such as critical earth metals.

I foresee that in 10 years' time the raw materials transition will be as high on the agenda as the energy transition is now.

The Circular Transition

The circular transition is the transition to a circular economy in which no more raw materials are lost. This is in stark contrast to our current economy, in which a large proportion of our products are thrown away or incinerated. That is pure pollution and waste. And above all a dead end because we make uninhibited use of raw materials to make those products.

A circular economy is natural and works on the basis of nature's principles, where the residual product of one person is food for the other. For example, nature has been designing, producing and innovating for 3.8 billion years without depletion, pollution and degeneration. We humans can learn a lot from that. By closing cycles, just like in nature, we prevent waste and pollution and we reuse raw materials and products endlessly. That sounds logical and simple, but is very difficult in practice because it requires a completely different way of thinking, organizing and working.

Thinking differently means learning to look naturally. Then you see each product as a collection of raw materials that we do not own but use temporarily and from which another product can be made after return. This also requires a different way of designing. The entire service life of a product must be taken into account right from the design stage. How can you design something in such a way that raw materials can be used again and again, without loss of quality, for another product? For example, Philips is working on a circular television whose various parts can be reused to make another product. And IKEA is transforming from raw material supplier to raw material processor and no longer sees a table or desk as an end product, but as a collection of raw materials, which are temporarily lent to customers, who then return them, after which IKEA can turn them into something else.

The circular transition also marks a radical change in our way of life, the change from ownership to use. Possession entails more disadvantages than advantages, such as acquisition costs, maintenance costs and waste disposal. That might be worth it for products that have a great emotional value to you and are therefore irreplaceable in a sense. But why would you want to own a lamp? You want to temporarily use the lighting function. Why would you want to own a table, desk and chair? You want to temporarily sit on it or work on it.

The transition to a circular economy not only requires a mental but also an organizational leap in scale. The entire chain is being overhauled. Circular entrepreneurs will organize themselves how they can get those raw materials back after use by others. In this way, companies will become raw material suppliers and raw material processors in the future. They then have depots everywhere where customers can bring their used products, that collection of raw materials. This requires a completely different logistics operation and organization of the raw materials chain. It also requires new business models, in which waste is seen as a raw material with which money can be earned.

All this is so drastic that we are only at the beginning of the circular economy. My estimate is that the circular transition is about fifteen years behind the energy transition. The circular transition is still in the conceptual phase: it is bursting with ideas and concepts, but little is being done with them in practice. Much more raw materials are wasted in the construction and food sector than in other sectors and there is still too little focus on reuse. Because the construction sector is responsible for 50% of the annual use of raw materials – while only 1% of the earth's surface and 3% of the land surface consists of urban areas – it is important that the construction sector in particular builds or renovates in a circular manner. That happens far too little. Fortunately, there are already some wonderful and inspiring examples.

The new headquarters of the Triodos Bank, designed by Thomas Rau, is made entirely of wood, with green roofs and a glass facade. The building is demountable, which means that the building can be completely dismantled, after which the materials can be reused. Each material used has a passport, which records which materials (wood, glass, steel, concrete and brick) are contained where in an object, the quantity and value of the materials and how they can be reused later. The building is a materials depot, where the materials can easily be detached and reused.

One reason why the circular economy is not yet making much progress is the confusion between recycling and circularity. The Netherlands recycles a lot, but it is far from being circular. The Netherlands is the European leader in re-using waste and products. Nowhere else in the world is so much waste collected and re-used, but that does not make the economy circular. Most attention is still paid to collecting used materials and raw materials and then recycling them. Recycling plastic, paper and glass is particularly popular. Companies pick out one element and want to produce cheaply by closing the production cycle, but they do want to continue to grow. And so, of all the products made and imported into the Dutch economy, less than 10% are made of recycled materials. This is an extremely low percentage, given that 80% of waste in the Netherlands is recycled.

Between 1900 and 2020, the extraction of raw materials (phosphorus, metals, minerals, biomass) worldwide increased from six to 100 billion kilos per year. It is expected that the extraction of raw materials will double to 200 billion tonnes per year by 2050. In the Netherlands, the use of materials is stabilizing due to an efficient infrastructure for recycling and re-use, and limited manufacturing industry. This is necessary because the Netherlands has an extremely ambitious goal: in 2030, raw material use must be reduced by 50% and in 2050, the Netherlands must be fully circular. These goals will not be achieved by a long shot if we continue as we are doing now. In the past 10 years, we have hardly made any progress with the circular economy. The share of circular companies even decreased, and especially for new products such as electronics, a circular culture is lacking. In January 2021, the Netherlands Environmental Assessment Agency (PBL) called for far more taxes in order to reduce the environmental damage caused by products. This immediately shows the biggest problem: as long as we want to continue growing and use more and more raw materials, we cannot create a circular economy. Moreover, recycling costs a lot of energy. Making the economy circular therefore also requires a great deal of energy, so much so that – unless the influx of new materials decreases dramatically – 100% circularity is actually not possible. An economy that builds on infinite growth can never become truly circular, not even if we re-use and recycle a lot. The real, overarching question is: should we continue to consume and produce as we do now? The answer is no, but companies and governments that are committed to the circular economy are still avoiding this question. A truly circular economy requires a system change that involves a number of steps: using raw materials more sparingly, designing, maintaining and repairing differently, re-using products, processing and re-using materials (recycling) and recovering energy from materials.

This system change turns the entire chain and the existing earning models upside down. There is still a lot to be done and changed to achieve a breakthrough in the circular transition. As I already stated, the circular transition is still in a non-committal phase, the same phase as the energy transition was in 15 years ago. Moreover, the circular transition is much more complex than the energy transition. Nor is there a clear measure of progress, such as CO_2 emissions in the energy transition. So different goals are needed for different parts of the circular economy. That takes a lot of time and research.

This Is How We Can Accelerate the Circular Transition

More pressure and coercion is needed through legislation and regulations. More coercive measures are needed, such as the obligation for companies to use a certain percentage of recycled materials. Or the obligation to make certain products repairable with public instructions, such as those which have existed for a long time in the car industry. Many of the current laws and regulations are rooted in the linear economy and thus form an obstacle to circular initiatives. For example, the Waste Substances Act in the Netherlands and other European countries prohibits the re-use of waste. This law dates back to the time when waste was seen as harmful to the environment. And because there are no rules or standards yet, biomass is hardly ever used as a building material. In fact, the existing standards favour building with concrete and disadvantage building with biomass.

A mental shift is also needed among consumers and producers. Social standards, as we have also seen in other transitions, can make a difference here. Measuring each other on wasteful and polluting behaviour can be an important impulse for a transition. At present, only a small minority buy recycled or second-hand products because the social norm considers them inferior, and companies do not use recycled plastic, for example, because they consider it undesirable. Entrepreneurs also do not yet sufficiently recognize that circular business models can be profitable. Think of leasing instead of buying (the shift from owning to using) electrical appliances, where the producer is responsible for managing and processing the raw materials.

Financiers also need more knowledge about circular principles and service models. The current forms of financing are still focused on linear companies and not on circular ones. So, there is not yet a financial level playing field. Investors make demands on circular companies which they are not yet able to meet. Circular companies pose a risk in the eyes of many financiers because they often have insufficient scale, while circular companies are looking for funding to scale up. They also need time to achieve a certain return, and that time is often not granted to them. There is enough capital, just not enough patient capital.

Alternative funding platforms such as crowdfunding are therefore indispensable for circular businesses.

The fact that circular earning models are so different from what investors are used to with the current linear earning models also makes it difficult to find investors. For example, in the case of the earning model 'product as a service', where companies offer products as services and consumers use washing machines and telephones, for example, is confusing for financiers: who bears responsibility for the product? Is it the customer or the producer? And how is this defined? It seems trivial, but investors struggle with it. Accountants who still think in terms of linear depreciation instead of revaluation also need a mental shift. They have to make the mental leap from residual value to harvest value. This also applies to lawyers, students and the government. This mental leap of scale is probably the most important thing to allow financial scaling up, so that circular companies and chains can scale up.

Finally, a particularly important accelerator for the circular transition is the reform of the tax system. The current tax system provides the wrong incentives by taxing labour and making it expensive, while leaving harmful pollution untaxed. For a long time, and in line with the 'polluter pays' principle, there have been pleas for tax reform that does not tax labour but rather pollution and consumption. It is also more logical to tax the extraction of value (pollution and use) rather than the addition of value (employment). By turning this around, and taxing smarter rather than more, some 23 billion euro will be freed up within a few years to reduce the burden on labour for both households and employers. If we do this intelligently, the lowest incomes will benefit the most in terms of purchasing power. In early 2021, The Ex'tax Project presented a Delta Plan for Tax Reform containing a roadmap to 2030 with a list of 20 measures that have been calculated, including a reduction in income tax, income support for the lowest income groups, payroll tax credits for circular innovation, a mileage tax, an air passenger tax, a shipping tax, a tax on industrial pollution, a water tax, a tobacco tax, an ammonia tax, a waste disposal tax and a CO_2 tax. These measures have been calculated and will lead to a substantial reduction in CO_2 emissions, give a boost to the circular economy and create significantly more jobs. The Netherlands can become a guiding light for this tax reform, but it will require courage, guts and leadership.

The Agriculture and Food Transition

The agricultural system we have created is completely economized. Everything revolves around productivity, volume and growth; it always has to be better, bigger, faster and more. Even more efficiency, even more optimization, even more increase in scale. But there are limits to better, bigger, faster and more. Dutch agriculture is a perfect example. While it is one of the most innovative sectors, it is not one of the most sustainable. The Netherlands is the second-largest food exporter in the world after the United States, which is amazing for such a small country (the Netherlands fits into the US 230 times) because it means you have to get an enormous yield out of a hectare. To do that, you have to use a lot of fertilizers and chemicals very intensively and unnaturally. This brings with it a number of persistent problems, such as the manure problem, environmental damage, greenhouse gas emissions, animal diseases and soil exhaustion. As a result, the agricultural system is running up against its limits and clashes with environmental standards (nitrogen), climate standards (carbon dioxide) and nature standards (biodiversity). Agriculture is digging its own grave due to sharply declining fertility and soil quality. If we continue in this way, the amount of agricultural land will remain more or less the same, but the number of farmers will be decimated, and they will earn even less. In 30 years' time, the last farmer will turn off the lights.

Almost everyone agrees that the current agricultural system is at a dead end. There is no escape; our agricultural system must change. Not just to be a little different, but really different. The time is ripe for a new agricultural paradigm: from agriculture at the expense of nature, the environment, animals and people, to agriculture that strengthens nature, enriches the soil, puts animal welfare first and pays farmers a fair price. Agriculture where quality is more important than quantity in every respect. In short, future-proof agriculture is natural, sustainable, uses biological pesticides and provides clean and healthy products at socially reasonable prices. This future-proof agriculture is modern circular agriculture, without wasting energy and raw materials and where all residual flows are used. Animal feed, for example, is then made from unused food. This future-proof agriculture is also high-tech agriculture, using the most modern digital tools such as sensors and drones for precision agriculture, big data analysis to dissect and use plans at a molecular level and to make them work optimally, and blockchain for conducting financial transactions.

This sustainable and digital circular agriculture is part of a new circular economy that is more regionally oriented. A region needs a scale of 50 by 50 km to circulate sufficient energy, raw materials, materials and food. Of course, global food chains will continue to exist, but the starting point is to provide people in the region with healthy food and thus make them healthier. So, it is no longer the mantra of large-scale export worldwide to feed as many mouths as possible but to provide knowledge and expertise so that countries and regions can do it them selves. That is more natural and also makes them more crisis - and shock-resistant. For arable farming, this means a shift from traditional to new crops and raw materials. Ultimately, arable farming will become the purveyor of raw materials for the biobased economy, in which high-quality bioproducts will be made from these raw materials. Examples of biobased crops are elephant grass (miscanthus) for making paper, hemp for making building materials, flax for making fibre or insulation material and lupins, which can be used as a meat substitute, among other things. In addition, medicinal crops such as cannabis, herbs, vanilla and turmeric may become popular because they respond to the current health trend.

At the same time, arable farming will continue to supply traditional crops for local and regional markets. I also see a great future for saline agriculture, especially in the Randstad. Saltwater seepage is creeping under the dikes as a result of the rising sea level, so it will not be possible to cope with increasing salination in the future. It would therefore be wiser to move with the salination process and focus on saline agriculture. Experiments with aquatic crops such as algae and seaweed, glasswort, sea kale, sea lavender and saline broccoli have been going on for years on a small scale. These are currently supplied as delicacies to top restaurants, but this fast-growing niche market could well become commonplace in all restaurants in the near future.

So, we are seeing a wide range of entirely new organic, medicinal and saline crops – and saline crops that can be used to make specialized, high-quality and healthy products. This also means completely new customers and new markets, such as the pharmaceutical, cosmetics, healthcare, clothing and packaging industries. This requires farmers to cooperate much more with experts from other fields such as IT, healthcare, construction, chemistry and pharmacy. For example, pioneering farmers are already collaborating with chemical engineers on biotech-crops, with data experts on blockchain applications, with food experts and health experts on healthy products and with builders on bio-building materials.

This Is How We Can Accelerate the Agircultural and Food Transition

Accelerating the agricultural and food transition starts with a new, big story, which we can then make small. In that new story, it is not humans who are central, but nature. People produce food together with nature instead of at nature's expense, and cultivate raw materials naturally, which then form the building blocks for the new, biobased economy. People also produce salty food on the water, moving with the water. Everything revolves around quality instead of quantity. Not wanting to feed the entire world but helping the world to do it itself and exporting knowledge and expertise. Local and regional is the basis for this, with high-tech tools such as robots, drones and advanced software. In a sustainable and circular way, in short: naturally. Half of the current agricultural land could then suffice, the other half could be used for nature, forestry, energy and housing. What a beautiful and natural story that is!

For this, we need mental system breakers who question the current agricultural system and dare to break it down. These system breakers (tilters, demolishers) react quickly and adequately to everything that is unnatural and show how it can be done naturally. One of the biggest barriers to making agriculture more sustainable is the European subsidy system. Every year, Europe spends about 65 billion euros on agricultural subsidies. That is 36% of the EU budget and is equivalent to about 115 euros per EU citizen. Of these subsidies, 80% go to 20% of agricultural holdings, which means that this money is used to maintain intensive agriculture in Europe, with all the associated disadvantages. According to the EU, subsidies are necessary to support farmers' incomes and to guarantee food safety and food security. However, as food safety is guaranteed by European legislation, we do not need to worry about it so much, and therefore no subsidies are needed for it. And the idea that we in Europe should feed the rest of the world is a chutzpah. Developing countries benefit more from the transfer of our knowledge and expertise so that they can grow their own food sustainably and efficiently. European agricultural subsidies are also intended to stimulate nature, but nothing is further from the truth: in the regions that have received the most European subsidies, biodiversity is at its lowest. According to the European Court of Auditors, this greening policy has already failed because there are no verifiable goals.

Radical reform of European agricultural subsidies can significantly accelerate the agricultural transition to sustainable and circular agriculture. Because agriculture is responsible for almost 30% of greenhouse gases, it would also be a major boost for climate policy. But because of an effective lobby by farmers and the agro-industry, the most recent attempt in Brussels to green the EU's agricultural policy failed. It illustrates how difficult it is to break the power of the existing agricultural institutions. It is a serious setback for the ambitious Green Deal, which was designed to reduce greenhouse gas emissions from agriculture and to better protect biodiversity by means of financial incentives.

The dismantling of intensive livestock farming is in full swing but can be accelerated by buying out livestock farmers with a fair price for their land, buildings and animals. The released agricultural land should then be given a new purpose in the form of nature, production forests or circular agriculture. The development of circular agriculture can also be accelerated by subsidies and interest-free loans for farmers who opt for new, circular revenue models and make their business operations sustainable. To give farmers a fair price for their products, the whole chain must change. This requires 'chain cutters', who cut through the long chain from production and distribution to sales and consumption. Take the example of eggs. After the eggs are laid, they are collected by a trader, then packed by a grader and sometimes sold on before going to the distribution centre which delivers them to a supermarket or restaurant. This way, a 'fresh' egg only reaches your plate after two weeks. As a result, farmers get too little for their eggs, consumers pay too little, and inter-mediaries and supermarkets pocket the profits. This can be done much easier, faster and cheaper, so the farmer can get a better and fairer price. That is why more and more farmers are delivering their eggs, cheese and meat directly from the farm to consumers, supermarkets or restaurants. It is so simple and so logical that you wonder why we have not always done it this way. Because international free trade agreements such as CETA and TTIP prevent farmers from receiving a fair price, the free market is failing here too, and the govern-ment must intervene. This can be done through price corrections with fiscal interventions, such as environmental levies and fertilizer taxes, and with financial incentives such as passing on sustainability requirements in product prices. Institutional incentives can also help, such as making agreements with supermarkets on better price policy, and governance incentives such as agree-ments on fair prices in international trade treaties.

The Spatial Transition

The integrated water, climate, nature, energy and housing challenge is extraordinarily complex and has far-reaching consequences for spatial planning. Nowhere in the world can you find so many people, activities, infrastructure and mobility on such a small, low-lying surface as in the Netherlands. Keeping this beautiful but vulnerable delta habitable and liveable is a major challenge in view of imminent climate change and rising sea levels. But also, the spatial claims that the economy, we humans and nature place on the urbanized landscape require a reassessment and redistribution of space. For example, the incorporation of wind energy, solar energy, geothermal energy, biomass, heat networks and hydrogen in the energy transition is a complex spatial puzzle. In the coming decades, more and more energy sources will emerge which, in spatial terms, will be at the expense of agricultural land, while at the same time more space will be needed for hummus, hemp and flax in order to make building materials from biomass. Much more space for production forest is also needed to provide the wood for the construction of wooden houses and buildings.

As if this puzzle were not complex enough, the Netherlands is also the first country in Europe to run into economic difficulties because it comes up against hard environmental and nature boundaries. In order to achieve the targets, set for climate (CO_2), environment (nitrogen) and nature (biodiversity), far-reaching and mutually reinforcing measures are needed. The recent PFAS chemicals crisis, which brought numerous construction activities to a standstill at the end of 2019, made the pain of the transition tangible. But for the reform of agriculture, industry, construction, traffic and transport, further painful measures are inevitable. This requires not only the agricultural transition described above but also a fundamental reform of industry, construction and transport. And even then, the spatial puzzle is not entirely solved. The sea-level rise associated with climate change is forcing the government to revise its water distribution policy as well. With an expected rise in sea level of half a metre to a metre this century, and further land subsidence in coastal areas of half a metre to a metre, parts of the Netherlands will be 7 to 9 m below sea level.

It is sacrilege to say this, but it raises the question as to what extent these extremely low-lying polder areas can still be kept dry by pumping and draining. There will come a time when, not only from a safety point of view, but also from a cost and benefits point of view, the polder areas must be flooded. This calls for a new Delta Plan, but one that is different from the current one: less of a blueprint against nature, more organic development in co-creation with nature. Zeeland in particular must once again become the testing ground for this unprecedented task, which we can tackle by searching, learning and experimenting.

But the total spatial task is so complex that the current laws and regulations are seriously inadequate. As we have seen with the PFAS regulation for the nitrogen dossier, legal palliatives no longer work. And because the Environment Act described in the chapter on government is not yet a solution, a Transition Act, with temporary exemptions from laws and regulations that obstruct the transition and new rules that stimulate the transition would be a good solution. Such a transition act could be more effective than new legislation in all sorts of separate areas because draughting and implementing new legislation is time-consuming and complex, while the urgency of the issues we face calls for acute legal action. For example, a transition act can create legal space to break the current deadlock on nitrogen, biodiversity and climate. In some respects, this transition act is comparable to the Crisis and Recovery Act of 2009, which created legal space for new infrastructure after the credit crisis of 2008. The difference, however, is that back then, the old paradigm was still to speed up infrastructural projects in order to give an economic boost to the construction sector. In these times of environmental, nature and climate crisis, this would be counterproductive and would only exacerbate the problem. In the new paradigm, the balance between economy, environment and nature should be restored, and this should be the focus of the Transition Act.

The integral spatial task, therefore, requires a different role from the government. Spatial policy is currently decentralized and fragmented, and this is no longer acceptable in view of the complex task ahead. More alignment and coordination at the central level is needed. But we should not want to return to the heyday of spatial planning, with top-down government control and detailed spot plans. We cannot go back to the old days, but we can go forward: back to the core in a modern way. The most important thing is that a new national strategy is drawn up, in which the transition tasks of climate, water, energy, nature and the environment take centre stage so that a new story is told which is aimed at redesigning a future-proof Netherlands. Perhaps with a Ministry of Space, not as an end in itself, but as a means to achieve better spatial planning from a symbiosis of top-down and bottom-up initiatives. In concrete terms, this means a coordinating and facilitating government that gives direction and offers space.

One thing is certain: the Netherlands is going to change drastically. There was once a scornful laugh when I said that the Netherlands would change more in the next 50 years than in the past 500. Now, more and more people see the necessity. If we let spatial developments run their course, we will continually run up against the limits. Nature will deteriorate, construction will come to a standstill, we will not become climate-proof and the landscape will become even more cluttered. That is why we need a new grand narrative, in which the balance between man and nature, between urbanization, infrastructure, energy and agriculture on the one hand and climate, water, nature and the environment on the other, is paramount.

The Financial Transition

Whereas the financial system was originally designed to support the real economy, in practice it has become increasingly detached from it. During the covid crisis, financial markets flourished and share prices shot through the roof as if we had never done better, while the economy was in deep recession. This shows that the financial sector is no longer a means, but an end in itself. As much as 95% of the money is used to create more money instead of spending it on products and services. So, the balance between the financial system and the real economy is horribly out of control. The financial sector consists of commercial banks, investment banks, insurers, pension funds and regulators such as central banks. The main markets are the money market, the capital market, the derivatives market and the foreign exchange market, with payment accounts, savings accounts, loans, bonds, shares and derivatives as the main financial products and services. All are aimed at the highest possible return in the shortest possible time. This is all about shareholder value and much less about added value for customers.

A wave of mergers in the 1990s created enormous financial conglomerates and a strong concentration of power. As a result, the complexity of the organizations has increased to such an extent that hardly anyone can oversee it anymore. In large banks, for example, one department often does not know what the other department is developing in terms of financial products and services, so they work completely independently of each other. This usually leads to more regulations, which only increases the complexity. This is a vicious circle that is difficult to break because there is a monoculture in thinking. The same books and models are used in economics and business schools around the world so that financial experts all have the same education and are brainwashed in the same way. This lack of diversity leads to introspection and tunnel vision. In such an environment, there is no place for fresh thinkers and cross-thinkers. This is also reflected in leadership that is traditional, top-down and masculine, and in employees who are more loyal to managers than to customers. This dominant structure, culture and way of working are deeply rooted in the financial sector and therefore difficult to break from within, although there are employees and initiatives within financial institutions that are trying to turn the tide. The power of ultra-short-term thinking aimed at shareholders is stubborn and difficult to break through. Outside thinkers are needed to break through the ingrained patterns.

In the chapter on the systemic crises, I describe in detail that there are three major flaws in the financial-economic system that cause persistent problems. The first problem is that the financial-economic system still lacks a brake on the size of the financial sector. The second problem is about money creation and the granting of credit. The growing mountain of debt creates instability and could degenerate into another financial crisis at any moment. The third problem is the allocation of money. As much as 95% of the money is used to create more money. Only a small proportion goes to the real economy. The conclusion is unmistakable: the financial system is sick, and no cure has been found yet. We have learned from the last financial crisis in 2008/2009. There is more control and supervision and there are larger financial buffers, but that is only dealing with the symptoms. The structure, culture and workings of the financial system have not changed substantially, so it is just a matter of time before the next financial crisis occurs.

My assessment is that the financial transition has not yet reached the tipping point. There is still no real urgency to actually change. But there is a growing awareness within the financial sector that things must and can be done differently. Also, the attitude of people within the sector has changed – partly out of necessity, partly of their own free will. Yet change is slow, because the 'old ways of thinking' still dominate, especially at the top of banks and financial institutions. So, there is no real breakthrough yet, but there are more and more hairline cracks in the system. There are also more and more bottom-up initiatives, such as cryptocurrencies with the wildly popular bitcoin, the rapid growth of sustainable and digital banking, the meteoric growth of crowdfunding, the rise of financial cooperatives and decentralized forms of insurance such as bread funds. All these initiatives are putting pressure on the system.

There is a growing distrust in the dollar in the current financial system, and this has been reinforced by the coronas crisis. Two developments feed this distrust: in the last year, almost 25% of all dollars in circulation have been reprinted (!), and there have been negative interest rates. The debt mountain is growing to a record height. These developments, which were considered impossible until recently, reflect the instability of the financial system. It has already passed its sell-by date, but nevertheless, it keeps being put on a drip. Two interlocking developments are accelerating the demise of the financial system. On the one hand, big capital and big tech companies are moving away from the dollar and towards bitcoin and other cryptocurrencies. On the other, there is a fast-growing, fanatical group of hundreds of thousands of young people who want to break the power of the big banks and see bitcoin as an expression of an alternative money system.

In the background, many entrepreneurs are building an alternative money system based on bitcoin. This is revolutionary because it enables global financial transactions without the intervention of a bank. So what Uber is to the world of transport and Airbnb to the world of travel, bitcoin can be to the world of finance. The recent surge in bitcoin's popularity shows just how volatile the financial system is. The fact that SpaceX and Tesla CEO Elon Musk has invested one and a half-billion dollars in bitcoin is a signal that this crypto coin is becoming mainstream and is paving the way for a new financial system without banks. Incidentally, Tesla has already stopped accepting bitcoin as a means of payment for its electric cars, out of concern for the enormous amount of (fossil) energy required for bitcoin mining. This is how the almost impossible seems to be possible after all: a decentralized and digital financial system and the collapse of the old, centralized, top-down financial system with powerful banks.

As an expression of this discontent and the growing resistance from below, an army of young amateur investors, organized via Reddit, recently turned the financial world upside down. They massively bought shares of the video game chain GameStop and pushed the price up to unprecedented heights in no time. As a result, large hedge funds, which had speculated on a price drop, suffered billions in losses. That was precisely the intention of the amateur investors, who despise hedge funds because they make a lot of money by investing aggressively with borrowed money. This action is not without risk for the amateur investors, because it is a kind of tulip mania. GameStop shares are artificially inflated, and they will also go down at some point, and then the amateur investors can lose out big time.

But there is more to it than that. The action also exposes the perverse structures of the stock market. It is a kind of David versus Goliath struggle: small private investors attacking the invincible Wall Street. It is a kind of protest movement, and the comparison with the Occupy movement is therefore easily made. Although this action will not topple the system, it does show how much impact a collective action by a relatively small group of citizens can have. This is a type of power that is underestimated and, as I have indicated before, I call it the illusion of powerlessness: citizens underestimate the enormous potential power they have when they act collectively. Ex-Unilever CEO Paul Polman recognized this, and once said that if any group of consumers united, they could bring down a multinational, which could even mean the end of such a big company. And indeed, if we really wanted to, we could bring down Monsanto, Shell or McDonald's within six months, but then we would have to stop buying their products *en masse*. I think that could actually happen in the future.

It is clear that the financial sector in its current form is not sustainable. A more diverse and decentralized financial system is needed because such a system is less vulnerable to disruption. Then the role of money and finance in society will also be brought back to normal proportions. Reducing and breaking up mega-banks, a financial transaction tax and banning certain financial products are necessary steps in this direction. Regulation is essential so that the financial market can once again serve the real economy and society. And facilitating customers instead of the shareholders should become the norm. This requires a turnaround in thinking. In fact, the financial system must be given back to the people, so that they again have a say in what happens to their money.

At the systemic level there are two alternatives to the present system of fractional reserve banking, namely full reserve banking and free banking. Full reserve banking means making money creation a public task and putting it in the hands of the government, and depriving banks of their money-creating capacity. Also, banks must fully cover their demandable liabilities with liquid assets. A clear demarcation between public and private is necessary to achieve financial stability. This way, the money system is democratized. Banks give individuals control over whether and how their money is invested. This reform could mean that bank runs are eliminated, total debts are reduced and the profits from money creation are collected democratically. Free banking means that anyone can start a currency and people can choose which currency they trust and want to use. It is a system in which banking is left entirely to the free market and banks are treated like any other business in a free market. They are then no longer subject to government supervision but must still meet their obligations. Both currents may reinforce each other in the future.

In any case, the financial transition that has been initiated is inevitable and irreversible. From a non-transparent sector to a transparent one. From overly complex to simpler. From the customer following, to the customer leading. The ultimate goal is to make money once again a medium with which we can create value that contributes to a better world, with financial institutions that become subservient to the real economy.

The Educational Transition

The covid crisis brought the future of education forward by 10 years. Suddenly, things became possible that had previously been considered impossible, and innovations were implemented at an accelerated pace. Digital education, tailor-made education, a flexible approach and better cooperation suddenly seemed possible, but sustaining them is difficult. After the crisis, there is a tendency to fall back into old patterns and structures, and it is precisely in these that education is stuck. For decades, our education has been trapped in the stranglehold of an outdated system. The excessive culture of measurement, testing and control is a clear symptom of this. Everything has to be measured in order to meet an imposed standard, and this puts constant pressure on everyone. Schools have to perform, otherwise, their reputation will suffer, and they will have fewer students. Teachers have to perform using compulsory teaching methods, with little room for individual initiative. Students have to perform, otherwise, they will fall by the wayside what could harm their careers. Parents demand performance from their children and from the school and criticize at the drop of a hat.

Meanwhile, education is constantly being tinkered with to make it better, without much result. Across the board, the quality of education has only declined in recent decades, as the State of Education report from the Education Inspectorate shows. This stranglehold, a vicious circle in which everyone holds each other captive, is rooted in an industrial nineteenth-century educational model with one teacher in front of the class who tells one story to 30 pupils. So, we treat every student the same and teach them all the same material. But if you treat every student the same, you get increasing inequality. Every person is unique and therefore unequal, but every person should have equal opportunities. The current education system, therefore, leads to more inequality (see the SER-report on equal opportunities in education). This means that an essentially different starting point must be leading in education, namely diversity and customization. Each pupil will have his or her own learning route (collective learning will remain important), the teacher will be given a great deal of room to develop, administrators will facilitate professionals and schools will be given autonomy. This is an enormous turnaround, which comes down to putting the education system back into the service of people so that people and the system reinforce each other instead of working against each other. Now it is the other way round and it is not the pupil or the teacher who is central, but the organization.

An illustrative example: when I entered my old secondary school a few years ago, I had to shake 15 hands. The hand of the rector, the vice principal, the education coordinator, the education planner, the education monitors, the research monitors, etc. 'Where are the teachers?' I asked because that was what I had come for. They turned out to be in the room next door. 'But what do you all do?' I asked. 'We organize education' was the answer. I said: 'When I went to school here, there was one rector, two vice principals (who also taught) and a caretaker. It was all about the pupil and the teacher. With you, it's all about the organization. 'Yes, but,' they sputtered, 'without that organization we can't exist. . .'.

The interference is huge, often with the best of intentions, but it's all exterior, all bureaucracy, all distraction. This goes to the heart of our education system, which has essentially outgrown itself. And this while education is absolutely the crucial link for the transition of the economy, society and all other transitions described in this chapter.

The core of the transition in education is a shift from standard to personalized education (not individualized education, because collective learning remains important), from yield to resource (pupil and teacher central), from control and management to space and freedom, and from subjects to themes that are offered in a multi- and interdisciplinary form, with a balance between theory and practice, between knowledge and competences. The goal is to give children and adolescents meaningful education that prepares them for a new economy and society, in which they develop throughout life. After all, young people need to become agile and resilient in order to be able to hold their own in a turbulent world. It cannot be that we train people for professions that will no longer exist in 10 years' time and that we do not include the professions that will exist then in the current curriculum. It is unacceptable that on our way from a compartmentalized society to a liquid society, we continue to divide education into compartments. You have to choose very early on at school whether you are an alpha, beta or a gamma student, and then you have to specialize again. At my university, the Erasmus University in Rotterdam, there are seven faculties, each of which has its own building. Seven silos. Within those faculties, you then have research and education departments, and they hardly work together, if at all. So, you have compartments within compartments within compartments. But the new generation of students has little use for these compartments. They are often interested in a wide range of subjects and mainly want to be educated and trained in a multi and interdisciplinary way.

The nice thing is that time does its work here. At a meeting with a number of CEOs of large companies, they told me what they were talking about in the boardrooms: leadership, sustainability, innovation, steering under uncertainty and transitions. 'Where do we find that at university? To be honest, you can't really study it yet,' I answered. 'Then we'll have to work like hell on it,' they said. But such a transition in education requires at least a generation, and many companies can't wait for that. They would go bankrupt. Not all companies are so agile and resilient that they survive the hurricane. That is why I am a passionate advocate of involving companies in education. In the future, education will belong to companies, and companies will sit at educational institutions, because learning, working and entrepreneurship are becoming increasingly intertwined. Fortunately, there are more and more examples of innovative campuses where companies and educational institutions work closely together.

Nature has taught us an important lesson with the covid crisis. It is diverse and resilient, and therefore crisis-proof. Our lives are so unnatural that we have turned away from nature, mentally and physically, and have even elevated ourselves above it. It is important that children learn that humans are part of nature and can learn a lot from it. By learning to experience nature again and getting to know its resilience, children and adolescents will also learn to deal with uncertainties and risks differently. Now we are proud and reward children when they do not make mistakes, but we should be proud of them and reward them when they make mistakes and learn from them. We are preparing them for continuity and stability when we should be preparing them for change and instability. They must learn how to deal with uncertainties and risks and be able to think and work together with others.

This requires a fundamentally different organization of education, flat and horizontal organizations with as little bureaucracy and overhead as possible. With administrators who steer by the main lines, who constantly connect the world outside the school with the world inside, who respond to changes and at the same time give direction and offer space. It requires room for teachers to develop, to be able to respond to the major current issues that we face with a dynamic curriculum that balances hard knowledge and soft skills, and in which children and adolescents themselves can also influence the curriculum. Give each school the space and freedom to figure this out for itself. Do not impose this collectively from above. We've been doing it for decades, and it doesn't work. It only creates more workload, more stress and more bureaucracy. Of course, you have a number of frameworks within which you need to work, and you set quality standards. That's fine. But there must be time and space for schools to work that out for themselves. In practice, this can be done through intensive cooperation between schoolteachers, pupils, parents and stakeholders from the surrounding area. This is also natural because human development never stops and is an integral part of life. This leads to inclusive education where everyone is welcome and receives equal and optimal opportunities. This makes education meaningful and increases the participation of future adults.

It is certainly hopeful that the field of education worldwide is changing enormously. The realization is dawning that society and the economy are changing faster and more fundamentally than education. There is a growing movement that realizes that education must change substantially in order to close that gap. This time, not top-down forced by the government, but bottom-up from the educational practice itself. In many places, new forms of education are being experimented with. The government can make the difference by embracing this educational innovation and by helping to scale it up, and not by putting the brakes on or thwarting it, as is currently often the case, on the basis of control and management. In the end, that only has the opposite effect. The growing bottom-up movement is a silent revolution that cannot be stopped, only slowed down. In order to accelerate this educational transition, it is important that all experiments are linked together on the basis of an overarching educational vision and thus reinforce each other in the same direction. That is why there is a great need for connectors who can link experiments and the networks behind them so that upscaling can take place. If that happens, a counterforce with the power to change can form, and systemic change in education can emerge organically. It will be exciting. We still have decades of work ahead of us.

The Health Care Transition

Like in education, the covid crisis has also shown healthcare to be resilient. The crisis has shown that we can count on the people in care in extreme situations. Although care workers have been put to the test during this lengthy period of crisis management and survival, they have done a heroic job, for which we are grateful. They have worked together across barriers and have accelerated the switch to online care services. The covid crisis also proved that we can look further than costs alone.

But the covid crisis also mercilessly exposed the systemic errors in healthcare. Decades of cutbacks, such as on the salaries of care workers and the elimination of some 10,000 hospital beds in the last 10 years, are now having their effect. Due to the long-lasting devaluation (not only financially) of the profession, many people have also stopped or are threatening to stop working in care. It has also become painfully clear how dependent we are on medical instruments and medicines from abroad. Because the current healthcare system is all about efficiency and profit – just in time, as they call it in logistical jargon – everything just works, but the healthcare system comes to an acute standstill when there is a disruption. Because every system that revolves around efficiency and profitability lacks buffer capacity, it is not crisis-proof. It lacks resilience and crashes with every disruption.

The fact that healthcare proved to be so resilient during the covid crisis is entirely down to the healthcare workers. But many care workers are at their wits' end and are dreading the post-covid period when much of the care that has been left behind will need to be picked up. And it is striking that, no matter how much praise politicians may have for care workers, doctors and nurses themselves (i.e., a bottom-up movement), they have taken the initiative for a national recovery plan (talking about resilience), for which they have to call on the Ministry, health insurers and other parties in the care sector to join them. Surely this is the world upside down? Thanks to the excessive market forces we have created a dehumanized care system: complex, bureaucratic and focused on profit.

Healthcare no longer belongs to people, but to large, unwieldy healthcare organizations and health insurers who stuff us into spreadsheets. It is a system where 'clients' and 'patients' are at the service of the healthcare system instead of the other way around. Being sick is rewarded, being healthy is not. The emphasis is still on cure, while it has long been known that prevention leads to more healthy life years. And, although the aim of care is to make people better and keep them healthy, the current care system makes people less sick, but not healthy. What is clear is that healthcare is not a market, but a public good. A hospital should not make a profit but provide the best possible care. For me, that's the heart of the care transition: making care of and for people again and putting the system back at the service of people. First and foremost, this requires a shift from control and management to trust, and from complexity to simplicity. For curative care it means a shift from curation to prevention, and from competition to cooperation. In long-term care, it means a shift from classic assistance to modern support, from 'taking care of' to 'taking care that'.

Looking beyond covid, what could a post-covid care system look like? If I had to sketch the rough outlines, I would come up with the following: in a new care system, the person should be central, not the large care organizations. It's all about trust, self-reliance, cooperation, cure and prevention. A care system that is more human, simpler, more affordable and more digital. More human means that people think and decide together with care professionals, that care is developed and delivered tailor-made, and that the human aspect (personal experience) comes first. Simpler means that funding can be much simpler, with multi-year agreements on insurance and that not everything is registered on an hourly basis. And less urge to control and manage also means much less bureaucracy. If we make healthcare simpler, we can also make it more affordable. It can save about a third of the money we currently spend on care. That's a formidable sum when you consider that in the Netherlands we spend 90 billion euros on care every year. The covid crisis has also underlined the importance of more digital healthcare. Digital care means that online contact with a medical specialist is possible and that diagnostics can also be done at the GP's surgery or at people's homes. But digital means much more than video calls and digitalization. It is mainly about the important role that digital technologies can play in organizing the process around the care client and the care provider, and innovative entrants must be given space to achieve this.

The organizational characteristics of a post-covid care system are on a smaller scale, with the local and regional levels as the benchmark. After decades of scaling up, it appears that this has not led to more efficient, better and cheaper care. On the contrary. In a new healthcare system, smaller-scale care will therefore be the starting point. Back to the human scale, in other words: forward to the past.

At the local level, the integration of education, care and welfare is increasingly taking shape and different cultures – such as socially driven primary education and commercially driven childcare – are coming together. An example of this is the integral child centres, where the child is central in everything and everything is under one roof: education, care and youth care. It sounds so logical that you wonder why we haven't always done it this way. Once again, it appears that integrated thinking and acting is a condition for a more balanced society. At the regional level, care parties are going to cooperate more closely. Healthcare providers, healthcare insurers, hospitals, GPs, welfare organizations, companies and citizens form a regional ecosystem that is focused on cure and especially prevention. This requires a comprehensive approach and intensive cooperation based on trust. A wonderful example of such regional cooperation is Vitaal Vechtdal, a coalition formed by entrepreneurs which set out to collaborate with companies and schools to make people healthy. Through training programmes, competitions, courses, lifestyle monitoring and a preventive package aimed at more exercise and healthier eating, they get people moving. Vitaal Vechtdal starts from the philosophy that care should be an integral part of our lives. Why have we turned healthcare into a separate silo, which is outside our daily lives? Instead, care should be part of where we live (at home), where we work (office and home), where we learn (school and work), where we recreate (outdoors) and where we are cared for. This is so logical and natural that it is incomprehensible that we have not made it happen. Vitaal Vechtdal is a success. A health movement began, and after a few years, it produced visible results, such as saving pharmacy costs and a significantly lower absenteeism rate. They saved the region millions of euros. If we were to do this throughout the Netherlands, we could save billions of euros of avoided health care costs.

In order to scale up the example of Vitaal Vechtdal, health insurers will have to turn their financing models upside down. The starting point would then no longer be to make people less ill, but to make them healthier. Not by financing illness, but by promoting and rewarding a healthy lifestyle. A few health insurers are already experimenting with this on a small scale, but in the future, all health insurers will follow this health path. Preferably in a cooperative form, as in the 18th and 19th centuries.

How Can We Accelerate the Health Care Transition?

The good news is that for years a civilized uprising has been taking place from bottom-up, out of discontent and frustration about the defunct care system. Nowhere else will you find so many loyal and docile people with a heart for their work as in healthcare. Before they revolt, there has to be something really wrong.

And there certainly is. For years, care workers have been frustrated about the high work pressure, low salaries, bureaucracy and cutbacks. In the Netherlands alone, there are more than a 100 innovation networks in the care sector. General practitioners, nurses, informal carers, young care professionals, pharmacists, care cooperatives, all want a more humane, simple and affordable care. The trick is to use the dynamics of the current crisis to accelerate the transition in healthcare.

There is a bright and different future for health care. But that requires a lot from us: patience, time, trust, a plan and leadership. The most important thing is to break through the existing power relations in health care. The current health care system is unsustainable; after 15 years the expiry date has been exceeded. But demolishing the current care system and building a new one will easily take 10 years. So, it would be wise to take an evolutionary approach to demolition and construction, by experimenting step by step on the basis of an overarching vision for a future healthcare system. There is already a great deal of experimentation going on in the health care sector, but one experiment after another is being piled up on top of another and not enough time is being taken to allow these experiments to take root. The current experiments, therefore, do not lead to structural change. To achieve this, it is high time to link the large number of experiments so that they form an organic whole, and a new structure is created. This calls for connectors and translators. Only when that happens we will see the systemic change in healthcare that we so desperately need right now.

The Social Transition

Our society is also in transition. The new society has a different structure and order than the current one, which still has a structure and order dating from the nineteenth century and is rooted in ideological and religious pillars. Despite the breakdown of religious pillars, the characteristics of this outdated structure and organization – top-down, vertical and centrally led – are still very much present in today's society. For a long time, the pillars dominated all social systems, from education and health care, trade unions, political parties and industry associations, housing corporations, broadcasters and newspapers to banks and water boards. This 'silo society' with a dominant, top-down, central role for the government resulted in a tightly managed society that functioned well into the twentieth century.

But in the 1980s, the first hairline cracks appeared in the silo. With the rise of neoliberalism, market forces made their appearance: the government withdrew and the (semi)public sector was privatized. Scaling up and merging were the starting points. People became customers, pupils became educational consumers and schools became educational factories that had to compete with each other. This excessive market function meant that everything revolved around returns, efficiency, effectiveness, costs and benefits on the basis of competition and rivalry. The social systems became unwieldy, bureaucratic and rigid, and instead of supporting people, they increasingly began to hinder them. This gradually led to the creation of two worlds that gradually grew apart: the system world and the living world.

In the system world, a clay layer of managers, technocrats and bureaucrats tried to steer by control and containment, while in the living world professionals and citizens needed space and trust. These two worlds are now diametrically opposed, which means that they are increasingly getting in each other's way instead of strengthening each other. If social systems become dysfunctional, there are two possibilities: either they die or they adapt and reinvent themselves. And it is precisely this process of demolishing the old and building the new that is now underway.

It is an evolutionary revolution. Every great transition is accompanied by a change of power. The old, established order (regime) has the power and is still dominant, but is threatened by a new order from below that is slowly but surely forming a new power. The old order is resisting the emerging new order with all available means in order to retain its power for as long as possible. What is happening now is a shift from established, conservative power to transformative power. Power is the ability to mobilize resources such as knowledge, material, money, lobbying power, rules and laws for a specific purpose. Transformative power is the ability to change the distribution of resources. See all research by Flor Avelino, who once graduated *cum laude* with me. This new, emerging power is no longer determined solely by size, scope or financial capacity, but equally by the ability to organize oneself cleverly, quickly, adequately and flexibly and to constantly respond to changes in the environment. Today, the established power is still superior in terms of protecting existing resources (knowledge, money, lobbying power, infrastructure, fossil fuels), but the question is for how long.

Just as unmistakably, but still chaotic, less clear and less structured, a new order is also emerging that is more adapted to the demands of modern society. This new order is currently still mainly moving in the undercurrent and is therefore still under the radar for many people. But this bottom-up movement has grown explosively over the past 10 years, and if you look closely you will see a fast-growing group of passionate citizens, entrepreneurs, social and economic entrepreneurs who are ready to take over power in this transition. It is a misconception that this movement consists of do-gooders or hippies. On the contrary, it is mainly business-minded, driven pragmatists such as self-employed people with their own companies (two-thirds of the self-employed choose to do this, a third are forced to do so) and citizens with social enterprises and cooperatives. They move in new networks, communities and cooperatives and thus create their own playing field, whether physical or virtual. In this arrangement, it is not the collective as one might think or expect, but the individual who is the starting point, albeit flexibly linked to and with each other. Not enforced from above, but spontaneously from below. Not from self-reliance, but from co-reliance. In this way, a new horizontal and decentralized social fabric is created from bottom up, in which everyone is unequal but has equal rights. This movement, as a response to the excessively profitable society, is driven by new values such as trust, togetherness, space for personal development and a greater eye for the long term. Human beings thus regain their central position. It is back to the core, the human measure, in a very modern, innovative way. It is forward to the past.

As part of the bottom-up movement, this new order is most visible in the form of the explosion of citizens' initiatives, 'the commons', that has taken place in the last decade. These citizens' initiatives cover almost all areas of society: from care to welfare, from energy to mobility, from food to construction, from security to integration and from culture to education and urban development. In the Netherlands alone, approximately 1 million people are directly and indirectly active in this movement. Worldwide, hundreds of millions of people are affiliated to it. This in itself is not surprising, because there is a lot of positive energy for change in society, and citizens can and want much more than before. The pioneers of this movement also have the knowledge, expertise and technical tools to do things themselves. There are already some 650 energy cooperatives in the Netherlands, but also hundreds of care cooperatives, bread funds and food cooperatives. There is therefore a growing group of citizens who are willing and able to actively participate in society. But there is also a large group of citizens who are still passive and expect the government to take care of things for them. Transitions, therefore, take place in phases and segments. It starts with a small group of pioneers, then the leaders of the pack join in, then the pack itself and finally the laggards. We are currently in the transition phase from 1 million pioneers and front runners to a pack of 2–2.5 million people. The tipping point is around 25%, which means 3 to 3.5 million adults in the Dutch population. If 25% of the population embraces a transition, the non-linear character of a transition will allow the remaining 75% to join relatively quickly. We are therefore approaching the tipping point, and things can suddenly go fast.

This Is How We Can Accelerate the Social Transition

This social transition is a complex, slow and autonomous process, but it can be accelerated by the government stimulating and rewarding active citizenship. To this end, citizens' initiatives must be facilitated by removing obstacles in the field of regulations and bureaucracy and, where possible, providing temporary financial support. The previously discussed Environment Act is a good example of how the government can promote active citizenship and place the initiative firmly in the hands of citizens and companies. Decentralization, or the transfer of government tasks, competencies and money from the state to municipalities, is also favourable for active citizenship in theory. In practice, however, things are more difficult, and we see that, in the social domain, municipalities have not yet really come closer to citizens and that there is once again a call for more direction from the national government. Citizens themselves can also be more proactive and use their latent power much more. A growing group of citizens are active and participate through numerous citizens' initiatives. But there are also a large group of citizens who are not yet ready for this and rather passively expect the government to take care of things for them. Complex issues such as sustainability and digitalization require citizens to adopt a more active attitude;

otherwise, they will suffer. For example, citizens are still barely aware of how carelessly they deal with their data, and how they indiscriminately give it away to data supercompanies. Citizens can be less naive and more proactive here and ensure that this data becomes and remains their property again. The government can stimulate them in this by means of cooperatives that collect and manage data for groups of citizens.

The Democratic Transition

The 'mother of all transitions' is the democratic transition. This transition is so far-reaching and complex that I have never dared to touch it before. But the democratic transition is more topical than ever, given the growing dissatisfaction with the way democracy works in many countries. The dissatisfaction is clearly visible in the United States, South America, Europe and in parts of Asia. Worldwide, democracy is under pressure and requires a fundamental change. Global research by the World Values Survey shows that there is less and less confidence in the practical implementation of democracy in democratic institutions. In Europe, about two-thirds of the population dislikes the democratic institutions in politics. Parties, governments, parliaments and the media are the most distrusted. Paradoxically, the same survey shows that the idea of democracy is embraced by more than 90% of people. Never before in modern history have there been so many democracies: 117 out of a total of 195 countries. Over the past decade, hand in hand with rising populism, the call for strong leaders has also risen sharply. Or, as the influential writer David van Reybrouck puts it: 'There is something strange going on with democracy: everyone seems to long for it, but no one believes in it anymore'. Indifference about politics is no greater or less today than it was in the past. It does keep people busy, but mainly in the sense of increasing frustration. There is a growing gap between what citizens think is necessary and what the politicians actually do.

Looking through the transition lens, you can see the symptoms of that dissatisfaction, such as the 'bashing' of politicians and politics in general, even though it is only a relatively small group that does so. Worldwide, the number of demonstrations is increasing for various reasons, including racism, discrimination, inequality, climate change, migration and autonomy. There is also widespread opposition to the self-absorbed political caste that operates in its own universe. In addition, numerous political scandals are widening the trust gap. In the Netherlands, we have had a series of affairs that speak volumes: the benefits affair, the Groningen natural gas scandal, the abolition of the dividend tax and the adoption scandal.

Looking at the underlying causes, you can see a number of cyclical shifts. For example, voter turnout has been low for some time now, and a relatively large group no longer votes at all. In the Netherlands, this is about 20% of those entitled to vote, but at the last Belgian federal election in 2019, where voting is compulsory, 90% turned out to vote and 6% voted blank. Only about 2% of the Dutch population is a member of a political party, whereas after the Second

World War the KVP (The Catholic People's Party) alone had more members than all of today's political parties put together. A large group of citizens therefore no longer feel represented – or rather seen and heard – by politics. They feel trapped between the coldness of the market and the bureaucracy of the government, and that is not a pleasant feeling to experience the worst of both worlds.

Therefore, a new balance between citizen, market and government is urgently needed. This is also part of the explanation for the explosive increase in the number of citizens' initiatives. Based on the adage 'If the government doesn't do it and the market lets us down', 'we'll do it ourselves', citizens are taking matters into their own hands. Also, in the field of new forms of democracy, there are numerous citizens' initiatives, such as citizens' councils, citizens' budgets, neighbourhood budgets and the citizens' summit G1000. These experiments demonstrate the need for new forms of democracy. When we look at the deepest roots of the growing gap between citizens and politics, we touch upon the uncertain world we live in today. In this in-between-period, which is characterized by chaos and great uncertainty, people not only have the profound feeling that they have lost their grip on life, but also that politics has lost its grip on society. This gives people a very uneasy feeling and makes them anxious: will I still keep my job? Is my pension still secure? Will my children still have a future? These are essential questions that people ask themselves and to which politicians have no answers.

Another dimension of the gap between citizens and politics is the horizontalization of society versus the verticalization of politics. Society has changed greatly in recent decades and is increasingly about horizontal relationships without hierarchy, as in networks, communities and movements. People, companies, social organizations, administrators and politicians interact with each other on an equal footing, on the basis of shared responsibility. Politics and government are still important, but no longer the most important actors. This contrasts sharply with the vertically oriented institutions of politics and government, which have not yet formed any real links with the new, more diverse, more complex and more horizontal society. This also applies to other traditional institutions such as branch organizations, trade unions, housing corporations and the traditional media. They are all still organized top-down, vertically and centrally, in line with the old order, and are now colliding with the new order. A power struggle is taking place, in which these old, traditional institutions have to adapt because they will die if they do not reinvent themselves. This clash between the old and the new order is also visible in our social systems, such as the labour market, the pension system, health care and education, which are all based on collectivism and egalitarianism, while society demands personalized systems that serve citizens according to their needs.

If this democratic system is not sustainable, what is? There is not really a clear alternative visible yet. There is also a big story missing. This transition is still at the beginning of the pre-development phase. Before we really see new democratic structures and institutions emerge, we will have to spend a long time searching, learning and experimenting. But it is possible to sketch a rough picture of a future democratic system. Because the present system is representative at a distance and gives people little say, the starting point for the new system is that people feel more heard and seen. I envisage a three-scale model, with local, regional and international (European) levels of scale.

At the local level, autonomy is the key concept. People manage their own neighbourhoods and districts via district cooperatives and cooperative district councils. Neighbourhood residents are responsible for the day-to-day running of their district, both financially and organizationally. Public tasks such as care, welfare and education are facilitated by the local government in close consultation with the neighbourhood cooperatives, in other words, the shift from 'providing for' to 'providing that'. At the regional level, regions with a scale of 50 by 50 km form the future fulcrum of the economy and infrastructure, so that raw materials, energy and food circulate as much as possible (30–50% would be nice) within the region. Within the regions, regional cooperatives, in which citizens and politicians are represented, steer the region together with regional organizations such as local authorities. Neighbourhood councils are the successors of water boards, the oldest democratic institutions in the Netherlands. This marks the transition from verticalization to horizontalization, a transition strongly encouraged by the Environmental Act. The regions are replacing the abolished provinces and states are also losing strength, because more and more tasks and powers are being decentralized to the regions and local communities and the regions are autonomous in economic, financial and organizational terms. At the same time, major issues such as peace, security, energy, raw materials, climate and migration have been scaled up to the European level. All these big, complex issues can only be solved at the continental level, with the European Union leading the way and having to do so together with other world powers such as China, Africa, Asia, South and North America.

This new democratic configuration also changes the institutional playing field. The traditional, compartmentalized playing field, dating back to the nineteenth century, with trade associations, trade unions, political parties and housing corporations is gradually making way for a modern, horizontal and fluid playing field with overlapping networks, communities, cooperatives and movements. This creates a much more diffuse field of liquid ecosystems, which enables us to analyze and solve extraordinarily complex issues integrally, using an integrated approach instead of the reductionist approach which no longer works. The democratic transition does not depend so much on money, investment or knowledge, but rather on courage, guts and leadership to dare to experiment with other forms of democracy, which in any case imply a shift of power. Both downwards towards the regions and local communities and upwards towards the European Union. That requires a change in the constitution.

Systematic experimentation with new forms of democracy is already taking place with citizens' councils, citizens' panels, citizens' juries, neighbourhood budgets and G1000s. However, this is now happening on an ad hoc basis, which means that many of these experiments are dying despite their beauty. This is because these new experimental forms of democracy are still embedded in the old structures and institutions. All too often, experiments are used as a cover to keep doing the same thing in the meantime. The fun, creative ideas and solutions that emerge from radical experiments must then be conducted by others, in bodies that, because of the existing power relationships and interests, do not benefit from radical changes. These change pretenders, who pretend to want radical change but in the meantime do not act accordingly, form an important obstacle in all transitions and hold back real innovation. That is why it is important that experiments take place systematically and are scaled up so that real structural change takes place.

To achieve this, and this is what distinguishes transition experiments from ordinary experiments, this must be considered from the start by anchoring the transition experiments in the existing institutions. By bringing them in like a Trojan horse, these institutions and structures can change more quickly from the inside. It would also help to involve experiments from other domains. Think of indirect examples of the new democracy, such as energy cooperatives, care cooperatives, food cooperatives and financial cooperatives. Connecting all these initiatives can lead to new ecosystems that in turn can form a movement. And this movement can exert pressure on the existing institutions and structures to really change, by adopting and anchoring these experiments.

Citizens Councils

Citizens' councils are gaining in popularity and are already applied in countries such as Belgium, France and Germany. A citizens' council is an instrument to give ordinary citizens the opportunity to participate in democratic decision-making. The composition of a citizens' council is determined by drawing lots so that it forms a representative cross-section of society. According to David van Reybrouck, citizens' councils would be better able to make decisions about complex issues and politically sensitive topics, especially with a view to the long term. Provided that these citizens receive support from experts and an appropriate fee.

This is certainly an interesting idea and worth experimenting with, and incidental successes have already been achieved. However, seen from a transition perspective, there is a major pitfall. A citizens' council is an instrument that is deployed within the existing democratic system. However, the instrument itself does not lead to system change. It ends up in the hands of people in a certain position of power who have no interest in changing the system. These change pretenders will use the instrument (temporarily), but at the same time, they will try to polish off its radical edges so that it becomes encapsulated in the existing system. And thus, it is rendered harmless. This is the rule rather than the exception. How many times have I experienced it myself? It can work, but only if the resistances within the system (mental, institutional, financial, etc.) are considered from the start so that they can be anticipated. This requires a transition approach. Only then will there be a chance of an instrument like a citizens' council being anchored in the existing democratic institutions.

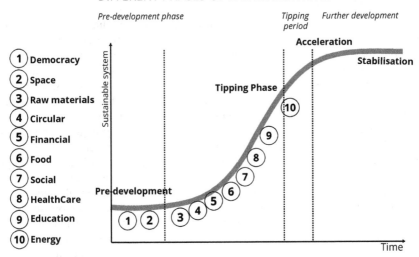

DIFFERENT PHASES OF THE TRANSITIONS

Keys to Accelerating the Transition

Looking at the transitions as a whole, one sees a diverse picture. What is striking is the cohesion, but the differences are also striking. You cannot see the entire palette of these 10 transitions in isolation, but neither can you see them in complete coherence. Each transition has its own context, rhythm and speed, and is also in its own phase. I use a transition index as a measure of the phase in which a transition finds itself. This index is determined by the degree of resistance, the degree of chaos in terms of protests and lawsuits, the relationship between niche players and the large dominant players, the presence of breakthrough technologies and break-through coalitions, and the degree of demolition of the existing and construction of the new. The following picture, which shows the S-curve of the development lens with the pre-development phase, the tipping phase and the further development phase, shows in which phase the various transitions are currently situated. For example, the democratic transition, the raw materials transition and the circular transition are still at the very beginning of the pre-development phase. The food transition, the care transition and the education transition are well underway. The energy transition is in the tipping phase.

We also see different clusters of transitions. First of all, the cluster of energy, raw materials and circularity. These are inextricably linked. Within this cluster, raw materials are a precondition for energy, and raw materials and energy together are a precondition for circularity. The financial and fiscal incentives, in turn, are a necessary condition for the success of this cluster as a whole. The second cluster consists of space, water, energy and circularity, because energy, water and circularity need to be fitted into the space in a smart and sustainable way. An enormous task. The third cluster concerns the 'soft' transitions, namely those of education, care, the social domain and democracy. They play a crucial role and are a precondition for the 'hard' transitions. Without reforming education, we cannot build a new economy. Making people healthier is an absolute precondition for being able to cushion and contain the adverse effects of the next pandemic and economic crisis. And democratic renewal is necessary for the success of the energy and circular transition. The importance of these soft transitions is underestimated, while in fact, they are at least as important as the hard transitions. In short, everything is connected. That is why I have tried to explain the connection in terms of the buttons you can press to accelerate the transitions as a whole.

So, what are the knobs you can turn? There are four key factors for accelerating the range of transitions: fiscal incentives (taxes and mortgages), financial incentives (subsidies and loans), legal incentives (laws and regulations) and mental incentives (social standards and behaviour). These impulses can accelerate or slow down the driving forces behind a transition, such as technological innovation, economic development, social innovation, government policy, social pressure and consumer behaviour. If we look across the palette, we can see a number of common impulses. For example, for the hard transitions (energy, raw materials, circular), which can only be tackled at the system level, the financial and fiscal impulses are of decisive importance.

Tax reform is inevitable. If we do not tax more but smarter, there will be financial room, it will bring a lot of environmental benefits and the lowest incomes will benefit the most. Tax reform has been hanging over politicians' heads for decades, but up to now nobody has dared touch it. Yet the moment seems ripe for a shift from taxing labour to taxing pollution and the use of raw materials. It is so logical: the polluter pays. If you extract value (pollute) you are taxed; if you add value (clean) you are spared. Effective tax incentives are CO_2 tax, air passenger tax, road tax, reduction of income tax and income support for the lowest income groups.

The financial playing field must also be changed. There is no financial level playing field because the current forms of financing are aimed at linear companies and not at circular ones. The focus is still too much on short-term financial returns with limited risk. Financiers demand return and scale, while in circular companies money is needed to create return and scale. To break this vicious circle, more patient and risk-bearing capital is needed. Capital that, especially with extremely low-interest rates, is available in abundance. The money is literally sloshing around, but a large investment fund such as Invest-NL must obtain a 'market conform' return from its investments. This excludes breakthrough projects with a radically innovative character and a radically different business model. The fund may not set lower return requirements than other investors. That would be unfair competition and the Netherlands would be violating European competition rules. I myself also have experience with the European Investment Bank, which had to assess a number of breakthrough projects in the Rotterdam region. I was surprised about the classic assessment frameworks they used, which were focused purely on financial return rather than on social impact. The government could and should be much more guiding in this by setting lower financial return requirements for breakthrough projects, granting more time to circular companies and looking at the positive social impact of breakthrough innovations.

Price is also an important key. As long as we do not pay a fair price for the products we buy, a fair economy is a long way off. A fair price includes the production costs plus the damage to people and the environment caused by the product. However, this is not the price you pay in a shop. For example, it takes about 8,000 litres of water to grow the cotton for one pair of jeans. Add to that the environmental costs of pollution and water scarcity caused by cotton production and the social costs of child labour, underpaid workers and unsafe and unhealthy working conditions, and the average pair of jeans becomes about 33 euro more expensive. In other words: the average pair of jeans is 33 euro too cheap. Fortunately, the realization is starting to dawn that we are deceiving each other with the current price system. We pass on all hidden costs to the next generations, who literally and figuratively have to pay the price.

Gradually, however, a global movement of companies, investors and governments is emerging that pleads for true pricing. More and more companies are embracing the idea of true pricing, even if it is only a small group of leaders. It is only the beginning of what is needed, but it is in any case hopeful. In the Netherlands, too, there are more and more companies that are starting to work with it. For example, there is already a True Price supermarket in the Amsterdam Pijp area, where products are offered at real prices and can be (voluntarily) paid for. And Tony's Chocolonely is working towards a real price for their chocolate bars. The prices of their bars are already higher than those of competitors, but they are transparent about their extra costs and are trying to reduce their environmental and social costs more and more. The success of Tony's Chocolonely shows that transparency about real prices and increasing sales can go hand in hand. The complexity of implementing this throughout the chain was demonstrated when the company was recently accused of child labour because they collaborated with Barry Callebaut, one of the world's largest cocoa producers, who make cocoa using child labour. Tony's Chocolonely indicates that it consciously works together with such a large cocoa player in order to make transparent where the problem of child labour lies and thus to banish it in the long term. Gradually, a global movement of companies, investors and governments is emerging to advocate true pricing. This is only the beginning of what is needed, but it is at least hopeful.

Governments can encourage companies, financial institutions and civil society organizations to use true pricing. It would be a breakthrough if a company like Shell would start working with real prices. The government itself, as purchaser, regulator and legislator, and in facilitating sector agreements, can also apply the concept of real prices, and has already embraced it for the sustainability of the food system, among other things.

The covid crisis could have been an ideal catalyst for making the economy more sustainable. But the 'Great Reset' loudly proclaimed by the World Economic Forum appears to be an empty slogan. What we are seeing is not a green recovery, but a black recovery. The government is pumping thousands of billions of dollars into the economy to keep it afloat. We keep everything going, including the fossil-fuel industry. So that money also goes to companies that we would be better off parting with because they are postponing investments in sustainability. With a black instead of a green recovery, we are missing a unique opportunity.

Research by international colleagues in *Science* (Andrijevic et al.) shows that if we were to invest approximately 10% of the covid aid in climate policy, we could achieve the climate objectives. This amount would not be at the expense of economic stimulus measures but would go towards sustainable energy, the stimulation of clean technologies and energy saving. Every euro that is spent on these areas generates three euros in terms of employment, innovation and strengthening the structure of the new economy. On the other hand, every euro you put into the fossil-fuel economy will cost you two euros because of the harmful side effects. True green recovery, therefore, entails the following.

(1) Phasing out activities that have no future, such as fossil-fuel energy and intensive agriculture.
(2) Strengthening businesses that contribute to the new, clean economy.
(3) Stimulating new, innovative and sustainable businesses.

Although this is so logical and truly a solution where everyone benefits, it is not happening. In fact, the opposite is happening. While the UN (UNEP) states that only a green recovery will lead to 25% less CO_2 emissions in 2030, the G20 countries, which represent 90% of the world's gross national product and 80% of world trade, have given 10 times more covid support to the fossil-fuel industry than to the sustainable energy sector. And yet it is precisely within this powerful bloc, which accounts for two-thirds of the world's population, that a radical change must take place. Despite the fact that this has not happened, there is still reason for moderate optimism. I will return to this at the end of this chapter.

The current legislation and regulations are more of an obstacle than a stimulus to the new circular economy. Most of the legal pointers are still pointing in the direction of the old, linear economy. The situation has improved compared to years ago when there were still dozens of laws and regulations that were diametrically opposed to the circular economy. But in the Netherlands, for example, we still have the Waste Substances Act, which dates back to a time when waste was seen as harmful to the environment and therefore prohibited recycling. Because of the current standards, building with biomass is also seen as more harmful than building with concrete. Thus, laws are solidified history. A transition act can offer a solution here because it is more effective than just making new laws in all sorts of separate areas. That is time-consuming and complex and takes years, while the urgency of the issues calls for acute legal action. A transition act makes temporary exemptions possible from laws and regulations that impede the transition, and new regulations that stimulate the transition.

It is important that citizens are given the space to contribute to solutions together with others. In Chapter 4 we read that citizen collectives such as energy, care and food cooperatives are a rapidly emerging informal power. There is a tremendous amount of change energy there, and the government can either encourage or stifle that change energy. A facilitating government gives space to these citizen collectives and removes obstacles. However, by forcing them into restrictive laws, rules, structures and institutions, this same government can also form the greatest obstacle to these citizens' initiatives. Radical experiments to give citizens more say and control, and therefore more power, all too often fail because of the existing power of the dominant structure and institutions. Structural change is therefore a necessary condition for upscaling these initiatives from bottom-up. This structural change cannot take place without democratic change. Indeed, democratic renewal is an absolute necessity for the success of the energy transition and climate policy. Finally, perhaps the most important key: the mental impetus. It is an uncomfortable message, but the systemic crises we are facing are deeply rooted in a moral crisis and are to be found in our attitudes and behaviour. We like to put the solutions outside ourselves and point at the system, blame others or seek refuge in technology, but the core of the solution lies within ourselves. This insight requires a personal transition, which I will elaborate on in the last chapter of this book. If you look at the most important hard transitions – the energy transition, the raw materials transition and the circular transition – they all come up against the same problem, namely infinite growth. A part of us is selfish and greedy and wants to grow continuously: more, faster, better! But if we keep growing infinitely, no hard transition will succeed, and we cannot become fully circular. If we do not reduce our consumption, we will hit the limits of raw materials, energy and circularity with a vengeance. We will have to use less energy and fewer raw materials on both the production and consumption side. The production side lies with companies, which still leave a lot to be desired, but our consumption behaviour plays a decisive role in this. This too is an uncomfortable message, but the transition path is paved with owning less, using less, wasting less and polluting less.

This micro-context of consumerism needs a macro-context. There is a need for a new story. A story that is not based on infinite growth and its measurement in terms of the gross national product. We will have to recalibrate the concept of growth. This could mean no growth, green growth, growth where we focus on sustainable progression and not on income growth or material growth, or regenerative growth, where economy and nature reinforce each other on the basis of a fair give-and-take between humankind and nature. I prefer the latter. In any case, infinite growth is impossible. There is nothing in nature that grows infinitely. Growth is a certain phase of an organism in nature, then it reaches maturity and stops growing, only to continue to flourish for a long time. In fact, everything that tries to keep growing in nature destroys itself or the environment in which it thrives. In our bodies, we call this cancer. In the economy, cancerous symptoms are climate change and loss of biodiversity, but also Covid-19 and other zoonoses. Be that as it may, the economy is crying out for a new, big story, with balance as its starting point. Balance between man and nature, balance between man and economy, balance between fellow men and balance between the head and the heart of the individual.

Mental impulses are also particularly important for soft transitions. This is not so much about money, because often the money goes to the clay layer of bureaucrats, and not to professionals such as teachers or nurses. In care and education, what is needed most is relaxation, time and space. This can be achieved by working more on the basis of trust and less on the basis of control and management (mistrust). Give schools time, space and trust to come up with their own solutions. The same applies to care institutions. Give citizens and citizen collectives the space to come up with their own ideas and plans and help them to realize these through a facilitating government, also by removing obstacles in laws and regulations. The new Environment Act should also make this possible. Provide room for experimentation with new forms of democracy, on the way to more direct control for citizens. Have the courage to break down existing institutions that no longer fit into modern society. Because society is also crying out for a new, big story, in which people once again take centre stage and systems support people. So, thinking and working on the basis of trust, in search of a better balance between people and systems.

At the meso level, we try to influence that behaviour. Behavioural research shows that it is a fairly long and rather difficult road to go from awareness and attitude change to behavioural change. According to others, it can also be done the other way around, by practising behavioural change and then creating awareness. In any case, it is a difficult road with many bumps that can take years, because most of our behaviour is habitual and permeated with routines. These habits and routines can be influenced by the impulses of influencing prices, shifting taxes, legislation, and regulations that are reviewed in this chapter. But, for a transition, we almost always forget the most important impulse: social norms. A transition does not require a minor change in behaviour, but a fundamental change in behaviour. A radical change, in other words. You can't really force or impose that, certainly not in the long term, because people often fall back into their old behaviour. This is why social norms are so important. People's behaviour is strongly influenced by their social environment. People observe others and create an image of what is normal or appropriate. We measure each other against undesirable behaviour and address each other on it, and in this way influence each other.

The Smoking Transition

Social norms played an important role in the transition from smoking to non-smoking. The transition took two generations, some 50 years. Fifty years ago, 90% of all men smoked, today it is just over 20%. Smoking used to be cool, social and sociable, and you were even challenged if you didn't smoke. Then a small group of front runners, who became aware of the harmful health effects, particularly lung cancer, stopped smoking. These frontrunners influenced a larger group, the frontrunners of the pack, and then the pack itself. The masses only stopped smoking when the health cult and the fitness craze emerged. Smoking no longer fitted in with a healthy life. This was the turning point and smoking was no longer seen as a cool, social and fun activity, but as dirty and unhealthy.

It was only after some 30 years of this transition that the government introduced laws and regulations to curb smoking. First in the workplace and in public buildings, and then in the hospitality industry, public transport and in aeroplanes. It was therefore first and foremost a change of culture, which was then tightened up by policy. This example shows the importance of social norms in a transition. If you still smoke nowadays you are considered a loser or a sucker. The same pattern, whereby social norms bring about a cultural shift, is already visible in the food transition. Slowly but surely, eating meat is seen as something that no longer fits in with a healthy and sustainable lifestyle. If you still eat a greasy fast-food hamburger in 10 years' time, you will also be seen as a loser. And if you don't have solar panels on your roof in fifteen years' time, you will be seen as a loser too.

If we want to prevent future systemic crises, all transition keys are badly needed. In the case of climate change, a climate crisis seems unavoidable, but the damage can still be limited. As already described for the energy transition, half a degree of temperature difference has an enormous impact. Therefore, we must fight for every tenth degree. The same applies to the impending nature crisis, which requires a radical change from a different paradigm: the balance between man and nature. And if we want to prevent the next pandemic, we will have to commit ourselves fully to better health.

Globally, there is a direct link between the number of covid deaths and the degree of obesity. Overweight and obesity are a rapidly growing problem that has not yet received sufficient political attention. If we really want to tackle this, then we must strive for a healthy food environment for people. This is only possible through an integrated approach with a coherent package of transition keys. By using fiscal incentives to tax unhealthy food products more and to tax healthy products like fruit and vegetables less. By introducing real prices, whereby the health damage of unhealthy food products is factored into the price. By using laws and regulations, for example, to regulate the amount of salt, sugar and fat in food products. Regulation of the food supply and the food providers is also necessary, as is information about and advertising of healthy food. By influencing lifestyles, people are encouraged to exercise more, engage in sport and eat more healthily. To stimulate and reinforce this, the infrastructure of regions, cities and municipalities must also be adapted so that people can walk and cycle more easily. For example, the construction of bicycle highways between cities stimulates people to use their bicycles rather than their cars. And finally, by adapting social norms, because obesity is not only a consequence of heredity or individual behaviour but is also determined by social norms. This can be done by telling a new story, with the framing that overweight and obesity are among the biggest health problems of our time, and that the best medicine against the next pandemic is good physical and mental health. And that by living healthily you are also being good to others socially, and not costing them.

What You Can Do

We are in a prolonged period of systemic crises. What can we, as individuals, do? At first glance, not much, because system changes are tough and complex and take a long time. That is too much to ask of a single person. But that's not true, because we are the system. The system is within us. We have conceived and built the systems ourselves and have benefited from them for a long time. At a certain point, the systems turn against us and become dysfunctional. Then they can die off, which happens regularly, or we can change them radically, with success or failure. When I was young and studying, there was a status quo. The word transition was not in vogue at all, and there was little or no urge to change. Not even when I started researching transitions. In such a stable phase of dynamic equilibrium, it is very difficult to change the system; small interventions have absolutely no effect. Now, things are quite different. We are in a transitional phase, full of turbulence and chaos. This is an unstable, vulnerable phase for a system in which small interventions can have a major impact. The old system is broken down and the new one is built up. In times of chaos, individuals and small groups of people can make a difference. So can you.

It starts with the realization that we humans have transformative power, the ability to really change systems. Of course, this is quite difficult and requires time, patience and perseverance, and of course, you will collide with the existing power, and often it does not work. However, we are able to break down systems and rebuild them. That might be the industrial food system, the fossil energy system, the sick healthcare system or the bankrupt financial system. But it could also be your city, your neighbourhood or your district. Or your company or organization. In times of chaos, all these systems are vulnerable and susceptible to disruption, but many people do not realize this and underestimate their potential power to change. We can only break down and build new systems if we do so collectively, but it always starts with an individual or small group. Transitions start small and then, under the right circumstances, can become big and bring about a change. So, the big is in the small. Currently, there are plenty of examples of small groups of people or individuals having a major impact. If you look closely, this is logical in times of chaos. Here are a few inspiring examples.

In 2010, a small group of students from Swarthmore College in Pennsylvania stood at the cradle of the worldwide divestment movement. They visited a coal mine on a field trip and were unpleasantly surprised by the pollution and damage to nature that resulted. When it turned out that the fossil-fuel company was a major sponsor of their university, the students successfully rebelled against it. This success spread to other American universities and eventually to Harvard and Stanford. Then universities on other continents joined in and the movement grew into a worldwide movement, with a simple but brilliant framing: disinvest in fossil fuels and invest in clean energy. The Divestment Movement, which is active in more than 75 countries on six continents, encompasses almost 700 institutions and has already succeeded in keeping five trillion dollars from being invested in fossil fuels. The movement is also very active in the Netherlands. Recently, a group of students from Wageningen University protested against their university's too close ties with banks that still invest in fossil-fuel energy. And with success: the university switched to a sustainable bank. The movement, which has doubled in size since 2015, puts pressure on fossil-fuel companies and is inspired by the successful South African divestment movement during the apartheid regime.

Urgenda, founded in 2007 by myself and Marjan Minnesma, is an action group that gained worldwide fame through the climate case against the Dutch state, which was instituted in 2015 together with almost 900 citizens and won, including two appeals. But Urgenda has done much more than that. The name Urgenda, once coined by me in the bath, stands for 'urgent agenda', a rough list of actions and goals to make the Netherlands more sustainable more quickly. It grew into a sustainability movement, with rituals such as the Day of Sustainability, regional tours and the walk to Paris, where the final agreement was made. Urgenda is still a Gideon's mob and not an organization, not institutionalized like other environmental clubs. It is an autonomous force. None of the goals on the original list have been achieved, yet Urgenda has had an undeniable impact. Here too, you see that the indirect impact is often much greater than the direct one. Like the climate court case, which was copied in other countries, and which gave many people worldwide hope that citizens can influence climate policy.

Not only groups can make a difference, but also individuals. There are plenty of examples of this. Take Greta Thunberg, symbol of the global climate movement. The Swedish teenager once decided to go on strike at school and to go to the Swedish parliament to protest there. She thus became a role model for climate change striking students all over the world. And that was in Sweden, which generates almost 60% of its energy from renewable sources and is, therefore, one of the best-performing European countries in terms of renewable energy. It is true that there is a lot of hydropower and biomass, but compare that to the Netherlands, where only 14% of the energy is generated sustainably. Greta Thunberg's strength is her authenticity and rationality. She makes no concessions and lives by what she says: as sustainably as possible. She doesn't eat meat, dairy or fly anymore. She also encouraged her family to buy solar panels and an electric car. By doing so, she is setting a good example for her tens of millions of followers on social media. The downside of this is that she can no longer go to school normally, and she is constantly threatened and needs security in public. She is therefore often angry and grimacing because, according to her, we are on a collision course with the climate. How long her angry tone will remain effective remains to be seen, as it is not very binding. But her impact is undeniably huge.

Roger Cox approached me in 2011 in connection with his book *Revolution Justified: Why only the Law can Save us*. He was enthusiastic about the role that the law could play in climate policy. According to him, the government could be legitimately held responsible for failing climate policy. To be honest, I didn't see much point in it. I have little interest in law anyway and certainly nothing to do with lawsuits, which I regard as a necessary evil. But his enthusiasm was infectious, and he convinced us to start a lawsuit against the Dutch state. Almost everyone advised against it, and I too had little faith in it, but we could at least try. At the end of 2012, we started the campaign and in 2013 the official court case began, with the aim of reducing greenhouse gases by 25% in 2020 compared to 1990. In 2015, the court in The Hague ruled in favour of Urgenda. This was confirmed on appeal by the Court of Appeal in The Hague in 2018 and reaffirmed by the Supreme Court in December 2019. This marked the ultimate victory for Roger Cox and his partner in crime Koos van den Berg. Thanks to the tireless efforts of these two lawyers, something happened that almost everyone had thought impossible: the State was forced to tighten its climate policy. Roger Cox then continued with a lawsuit against Shell, together with Friends of the Earth Netherlands, which hardly anyone believed in either. But again, he won again, a heroic achievement that can have a global impact on other fossil-fuel companies. He himself remains modest, but the impact of his legal interventions can hardly be overestimated.

Boyan Slat is an avid diver, and during one of his diving trips in Greece, he realized that he came across more plastic than fish. That was reason enough for him to do something about the problem. He stopped his studies at Delft University of Technology and came up with a plastic catcher with which plastic could be fished out of the ocean. Thus, the Ocean Clean-up was born. He collected tens of millions of euros in donations and started experimenting with the plastic catcher, a 600-metre-long U-shaped tube with a metres-deep plastic screen attached to it. He gathered a whole team around him, attracted attention worldwide and in the meantime came up against numerous technical problems. At first, the plastic trap did not seem to work: the plastic was not really held, but eventually, a version that did work was developed. Then came the criticism from the scientific community. Biologists and ecologists warned that in addition to plastic, all sorts of creatures were also caught: jellyfish, snails, crabs, all animals that form an important source of food for fish and birds. They float in exactly the same places as the plastic, with the risk that you clean up an entire ecosystem in addition to the plastic. It's like having a bulldozer mow down a forest because there are 'pieces of balloon in the tree branches', says biologist Rebecca Helm. However, the Ocean Clean-up campaign denies this and says that there is no evidence for it. Other experts say that the Ocean Clean-up only cleans up a fraction of all the plastic that ends up in the ocean. In the best-case scenario, the Ocean Clean-up cleans up 8,000 tonnes of plastic a year. That means 0.1% of the plastic that we dump into the sea every year. So, we need thousands of projects like this to really tackle the plastic soup, which costs about 600 billion euros. A gigantic sum.

For me, the value of the Ocean Clean-up lies in something completely different, namely not in the direct, but in the indirect effect. Boyan Slat has put the problem of plastic soup high on the agenda. Ten years ago, hardly any attention was paid to this problem, but now it is high on the agenda worldwide. An enormous step has been taken in raising awareness. Moreover, the Ocean Clean-up has grown into a movement worldwide that is enormously popular among young people. In five years', time, they want to ensure that 50% of all the plastic in the ocean is removed. Whether they will succeed is uncertain, but the impact of this global movement is immense.

These are examples of successful change agents with the necessary impact. There are thousands of such examples all over the world. Of course, you could argue that there are many failures on the other side, people who didn't succeed. But it's not so much about succeeding or failing. It's about trying and showing leadership. Of all the great things I have tried in my life, about half of them have failed. So be it: *you won't be remembered for your failures; you will be remembered for your successes.* When it comes to systemic change, it is fashionable to play down the role of the individual. It is dismissed as marginal consumerism or naive idealism. First we have to tackle the big companies like Shell, that's the way to go. Or the government must first implement stronger policies. Or first the systems must be changed. 'With eating less meat and flying less will get us nowhere' is a popular saying, as is 'a better environment does not begin with yourself'. It is even said to stand in the way of a real approach to climate change.

From a transition perspective, this is all nonsense. Anyone who debates this kind of thing does not understand how transitions work. Actions and interventions of individuals have an impact at different scales. Actions at the micro level have an impact at the meso level and ultimately at the macro level, and interventions at the meso level in turn have an impact at the micro and macro level. The indirect effects of our actions are often greater than the direct effects. It is only in the longer term that you see the knock-on effects of these indirect effects. Every intervention in a complex system must be placed in the light of complex system dynamics. This is how transitions work. In a phase of chaos, small interventions can have a major effect. A ripple can cause a wave. If you take a brief, superficial look, you won't see any change. Those who look long and hard will see change. First under the surface, then above it. First small, then big and then a wave. It is the difference between a photograph and a film: if you put in your transition lenses, you see a film, but with stationary spectacles, you see only a photograph.

People underestimate their own power to change and overestimate that of politicians, policymakers and CEOs. Through stationary spectacles, you see people fighting powerlessly against the system. With transition spectacles, you see them influencing and changing the system. I have already mentioned the example of a random group of consumers who can bring down any multinational, provided they unite at the right time. This is not the age of movements for nothing. Radical ideas for change are going viral. Think of the yellow vests and the MeToo movement. Think of Black Lives Matter and the climate movement. Think of Kick Out Black Pete. Whatever you think about it, the latter has unmistakably changed the way we think about Black Pete. Things that were scorned 10 years ago can no longer be ignored. The social norm has definitely changed: Black Pete is out. The appearance of Black Pete has changed and there are now numerous coloured alternatives. For many people, this is unexpectedly fast, but for those who wear their transition spectacles, this is logical. Things have been brewing in the undercurrents for some time, but this is not yet visible to many. Then incidents take place, and the attachment grows, and with it the resistance. Until 25% of the population embraces an idea, then the tipping point is reached. The remaining 75% then goes relatively quickly because of the exponential growth that takes place.

That is the hope I want to give you. On climate, we have not yet reached the tipping point of 25% of the people, but my estimation is that we are close to it, between 15 and 20%. That means that with the next systemic crisis we could reach the tipping point. And then we will enter the acceleration phase, in which developments can happen very quickly. Ten or 20 years ago, Greta Thunberg would not have had such an impact, and Urgenda would not have been able to win a climate case. Today, everything matters. Every action, every intervention, of every human being. Systems are fragile and faltering, and people can accelerate that in a targeted way. People not only influence systems but also each other. Social norms play an important role in our behaviour, and it is these that change during a transition. Smoking used to be cool and cosy, now it is dirty and unhealthy. Black Pete was popular, now he is out of favour. A weekend flight to New York was once cool, now it is not done. Solar panels were once for alternative types, now they are hip and cool. In short, things that were once seen as normal can no longer be done at a certain moment and become unacceptable. Or the other way around, things that were once nerdy are now fashionable. Think, for example, of the electric bicycle or the electric scooter.

So, as an individual you can do all sorts of things to make the world a better place. You can join the global climate movement with all kinds of branches, such as the Youth Climate Movement, The Divestment Movement and Extinction Rebellion, which also has a scientific branch, Scientists4xr. In the Netherlands and Belgium, there are the Young Climate Movement and the Grandparents for the Climate. There are also similar movements in the field of food, plastics, etc. You can also participate in specific action groups, for example, to ask for more attention for climate and sustainability in education, such as the initiative Education in Transition at Erasmus University Rotterdam, or the Rethinking Economics movement. You can also set up your own action group for a specific topic, as more and more students are doing. In short, you can turn your anger into action. Recent research by Australian researchers (Stanley et al.) shows that there are three types of emotions in reaction to the ecological crisis hanging over our heads. People get depressed, which has a paralyzing effect. Or they become anxious, which leads to collective fear. Or people become angry, which turns out to be the most activating emotion, leading to both individual and collective action. So, anger is an emotion that can be effectively translated into action. You can do all kinds of things, such as starting your own sustainable business, preferably together with others.

And you can make your lifestyle more sustainable. More and more people are becoming flexitarian; in the Netherlands almost half of the population already is. If you do not eat meat two or three times a week for a year, you save just as much CO_2 emissions as if you did not drive a car for a year. Eating and producing meat is one of the most climate-damaging activities there is. If we were to switch to a plant-based diet worldwide, 30 million km^2 of land would potentially become available. That is about 750 times the Netherlands and three times the United States. Stopping eating beef and pork also helps enormously. Chicken and fish are much less harmful. Try also to waste less food. One-third of our food is wasted during production and another third during consumption. Flying is also a very climate-damaging activity, so try to travel by car or train. And driving electric is in all respects less climate-damaging than driving a petrol or diesel car. And the less you own, the less CO_2 you emit. The clothing industry, for example, emits more CO_2 than aviation and shipping together, about 8% of global CO_2 emissions. Fast fashion chains like Zara, Primark and H&M are the main culprits, with tens of new collections and tens of thousands of new designs each year. We buy this junk *en masse* and throw it away after wearing it maybe 10 times. A solution to reduce this waste is to buy fewer clothes, and, if you buy clothes, to buy better quality clothes that last longer. So, there is a lot you can do. Nowadays, there are even whole handbooks on how to live more sustainably, by Babette Porcelijn, among others.

That is why, after all these years, I am and will remain optimistic, even though I foresee more chaos in the short term, with increasing resistance, protests and conflicts. The next 10 years will be difficult and laborious, but in the longer term, I am optimistic, because we are reaching the tipping point and things can go very fast then. A climate crisis will speed things up. The covid crisis brought time forward by 10 years and made us do things we thought were impossible, such as digital working, remote collaboration and flexible working. A climate crisis will bring time forward even more, perhaps by 20 years. We will come up with solutions that we did not think were possible. So, solutions that are not yet in sight will suddenly emerge.

On balance, we have everything in place to become carbon-free within one generation. We have the knowledge, the expertise, the power and the institutions. A lot is already technically possible. It depends mainly on ourselves, on our willpower. If we don't really want it, we flee into excuses. But the time for excuses is behind us. If we really want it, it is possible! I am not asking you to carry the world on your shoulders. I am not asking you to stop having fun. I am not asking you to raise money. I am only asking you to stand up and act.

The Netherlands as a Laboratory for the World

Together with the design and architecture agency KuiperCompagnons, I worked for more than a year on a vision of the future for the Netherlands over the next hundred years, 'The Netherlands in 2121: a land with a plan'. We tried to make a complex puzzle out of the interrelated transitions that are coming our way, you can find the vision here:

https://www.kuipercompagnons.nl/nl/projecten/nl_2121_land_met_een_plan/

Starting point of this vision of the Netherlands in 2121 is 'humans and the environment in balance'. This is precisely because there is now an imbalance, which is a major cause of the crises we have had in recent decades, and which are discussed in previous chapters. Restoring this balance means that we will have to deal with energy, water, climate, nature, mobility, housing, health and education in a radically different, smart and innovative way.

We see the Netherlands as a spatial-planning laboratory for the rest of the world. The Netherlands must do what has never been done before. We're talking about a formidable spatial-planning challenge, involving energy, water, climate, nature conservation, agriculture, housing, and transportation. The country will be completely transformed in the coming decades, and more will change in the coming century than over the past thousand years. Every square metre will be revamped. Sustainable energy will grow rapidly and must become an integral part of the landscape. Water will get far more space, and it will become one of the main elements of spatial planning. The climate will have a profound influence. We can expect increasingly frequent droughts, rising sea levels, and rising water levels in major rivers. The damage done to nature must be restored, and nature will demand more space. In addition, demand for new, affordable housing will be enormous, and many existing houses and buildings will be renovated and transformed to secure them for the future. Finally, the Netherlands suffers from permanent traffic congestion, so we will need a new, modern transport infrastructure.

(Continued)

(*Continued*)

This complex special-planning transition requires a mental transition that will enable a leap in the scale of our thinking. Take, for example, the way we deal with water. The pressure of water on land is increasing and vice versa, which is further aggravated by climate change, rising sea levels and subsidence. In our baseline scenario for 2121 we presume a global temperature increase of 2°C, a sea levels rise of 1 m and further land subsidence of 1 m in the coastal areas. That means that parts of West Netherlands will be situated 7–10 m below sea level. This is no longer tenable. We can no longer keep pumping and draining the water. That would also be too expensive. The only solution is for us to relate differently to water and to create more space for it on land. Water as a development partner and companion on a journey; that is the mental leap of scale we need to make.

The same mental leap of scale is needed with regard to our attitude to nature. We feel superior to nature and feel that we have the right to ruin nature. We are beginning to realize that in doing so we are actually destroying ourselves, because nature is the source of key functions that are vital to human beings, such as clean water, clean air, clean energy, food and health. Restoring nature is therefore a prerequisite for our continued existence. Nature as an ally with whom we humans pull up together from co-existence is then the mental scale leap. The same applies to other themes such as energy, climate, housing and transport, which call for a similar jump in scale. Because of the rapidly growing claims on space for these themes (energy, water, climate, nature, mobility, housing and transport), we will have to deal with space in a very smart and innovative way.

Chapter 6

Personal Transition: The Journey Inside

The Journey to the Outside

After the palette of transitions we have seen, it has probably become clear to you that a lot of things are changing in many areas, and it's all happening extremely fast. Many people feel this, too, because the unrest in the world reflects the unrest in ourselves. We feel chaos and unease, and we have the feeling that we have lost our grip on life. And rightly so. We also feel that politics has lost its grip, and that is true. In times of chaos, everyone loses their grip, and no one is in control. That creates uncertainty and we humans don't like that. We like stability and certainty. But, after the chapter on systemic crises, it has become clear that chaos in a complex system drives the search for a new balance. Chaos is an integral part of a major system change, and therefore, we are not living in an era of change, but in a change of era. The economy is being given a new foundation: from polluting and wasteful to clean and circular, and from profit-driven to value-driven. Society, too, will have a different basis: from pigeonholes to fluid systems, from vertical to horizontal and from exclusive to inclusive, with equal opportunities for all.

It is rare for a total revolution in the economy and society to take place more or less simultaneously. The last time this happened was in the nineteenth century during the Industrial Revolution. Because such a period does not occur in every lifetime, we are lucky to experience it. I sometimes say to my children: 'How often does it happen that you are part of a revolution?' I call a transition an evolutionary revolution, and there aren't that many generations that get to experience it. You have to embrace the chaos and accept that it is restless for a long time and try to find peace in the turmoil. But you can then contribute substantially to a new society and a new economy. How beautiful is that!

In this age of change, every individual and every initiative counts. You can make the difference right now. In all the years that I have been working with complex systems, I have increasingly come to realize that people determine the course of transitions. Even though the emphasis today is often on technology, at the heart of transitions is the work of people. The fact that people actually change is an absolute precondition for systemic change. We are not talking about an

Embracing Chaos, 135–155

Copyright © 2023 Jan Rotmans and Co-Writer Mischa Verheijden

Published under exclusive licence by Emerald Publishing Limited. Translation by Michael Gould. The moral rights of the translator have been asserted. Copyright © 2021 Jan Rotmans en Mischa Verheijden. Original title Omarm de Chaos. First published in 2021 by De Geus, Amsterdam

doi:10.1108/978-1-83753-634-420231012

ordinary change, but about deep, fundamental change. But many people say: 'I do want to change, but the system is holding me back'. If you blame the system, you put the change outside yourself. In fact, you are looking for an excuse because you don't dare to change anything yourself. People are deeply afraid of losing their income, status, position of power, and ultimately their identity. Everyone knows this fear, right? But transitions are people's work and require, above all, a personal transition by daring to search, look and feel very deeply inside yourself. By not denying your fear, but rather by looking for it and naming it in depth, you can transform your fear into something positive. I call this search the journey inwards.

The Inner Journey

In my book *Revolution*, I have given 10 examples of people who have gone through such a personal transition. These 10 stories are representative of the thousands of people I have spoken to in recent years who have undertaken the same quest. These thousands of people in turn symbolize the millions of people worldwide who are engaged in this quest, which in turn symbolizes society and the economy as a whole, which are in fact also engaged in searching. Many people are at a crossroads in their lives: they feel trapped between the rigid systems of society. For many, this is a reason to step out of the system. They take the leap and start their own journey inwards. This requires courage, guts and leadership because there is no compass for the most fundamental decisions in your life, your own personal transition. You just have to face it. The stories I hear are all very intense, but all these people tell me: 'It was worth it, I wouldn't have done it any other way'.

I myself have also gone through an inner journey. It was triggered by a personal crisis: a cycling accident in the French Pyrenees. On 23 August 2004, I crashed while descending the Aubisque and hit the asphalt with my face. I broke just about everything in my face: my lower and upper jaws, cheekbones, nose, eye sockets and my jawbone. Some of my teeth were also knocked out. I was lucky that I was wearing a helmet, otherwise, I probably would not have survived. I had to rehabilitate for about a year and underwent several operations. Just before my first operation, I wrote on a note: 'I'm in a hurry, I have to start next week'. On 1 September, DRIFT, the transition research institute I had founded, was due to start. The surgeon said, 'Hurry? You may never be able to work again'. After a jaw-fixing procedure and months of lying at home, I wanted to do something again. I was able to write an e-mail again and thought, 'There, I can do that again'. Then I got a few e-mails back and everything went black before my eyes, after which I had to lie down again. I became so incredibly angry, and later I wondered why.

That's where – first unconsciously, then consciously – my journey inwards began. I always wanted to perform and be the best. I asked myself, 'Did you become who you wanted to be?' My immediate reaction was: 'Yes of course!' I was a professor at a very young age, I was successful, and I had founded my own research institute in Maastricht. But that was all on the outside. I was not sufficiently occupied with the inside. Then I started to look very deeply into myself, and I realized that I had been developing and transferring knowledge about climate, sustainability and transitions for decades, but that I had only reached a thousand people at most. Scientifically, I may have been successful, but I had little impact from a societal point of view, while I was trying to get people moving based on the urgency I felt. As a little boy, I wanted to study mathematics and, as a professor, make the world a more beautiful place. When asked what I wanted to do, 'Making the world a nicer place', I seem to have said as a 5-year-old. While lying flat in a hospital in Pau and later in Maastricht, I asked myself the question: 'Are you really doing what you want, or do you want what you do?' Only after months did I realize that, although I told myself I was, I was not really doing what I wanted. This was not what I had promised myself as a little boy, and while the outside world thought I was successful, I was failing myself.

Apart from my children's illnesses, that was the hardest thing I have ever experienced in my life. And yet that is the way to go. I realized that if I wanted to remain loyal to myself, I had to become more activist and share all my knowledge with people in society. That was scary and confrontational. I was afraid of resistance and afraid of losing my scientific reputation. On the one hand, I had to return to my old level as a scientist and, on the other hand, make the change to an activist. That didn't really happen until 3 years after my accident with Marjan Minnesma when we founded Urgenda. And there was resistance: scientists were angry, and activists thought I was too scientific. That was mainly because I didn't connect and communicated from my head. People find that interesting, but it doesn't prompt them to act. Only when you touch people in their hearts and stomachs do you get them moving. Apparently, I had no connection with myself either. In order to get others to move, I first had to come to a standstill myself. This is how I learned that whoever wants to change in a fundamental way must first come to a standstill. I connected much more with myself, and only then did I connect with others. I started giving lectures from my heart and people became emotional, some even cried. I can't stand people crying, but I also got emotional when I told them about my accident or my children's illnesses. I got all worked up and I was ashamed of it. Until someone said to me: 'It's beautiful that you dare to be so vulnerable'. That's how I discovered that toughness lies in showing vulnerability.

So, I compare a personal transition with a journey. Not a holiday trip; that's external. It is a journey inwards, deep inside yourself. An exciting journey, for which there is no travel brochure and no compass. The destination is unknown. Yet, for many people, the adventure of taking the journey inside beckons. They cherish hope and desire. Others do not yet dare to do so. They wait for the right moment, which may never come. Others, blocked by fear, do not embark on it at all. Fear of real change is quite normal. After all, there is a lot to lose; in the end, it is all about you and everything that is attached to it. You know what you are leaving behind, but not what will take its place. You have a lot to lose, but what can you gain? Letting go of the familiar and embracing the new is therefore the core of the journey inwards, and that is easier said than done. Yet it can be learned, by learning to deal with the fear and learning to accept uncertainty.

Despite the fear, I notice that, as a seismographic sign of the times, more and more people are engaged in the journey inwards. People are complex beings, too complex to fully understand. My whole career, trained as a mathematician, I have been working with complex systems, such as the energy and climate systems. Until I realized that the most complex systems are people themselves. That's how I came up with the idea of applying the transition theory to people. If you look at people's personal transitions through the development lens, you see that every personal transition is unique. Everyone has their own journey inwards. There is no absolute beginning or end, but in a continuous process of real change, common patterns and different phases can be distinguished. However, these are not strictly separated from each other. You do not go smoothly from one phase to the next. A personal transition, just like any substantial change in a complex system, has an erratic course with phases that overlap.

This is the evolutionary nature of a (personal) transition: sometimes you make a great leap, then you fall back, and you feel like you're going backwards. You can get hopelessly lost, and sometimes you come to a (temporary) standstill. You try, stumble, fall, get back up and go on again. Again, and again. It's all part of the process of shock-induced change. In the chapter on systemic crises, I said that the s-curve depicted is the ideal image of a transition, but in practice, it is never like that. A personal transition, therefore, requires courage, guts and leadership to repeatedly choose the most difficult and challenging path and to constantly work on overcoming fear. Courage means that something else is more important than your fear. So, all things considered, the journey inward cannot fail. You always learn from it. What matters is that you try and live it consciously. It is searching, learning and experimenting, and that always brings you further in your evolutionary development as a human being.

In the first phase of a personal transition – the pre-development phase – you become aware of a feeling that you really have to change; only the necessity is missing. Your fear dominates, and that which demands real change is pushed away or shouted down. I meet people who tell me that they have already gone very far with their personal transition. Usually, this is a sign that they have not yet begun their journey inwards. They over-shout their fear. Those who are really on an inner journey generally do so in sheltered conditions. When the urgency for deep change is still lacking, additional stimuli are needed. These can come from within or from without. Moments of deeper insight, life experiences, knowledge from training and courses and inspiring encounters are examples of external stimuli. However, experience shows that, however traumatic it may be at times, it is often personal crises that are the decisive factor in arousing the urgency of the journey inwards. An accident, death or serious illness often forms the springboard for a personal transition. I have experienced this myself. So, a personal transition starts with feeling differently, with a deep sense of urgency that the moment has come, and that real change is inevitable. When you have decided to start the journey inwards, you do not yet know what you are getting into and how the journey will go. You have no route and what you see is mostly fog. And because fear still prevails and lurks everywhere around the corner, there is no beckoning prospect yet.

In the next phase, the tipping phase, you acknowledge your fear and embrace the necessary deep change. Embracing your fear, and with it, the change, is a crucial point, a tipping point. It is the beginning of letting go of the old and familiar, of everything that felt so comfortable. Your familiar way of thinking and your habitual behaviour. These are steel frames of mind and ingrained patterns that are deeply embedded in your consciousness. But if you do what you always did, you get what you always got. Breaking this status quo requires you to leave the beaten track. This is extremely difficult and takes a lot of practice. It is a process of trial and error, but from the feeling that you really have to do this and that you dare to do it, a new kind of thinking and acting carefully emerges. The philosopher Henk Oosterling calls it 'doing thinking'. The fog slowly lifts, and a new perspective gradually begins to appear. Not immediately crystal clear, but rather vague contours. In time, the perspective becomes sharper and clearer. This requires a lot of practice, time and patience. People underestimate this. A personal transition, the journey inwards, does not come naturally and is a matter of serious and hard work. As Peter Sloterdijk, one of my favourite philosophers, pointed out: du mußt dein leben ändern (you must change your life!).

You get further on your journey inwards by practising daily to break through your stubborn patterns, routines and habits and develop new ways of thinking. To be able to do that, the balance between the mental and the physical is important. If you are not physically fit and healthy, you will not be mentally balanced, and vice versa. Many people need a boost, and a mentor or trainer can certainly help with this. I myself have a personal coach to stay physically fit. I work on my physical condition two or three times a week to get and stay in shape, even though it's not always fun. I also do exercises for my mind to achieve balance. For example, I have taught myself to zoom in and out regularly. Zooming in has an eye for detail and honours the small, but you also experience slowness because you are in the middle of complex, viscous processes. Those who zoom out take a step back and oversee the whole, and thus perceive real changes more consciously. From overview to insight. Every few days, I take a quarter of an hour to zoom in and out so that I can put everything into perspective and feel it through. I prefer to do that at the end of the day when it is dark. Every few months I do it a bit longer and after each year I do it more extensively. The most important thing that these exercises of zooming in and out bring me is peace. And, as I said, peace in the midst of unrest is worth a lot. It gives you confidence that things will turn out all right.

Then you come to the acceleration phase, in which you overcome barriers and create breakthroughs. This is a fierce and challenging phase. Acceleration does not mean speed, but a number of things do accelerate. In this turbulent phase, you try to break down a number of fear barriers, which you started to do in the tipping phase. See it as a layered system of barriers that you have to overcome on your journey inward. The outer layer you have to pass through is that of the world. Many people suffer from the illusion of powerlessness: what can I do in this big, complex world? What difference can I make? Do I matter at all? Shouldn't others change first? Why should I start? So, there are plenty of excuses not to really change, because it would not really make a difference. But if everyone thought like that, nothing would ever change. Only when you realize that every essential change matters, and that every person matters, can you get over this hurdle and try to get over the next barrier.

That next barrier is the system. How often have I heard people say: 'I want to change, but the system is against me'. But if you blame the system, you also put the problem outside yourself. Then it is laws, rules, procedures and protocols that stand in the way of your change. That is understandable in itself, but, if you really want to change, then you look for the change in yourself and not in rules and procedures. We are the system ourselves and we can influence it. The fear barrier that comes your way next is therefore you yourself, and specifically, your ego, status, power and income, which you feel are at stake. After all, there is a lot to lose: you have a nice job, a nice department and work with nice people. Your deepest fear is to lose all this. People naturally associate major changes with decline, but the fear of going backwards dominates the perspective that you can also go forwards. The trick is to learn to see that your job can become even more enjoyable and that the change can also bring benefits for your position and status.

At some point, you will realize that it is not at all about your ego, status, position of power, happiness, well-being and health and that your connection with your friends and loved ones is much more important than all the external appearances. This fear barrier is a very tricky one, and many people get stuck on matter, power and appearances. But, if you finally dare to step over your ego, you will reach the deepest barrier in yourself: the core of your human and world view. How do you look at others, the world and especially at yourself? These are deeply rooted, ingrained ideas that are quite difficult to change. However, this is possible in this phase, because a new perspective has now taken root in your brain and feelings. You feel and think differently. It just has to become tangible and clear by asking the right, honest questions to yourself: Have I become who I wanted to be? Do I do what I want, or do I want what I do? What is my inner compass? These are confrontational questions with which you mirror yourself against your own core values and starting points. I call it reflexivity, and the answers can hurt. Putting it outside yourself is also easier, but then you avoid the confrontation with yourself.

The only way to move forward in your personal transition is by confronting yourself. Step by step, you can learn to let go of the fear of this painful confrontation by experimenting with something new. A new thought, a new idea, a new project. Something exciting and contrary to what you thought or did. After reaching this tipping point, there is no way back and your personal transition, just like any other transition, becomes an irreversible process. If you feel deep inside that the old does not fit anymore, you cannot go back and really want something different. Another life, another partner, another job, other friends, sometimes even everything at once. These are major events, which are the result of radical choices arising from who you are and want to be in the undercurrent. To be able to take this step, it helps to concretely imagine the new perspective that has nestled in your head and heart. But don't underestimate it: this also requires a lot of practice and perseverance. It pays to work because that can also produce something beautiful. It makes you lighter, it makes you cleaner, it gives you energy and it gives you a lot of satisfaction.

In the last phase of the journey inwards, the new perspective sinks in further and you start to act accordingly, first consciously and later unconsciously. This requires a change from thinking differently to doing differently, from 'doing as usual' to 'doing uncommonly'. Despite the fact that the transition is now almost complete (although it is never finished), this phase is also a difficult one. Thinking differently does not automatically mean acting on it. Cognitive dissonance, a phenomenon from social psychology, exposes the tension between thinking and acting. As an example, I mentioned earlier the change pretenders, people who say 'yes' to change and then do 'no'. Here, too, practice makes perfect through experimentation on a small scale. By putting a new idea into practice and reflecting on yourself that you are also carrying this out consistently in, say, 3 months, with all the resistance and pain that this may entail. If this succeeds on a small scale, you can try to scale it up and start with an experiment of, say, 6 months. Through frequent practice, you will start to translate it more consciously into practical action, and as a result, you will start to act on it more and more subconsciously. This last step, from consciously acting differently to unconsciously acting differently, means that the perspective has finally landed in your subconscious. This is certainly not the end of your personal transition, but this journey inwards stops here for the time being, until the next insight or personal crisis sets you on a new journey inwards.

I am Going on a Journey, and I am Taking With Me...

You don't need that much on your inner journey. So go as lightly as possible and take four essential things with you: time, space, trust and a plan. That is all. And, by time I do not mean linear clock time. This usual clock time only hurries you along. In the hectic of everyday life with deadlines and milestones as part of the planning and control cycle, you cannot really change. Kairos time is the time you need for your journey inwards. Philosopher Joke Hermsen wrote a wonderful book about it. In Greek mythology, Kairos is the youngest and most rebellious grandson of Chronos. Kairos managed to bring about change and insight. Kairos is the time of the right moment and concentration. Time for yourself to deepen and still yourself. It can be a few hours, a few days, a few months or a year: Kairos time cannot be expressed in chronological terms. The lesson we can learn from the ancient Greeks is that whoever wants to change (transform) must first come to a physical and mental standstill. It seems contradictory, but you only start moving from a standstill. On your journey inwards, movement arises from a standstill, and you come to standstill from movement. During your time in Kairos, you will search for your inner compass and take the time to ask yourself essential questions and find the answers deep within yourself: why do I do things the way I always do them? What are my deeper motivations and where do they come from? Do I do what I want, or do I want what I do? And what am I really afraid of? Answering these questions goes far beyond the notion of reflection. It requires reflexivity, mirroring yourself against your own starting points. It is a reflective process in which you dare to question your own assumptions. It takes courage. And perseverance.

On your journey to the inner world, you will also need mental and physical space. The trick is to create space in your head and heart for your Kairos time. This usually works best in a special place. Not at your workplace or at home, where chronological time determines the rhythm of your life. Find a quiet place where you can isolate yourself in peace. That is different for everyone. For me, an island is a special place to find that space. An island forms a closed entity from which you cannot just leave. The energy is different there. I also become calm on the coast or in the mountains. That gives me the mental space to come up with new ideas and thoughts. So, look for a place where you feel at ease and grounded. A place that gives you the mental space to come to new insights.

The journey inwards starts with trust. Trust in yourself. It strikes me that this trust is often lacking in people. People have a certain fear and insecurity, and a tendency not to really trust themselves. Trust cannot be imposed or forced, but it arises from within, from the connection between head and heart. This connection, this trust, is crucial because only when you have trust in yourself will you also have trust in your journey within.

Finally, every journey stands or falls with preparation, and a plan is an important part of this. Not a well-defined, elaborate plan, not a roadmap with markers, not a blueprint, but rather a direction, an idea of where you would like to go, a sketch of what you would like to achieve. People generally spend little time on a plan for their own future. The idea is that it makes little sense anyway because what the future holds is uncertain. But do not underestimate the power of such a plan. Not that a plan is a guarantee for success, but at least with a plan you have something to go on. Make a plan for a period of 5 years. That is far away and yet close enough. Long enough for a transition period and short enough to make it concrete and practical. I myself develop a plan for a new route every 5 years. Not that such a plan necessarily comes true. On the contrary, more often than not it does not. But these plans do function as a kind of compass and give me a guideline and a perspective for action. You then undertake actions in the spirit of your plan, which makes your route go in the same direction.

Time, space, trust and a plan, that is all you need on your journey inwards. It sounds so simple, and in fact, it is. At the same time, it is also difficult and hard work. Much practice and perseverance are needed. Do not ask too much of yourself, but do not ask too little either. Wanting it too soon is counterproductive. Here, too, it is a question of balance. Being ambitious, but also having an eye for what is feasible. Towering ambitions often die in beauty because they are practically unattainable, and that is at your expense. So, think big, but do small, and try to connect those small steps to the higher goal again and again. As I said, it is an evolutionary process. The outcome is radically different, but the way to do it is in small steps. When you have made another step, be aware of it and celebrate it explicitly. Celebrating success gives positive energy and is very necessary to overcome fear and resistance permanently. In the end, it is all about getting the best out of yourself and making the most of your potential. That takes time. Trust that it will work out. Do not think you are the only one on a journey. In a society that is at a crossroads, there are masses of people all over the world looking for meaning and purpose, for new values. It is about getting the best out of ourselves and sharing that with others. That we learn to search together. Because up to now, the journey has been highly individual, and not collective. There is a wild and unfocused search. It still lacks a binding force, but that connection can arise from shared core values, symbols and rituals so that the individual journey inwards can grow into an unstoppable global movement.

Transition Expedition

'This week can change your life', I say at the beginning to the participants in a transition expedition. They look at me in disbelief, but at the end of a stormy week, they realize that a lot has been set in motion. Since I have experienced the importance of the journey inwards myself, I have been organizing transition expeditions together with born connectors Emmely Lefevre and Lotte van Hal. With a small group of 5 to 7 people, we travel for a 5-day programme to an island at home or abroad. A journey, but not a holiday: the participants will work hard on their personal transition. It is a week of Kairos time to reach inner depth. Participants are usually about to start the journey inwards, or have already started, but are stuck. Or they are at a crossroads in their lives and want to make a jump, but do not dare to do so yet. Such a week is therefore extremely exciting and very intensive for them. For us as well. Exciting things happen, many emotions are released, and an atmosphere of fraternization grows because people open up more and more.

Each morning of this 5-day journey starts with physical or mental relaxation, after which I give a penetrating talk about various aspects of transitions. I teach participants to use the transition lenses so they can position themselves and get to know and understand themselves better. After that, the participants are given assignments to work on themselves. In the afternoon, they set off on their own or with someone else, without a compass. They are then allowed to consciously get lost, both mentally and physically, and experience shows that this has a very liberating effect. Getting lost helps you on your journey inwards. At the end of the day, there is individual coaching and a feedback session in which participants share their experiences with each other. By listening to each other's stories, they help each other. People recognize things in each other and find it reassuring to know that they are not the only ones struggling with something. The group's reflection is encouraging, comforting and deepening. After dinner, there is another evening session with a group discussion and time for relaxation. At the end of the week, the participants present their own transition plan, on an A4 sheet or on the back of a beer mat, and they recite a letter to themselves. These are very emotional moments and the ultimate reward for all the efforts during the transition process.

Emmely, Lotte and I create a safe environment for the participants so that they can feel at ease and there is room to express their feelings and emotions.

(Continued)

(*Continued*)

Therefore, there is a lot of laughter and plenty of room for relaxation. In such a safe environment, people come to certain insights and make decisions that they would otherwise not readily make. This can lead to radical decisions. It can happen, for example, that people decide on the spot to quit their jobs because they want a completely different job, to start their own business or even to lead a completely different life. Of course, this does not come out of the blue that week. These personal transitions have been slumbering under the surface in the undercurrents for a long time and come to the surface during such a week. By being so intensely involved with yourself for a longer period of time in your own Kairos time, you can more easily achieve breakthroughs. And when that happens, it is enormously refreshing. Again and again, it turns out that people are looking for something that is already there, only they didn't see it because they didn't take the time and space to be conscious about it. As Johan Cruijff once said: 'You only see it when you get it'. Once you see it, it turns out to be surprisingly simple.

The journey inwards continues after that week and also translates into a journey outwards. For example, there was a director of a large company who found insufficient satisfaction in what he was doing. He wanted to stop but wondered what he should do next. In the group, he naturally functioned as a coach and mentor for others. It was actually quite obvious that he should do that professionally, but it did not occur to him to do so. A small touch was enough to make him realize this, and his choice was made. Someone else wanted to write a book about the experiences in her work. She couldn't do it herself, she thought. She had already hired a ghost-writer once, but that did not produce the results she had hoped for. During the transition expedition, she decided to do it herself, which yielded a nice result sometime later.

There are countless other good examples of people who just needed a little push to make a radical choice. Of course, this remains a scary and exciting process, with ups and downs after the week. That's why we stay in touch after the expedition and why we organize follow-up meetings to exchange experiences. Without exception, they are positive, and no one regrets the choices that were made or the path that was taken. It hasn't always been easier, but the satisfaction is all the greater, as is the pride that one has dared to do this. And rightly so! We travel with these courageous people and keep them in our hearts forever.

What Type of Changemaker Are You?

Twenty years of transition research have shown that transitions often arise through radical initiatives of small groups of people. Groups of three, four or five people who take a different path and have the distinguishing competencies to create the movement that will topple the system in which they operate. I currently distinguish 6 different types of changemaker:

(1) Frontrunners
(2) Connectors
(3) Builders
(4) Demolishers
(5) Tilters
(6) Followers

Not to pigeonhole people, because all these types of change agents are needed to realize real change. There are roles that overlap and there are people who fulfill multiple roles or grow from one role to another. For example, I am a natural frontrunner, later developed into a tilter and only in recent years have I become more of a connector. In the first years of my career, I also demolished quite a lot before I was able to build anything up. I am not particularly good at following others.

Many people are not aware of the role they play, nor of the complementary roles they need around them. I know quite a few people who, in their urge to change, take on a role that does not suit them. For example, I know someone who is a natural connector, but who played the role of frontrunner for years and got burnt out as a result. You, therefore, need different types of changemaker in the various phases of a transition. In the pre-development phase, you need frontrunners, inspired and content-driven people who create space and want to distinguish themselves by contributing to a system breakthrough. Frontrunners see the solution and cannot imagine that others do not understand them. As a result, they are often too far ahead of the troops. At some point, they look back and see that no one is following them. This is the pitfall of frontrunners: on their own, they have no chance and they become overworked or frustrated. Because they are not so good at connecting, they are not able to create a movement. Therefore, their direct effect is not so great. The indirect effect of frontrunners, however, is great: they have innovative ideas and start projects that often lead to new insights and system breakthroughs. Frontrunners overlap with builders, only builders have more ability to work with others. However, builders are not necessarily content-driven or visionary.

In the breakthrough phase, there is a need for connectors to connect the old with the new. They connect people, ideas, projects, networks and processes. Connectors can mobilize a crowd to have an impact. To illustrate this, I once had a penguin film made. An endless procession of penguins waddles along until one penguin gets out of line because it realizes that this is a dead end. The rest waddles on tireless until a second penguin follows the example of the first. Then come penguins three, four, five and the rest, until a substantial group separates and takes a new path. Under the influence of a tilter, a new order emerges, and finally, the whole penguin colony takes a new path that does offer prospects.

Without connectors, you get all these little islands. Then everything is too fragile to stay upright. Connectors have an important role in the in-between-period, the phase between 'it is' and 'it will be'. In this vulnerable phase, where old systems crumble and new ones emerge but are still fragile, connectors ensure that new networks and communities emerge that also need connections. Connectors are process-driven, think in terms of possibilities and similarities and look openly at everyone's qualities. They are social, strong-minded, empathic and subordinate their ego to the greater whole. They do not need to be in the foreground themselves, and therefore form a natural link with leaders and tilters.

Then you need the builders and demolishers, those who build something new and those who demolish the existing structures. We prefer to build rather than demolish. People also like to create something new. A builder builds new structures and organizations for a higher purpose and creates a lot of energy to put his or her shoulders under them. The ability to create something from nothing is an important characteristic of a builder. Builders are driven to show growth and enjoy the building process itself. Because demolition has a negative connotation, demolishers are less popular. They do look for allies, but they don't need to be loved because they get used to the resistance and opposition in their path. It will not stop them from continuing. In any case: the new is leading, the old is following. Building is also relatively faster than tearing down. When you build something new, it becomes clearer why the old has to disappear: 'Everything new', Stef Bos sang, 'makes room for the old to disappear'. But if we demolish too little, we can also build less. Without demolition, all space is still taken up by the old. So, demolishers are crucial and indispensable. Just as builders with a higher purpose create the new, demolishers with a higher purpose demolish the old and enjoy that demolition process. And there is still a lot of demolition work to be done: everything that functioned well but is no longer appropriate to the new age must be demolished, including institutions, organizations, structures, laws and regulations. And when that happens, things can happen fast.

From that point on, you need the tilters, because resistance increases and tilters are good at dealing with it. A tilter can even enjoy that resistance, and that is an important characteristic for someone who wants to realize something special, namely the actual change of a company, organization, sector or system. But tilters are scarce. Examples of political tilters are Nelson Mandela, Martin Luther King, Gandhi and Gorbachev, and in Europe Frans Timmermans, with his radical greening agenda, and Angela Merkel. In the Netherlands, perhaps Pieter Omtzigt. But within companies, sectors and social domains, we also find tilters, such as Jos de Blok and Roger Cox. Just like frontrunners, tilters are driven by content, but they are also strategic players and can act on several stages at the same time. When there is a storm, a tilter remains upright. They have the ability to mobilize people and get a movement going. In the phase of a transition where a new order is being created, followers are an indispensable link. They help a tilter to create a movement and thus achieve a breakthrough. A tilter without followers will never be able to achieve great things. Followers are supporters and thinkers who support a higher goal but do not want to be in the spotlight themselves. They operate in the background, see where there are gaps and fill them.

As you can see, combinations of different types of change agents can play a decisive role in the different phases of a transition. Smart interventions at suitable moments and by the right combination of change agents can speed up a transition. The trick is to find the right combinations of change agents in society, in companies, in government and in social organizations. Until now, I have seldom seen the right mix of change agents from close up. Often, change agents still operate on their own and do not form coalitions with complementary change agents. This will be one of the great challenges of the transition tasks we are facing. One thing is certain: on your own, there is little chance of success. It may go faster, but together you can get further. An African proverb tells us, 'if you want to go fast, go alone. If you want to go far, go together'. This is why you should reflect on your own role as a change agent and ask yourself reflexive questions: what role do I play as a change agent and why do I play this role? Does this role suit me? What other roles do I see myself playing? And what other roles can I not fulfil, but do I need? This brings you to people with complementary qualities, with whom you can work together on the essential change. Whichever change agent you are, each type requires courage, guts and leadership, because you will meet a lot of resistance along the way.

Resistance

Learning to deal with resistance is crucial if you want to implement a substantial change. Suppose that you want to change something substantially on the basis of your mission, then you start an intervention with a certain goal in mind. Based on the awareness that you will evoke resistance, try to estimate in advance what kind of resistance your intended change will evoke and where it will come from. The point is to learn to recognize that resistance to change is quite normal. In fact, it is a good sign: if there is no resistance, there is no tension or resilience, and your intervention does not really matter. Yet changemakers find resistance annoying because it slows things down and slows them down. You can also see it differently: if you are not met with resistance, it means that what you are doing does not really matter. You are not a factor of importance. That is painful because then you yourself does not really matter.

I have experienced this myself for years. I did research on climate change and hardly anybody took it seriously. Later, it was the same with sustainability, and when I started working on transitions, people wrote that I would perish under my own hype. I kept it all in my archive. Now I can enjoy the resistance, but during the first decades, I often felt misunderstood and alone. Resistance is a good sign. It is the beginning of contact and interaction; you touch something in someone or in an organization. From that experience, I try to help people enjoy the resistance they encounter. Resistance is healthy. Our immune system also provides resistance to outside influences in order to prevent disease. Just like the human body, resistance also has a function within an organization. Imagine that within an organization there was no resistance to essential change. That would show a lack of resilience. Resistance is a sign that people want to maintain the familiar. It can also be a natural corrective mechanism if the proposed change is too great or too violent or too fast.

There are various reasons for resistance. Deep down, resistance stems from fear. Fear of losing control, or fear of the uncertainty the change will bring. It touches on a deep fear of saying goodbye to the existing and embracing the uncertain new. You know what you have and not what you will get. Substantial change also hurts, and avoiding the pain is postponing execution because it comes back like a boomerang. In retrospect, it often turns out that the fear of the pain is greater than the pain itself, and people wonder what it was they were so afraid of. Try to find out what kind of resistance it is. There is direct resistance, for example, with direct communication and an open attitude. If this is done constructively, it can be positive, but a lot of resistance is indirect and less easy to recognize. In the case of indirect resistance, people mean or think something else than what they say. The real message is then unrecognizable. This may be because of fear. Fear for their own position, status or power. There may also be group resistance. This is even more difficult to deal with because people can then hide behind each other. It is usually a sign that one does not feel safe in the organization. And then there is systemic resistance, which often translates into personal resistance. Transitions are systemic changes that are accompanied by intense systemic pain. This is logical and understandable because it undermines existing interests and leads to a shift in power. After all, you don't ask a turkey to put itself on the Christmas menu. And the closer we get to the heart of a transition, the deeper the pain and the greater the resistance. This means that the tipping point has been reached and that the transition is accelerating.

Take, for example, the transition from coal to natural gas in the 1960s. Although the advantages of natural gas – cleaner, cheaper and economically more advantageous – were evident, there was fierce resistance to natural gas. Two thousand coal traders protested against the introduction of natural gas with the slogan 'Coal trade in the cold with natural gas heat', and the Solid Fuels Foundation advertised with 'Cosy people burn coal'. People also took up the cause of their local coal merchant because they could have a friendly chat with their coal merchant, whereas natural gas is anonymous and comes out of invisible pipes. Many housewives did not like cooking with gas: wasn't the flame from the burner too bright? Wouldn't the meal burn? 'I'll stay who I am', said one housewife who did not like cooking with natural gas. In order to take away the fear of gas, housewives could learn to cook on natural gas during information evenings. A large group of households had to pay to be able to participate in the transition. People had to get rid of their old cookers and buy a gas boiler and cooker, which for some was quite a financial blow. The headline in the newspaper The Telegraph was 'Those who have to pay the price'. Much of the systemic resistance was directed at the Minister of Economic Affairs, Joop den Uyl, who announced the closure of the coal mines in Limburg in 1965. This led to furious reactions from the coal lobby, as it involved big interests and a lot of money, and 45,000 direct and 30,000 indirect jobs were lost. Replacement jobs were promised, but this was of little consolation.

There is much to be learned from this coal-to-gas transition. That transitions go against vested interests and initially cost money (investments) that are only recouped years later. That those directly involved feel the pain and others feel it because they have to get used to something completely different. That the media are often critical and 'against'. That clarity of approach and information provision are required (a big new story needs to be made small). That the role of the government is crucial (the market will not do it alone). And that people often get carried away with taking too big steps, whereas taking small ones, in the beginning, can be highly effective. Afterwards scaling up can then take place. It is therefore not so much about solving resistance immediately – that is usually not possible. It is more about recognizing resistance, discovering where it comes from and then trying to anticipate it. Going straight through the resistance makes no sense at all, it only increases the resistance. Often resistance needs time, time to overcome the fear. I know this all too well from my own experience. The more subtly you deal with resistance, the greater the chance that it will subside. If the support for your interventions increases in a natural, organic way step by step, resistance will decrease. In addition to having the courage to deal with resistance, a transition requires leadership.

Leadership

Especially in a period of chaos and instability, such as the one we are living in now, there is a need for leadership. Just not traditional leadership. During the covid crisis, we have seen authoritarian leaders fail on all sides of the world, from Bolsonaro in Brazil and Trump in the US to Putin in Russia. All men who seem to know no doubt, operate from certainties and steer top-down in order to control. However, this control is fake because the covid crisis was forcing us to steer away from uncertainty. In the beginning, we knew virtually nothing about the covid virus and how to combat it. Gradually, we developed knowledge and experience: it is learning by doing and doing by learning. Classical leaders fail in this respect because they refuse to admit their mistakes and learn from them. They do just the opposite. It is therefore not surprising that it is precisely populist leaders who could not cope with the covid pandemic.

In times of chaos there is a lack of trust in leaders and therefore we need authentic leaders: people who do and live up to what they say. And when society falls apart, there is a need for connecting leaders: people with great empathy that can connect people, groups and ideas. Modern leaders dare to go against the grain, dare to take unpopular measures, can deal with resistance and give direction and offer space.

Feminine Leadership

Research shows that female leaders are not so successful in crisis management because they are women, but because they lead countries that are more likely to place a woman at the top. This cultural context gives female leaders the power to make a difference. However, the covid success of these female leaders is the prelude to an era of female leadership. In the current era, you see that masculine leadership, dating from the industrial era, is still dominant in many multinationals and large, complex organizations. These masculine organizations are characterized by hierarchy, top-down decision-making, control, proficiency and a performance-oriented culture. Masculine values are goal-oriented, decisiveness, willpower, perseverance, confidence in one's own abilities and a reliance on facts and logic. But when there is too much masculine leadership, people are no longer central. There is a lack of care for people and a chilly environment arises, in which performance is central and excessive stress and fear arise. The soul then disappears, and the organization becomes sick, and ultimately deathly sick. Until things escalate and the organization dies or reinvents itself and takes a different course.

Connecting Leadership

Do you recognize the mirror of our society in this? What is happening now, in this in-between-period, is that society is falling apart due to increasing polarization and conflicting interests. It is precisely then that there is a great need for connecting leadership, for leaders who give direction and offer space, who lead from a great capacity for empathy, who subordinate their ego to the greater whole, who are good listeners and show sensitivity, who motivate people intrinsically and who create connections at all levels. These are the typical characteristics of feminine leadership. It also fits the trend of feminine organizations: flat network organizations with a people-oriented culture, with an eye for work-life balance and open communication, aimed at connecting people. This fits well with the 'softer' sectors such as education and care but is also becoming increasingly visible in the business world. And it will become clear that if feminine values – connection, care, attention, patience, and the like – are to be valued, they have to be considered.

You can understand that when feminine values – connection, care, attention, patience, trust that things will work out, an eye for process and context and starting from feeling and intuition – become more and more important, leaders with big egos have, or will have, a hard time. But also on the feminine side, the balance can tip. When there is too much feminine leadership, there is a lack of clarity, the course and mission are not clear, and it takes too long before decisions are made. So many concessions are made to people that this is at the expense of the company's results. The organization gets into trouble and needs clarity, rigour and entrepreneurship.

So, a balance is needed between masculine and feminine leadership. This balance is far from being achieved within organizations, but society is slowly but surely feminizing, and new generations need different forms of leadership. A better balance requires much more feminine leadership and many more women, especially at the top. You cannot force this, not even through women's quotas. You have to create the circumstances in which women feel comfortable. This is in the culture, the emotional climate and the mindset, and it takes a lot of time to transform this within existing organizations. It is not a rule that feminine values are exclusively reserved for women. There are also female leaders who lead organizations based on masculine values, just as there are men who lead organizations based on feminine values. In this time of transition, we also need connectors here. Connecting is a form of informal leadership, right across the formal organization. Connectors in an organization are people who connect the old with the new, the outside with the inside, and who can translate successes from one context to another.

People who can do this can be found in every conceivable position in an organization. But, when it comes to leadership, people still automatically look upwards, to the top. It is a classic reflex. But leadership is not only found at the top of the organization; leadership is everywhere. There is potential leadership in a great many people, only they don't realize it themselves and not enough space is given to developing that leadership. So don't immediately look upwards, but first to yourself. What kind of leadership is hidden within you? What is needed to develop it? Leadership is also found in small things: being proactive, taking the initiative, denouncing something, addressing someone, using space instead of sitting back and waiting. The awareness that it starts with you is the most important thing. 'Don't wait for the revolution. Do something now', as the Croatian philosopher Srećko Horvat says. This can be done at any level: in the organization where you work, in your circle of friends, in your sports club. If you think things should be done differently, speak up and try to make things better. To me, that is a form of leadership. Just by being yourself.

Authentic Leadership

Authentic leadership is therefore becoming increasingly important. If you are not an authentic leader in this day and age, you will be tackled and punished mercilessly on social media. The difference between what you say and what you do is immediately exposed. An authentic leader is sincere and honest, dares to show his or her true nature and also knows his or her qualities and limitations. But above all, an authentic leader stands upright in the storm. That requires courage, guts and authenticity. Angela Merkel said 'Wir schaffen das', ('we can make it'), which to me is a striking example of an authentic leader. She sometimes failed and was sometimes wrong, but she always stood up straight and never wavered. What a strength she radiated. In times of crisis, agile leadership is also important. Not sticking rigidly to well-defined ideas, plans and strategies, but constantly responding to changing circumstances. Continuous learning, adapting and anticipating. Stimulating a culture of searching, learning and experimenting. Dare to make mistakes, dare to admit them and learn from them. The art is to combine giving direction with offering space. Mental space, organizational space and also financial space. This is still difficult for many leaders because they appear to be opposites, but nothing could be further from the truth. It is essential that leaders should not want to organize and arrange everything themselves but leave this to others on the basis of trust. In other words, they should not organize things themselves, but enable others to do so.

Inspired Leadership

Modern leadership is also inspirational leadership. An inspirational leader is driven by principles and thinks and acts with heart and soul on the basis of positive, stimulating values, and wants to have a positive impact on the world. Based on the urge to manifest his or her dream, an inspirational leader leads others along in the dream. This can go far. Sometimes too far, which can cause people to lose themselves. Inspired leaders are often front runners, and they tend to go too far and lose others around them. They are so far ahead of the troops that they lose contact with those who lag behind. Without connectors around them, they are not really effective. Paul Polman, the former CEO of Unilever, was an example of such a leader. A visionary and inspired leader, who had a positive worldwide impact, but lost the people around him and fought a lonely battle within Unilever, as aptly described by Jeroen Smit in the fascinating book 'Het grote gevecht en het eenzame gelijk van Paul Polman' ('The big battle and the lonely truth of Paul Polman'). A spirited leader who is also authentic feels his surroundings and is also felt by those surroundings. This is only possible if you are connected to yourself. Only then can you connect with others around you. This requires the courage to make yourself vulnerable and to show your emotions and feelings, your qualities but also your shortcomings. Then you become approachable and accessible, and you get closer to people. That sounds easier than it is. Many leaders still have difficulty with this because they consciously create distance out of fear of showing themselves as human beings.

Transformative Leadership

Besides connecting, feminine, authentic and inspired leadership, transformative leadership is also needed. Transformative leaders are charismatic people with a vision who can touch others in a specific, emotive way. They radiate power. Not only mentally, but also in the way they present themselves publicly. They are able to arouse a collective feeling of optimism and to bind many people to them. Especially now, in this time of chaos and turbulence, we need transformational leaders who can create a movement by mobilizing groups of people and by giving them a voice and a direction. These leaders have the ability to break down systems and rebuild them. They can transform organizations through inspiration. But transformative leaders are rare because it requires a lot: a lot of energy, passion, perseverance and the ability to overcome resistance, and at the same time empathy, connection and sensitivity. A synthesis of masculine and feminine leadership. A transformational leader is a connecting tilter, or a tilting connector. Research shows that this type of leadership leads to demonstrably better results within an organization in the long term.

But, as I have said, these leaders are rare. In politics, you have to look far and wide for transformative leaders. Transformative political leaders do not act from political motives but from a social ideal that they want to realize. Do you see them? Transformative leaders are also thin on the ground in the business world. Feike Sijbesma, the former top executive of DSM, who now dedicates himself to public affairs, is an example. You find transformative leaders more in society. Internationally, I think Greta Thunberg is an example, because she became an icon for millions of young people all over the world. But I have my doubts about her style: she is often angry and provocative in public, and this arouses a lot of resistance. I recognize that from my early days. I used to be a frontrunner, builder and demolisher all at the same time, but now I'm trying to be a transformative leader myself more and more. In times of unrest, I try to radiate calm and confidence, based on the deep sense that things will eventually turn out all right. That doesn't always work out either, like in the period of the first covid lockdown that first paralyzed me, until my wife Inge said: 'This is what you are always talking about, isn't it? A period of chaos, which we must embrace'.

But I could have gone further if I had fought and struggled less and moved a little more and operated a little more subtly. I have always missed a mentor, although I never really showed that I needed one. Someone who would have made me feel calm could have helped me a lot. So now I try to be a mentor for people who are looking for a beacon in turbulent times. I try to give them peace and confidence so that they try things that they otherwise would not dare to do. It gives me great satisfaction to see that people develop faster as a result. I also try to inspire people and get them moving. That is only possible from a connection. Only when you are connected with yourself you can connect with others. Thinking, looking and feeling from connection, so that head, heart and hands merge together. Only then you can touch others on an emotional level and get them moving, from peace and trust in yourself and others. I also try to light the fire of change wherever it is needed. I try to mobilize people for a 'civilized uprising', in healthcare, education and construction, but also in regions, cities and districts. I myself would like to do this more internationally in the years ahead. What matters to me is not so much that I will succeed, but whether I have done everything possible to make it work. I cherish my failures as much as my successes. The road to mastery seems to me to be a fascinating journey. That you rise above time, as it were, and are no longer part of a 'for' or 'against' but are lifted above all doubt. There is still a way to go, but isn't that a wonderfully challenging journey?

Step Into the Arena

Can we connect the journey inwards with the journey outwards? We human beings are on a destructive journey. We are destroying the environment for our own growth. This may go well for a long time, but eventually, it will come back to us like a boomerang. The signs that we have reached a tipping point are already there. Covid-19. Climate change. Biodiversity loss. But that is only the beginning. Nature is our lifeline and provides us with the resources for our existence: clean water, clean air, clean soil, food, raw materials, energy and medicines. If we continue to pollute, waste and destroy these sources of life, we will eventually destroy ourselves. But if this destructive journey is a dead end, why don't we take a new path? Because we are stubborn, and we only do it when there is no other way. A new path does not come about by itself. The path is paved by a beckoning perspective. In this time of uncertainty and chaos, we need above all a new, big story. A positive story that inspires us, stimulates us and binds us. A natural story, in which balance is central. The imbalance between man and nature reflects the imbalance between our head and our heart. Only when we heal our relationship with nature we can also heal the relationship between our head and our heart within ourselves. And ultimately between humans and fellow humans.

If we did this in every aspect of our lives, what would our world look like? We would grow our food in a natural way that strengthens and enriches nature. Animals would be treated kindly. We would eat clean and healthy products without wasting food. We would pay a socially fair price. We would create and distribute clean and sustainable energy and not waste it, by exchanging energy naturally between homes, neighbourhoods, districts, regions and countries. Like a cascade, just like in nature. We can then live together in communities that share core values and take care of each other in a natural way. Care is an integral part of our lives and is part of how we live, work, recreate, play sports and move around. Prevention and making people healthier is the starting point in everything. We teach children to develop and use their potential in a natural way by providing a stimulating and challenging learning environment in which they can make mistakes and learn from them. Search, learn and experiment is the motto. We design our country in a natural way. A green-blue oasis where communities live together with nature in the greenery and on the water. Just like nature, companies produce clean products and services in a regenerative and circular manner, add value to the earth and to people with a positive impact and ensure a fair distribution. People are satisfied with what they have and who they are. They are in balance and mostly happy. Their level of happiness is measured annually and is the starting point for policies aimed at the long term. A Minister for the Long Term is appointed to be able to adequately anticipate and respond to crises. Every large company also appoints a long-term director who, like the Ministry, makes scenarios and risk analyzes based on structural uncertainties. Politics is embedded in a democratic system in which people feel heard and participate in the decision-making process at the local and the regional level.

How does that sound to you? Like a utopia? Far away? Naive? And yet, if you let it all sink in, it is all there already. Everything in this utopian story already exists on a small scale in experiments. We just overlook it. And when we see it, we find it almost impossible that it can also be done on a large scale. This is a sign of our lack of imagination. I call it ingrained impossibility thinking. We mentally make the possible impossible. The trick is to make such a big utopian story small. So small that it becomes practical for everyone and offers handles to make choices for his or her own life and environment. All those small stories then add up to a big story. The greatest challenge for all transitions we are facing, therefore, lies in the mental leap of scale. Even more than in technology, politics or institutions, it is in our minds and hearts. It starts and ends with ourselves. The question that triggers me is: what are you doing with your possibilities in the time that you are living on earth?

Do you try to use your talents in the best possible way for something political? Do you try to contribute to the big story with your little story? Or do you let it pass you by and keep floating around without a compass? Are you really doing what you want, or do you want what you do? Will you become part of the revolution and contribute to it? Or will you let it pass you by and just experience it? Do you travel outside and inside with it?

As far as I'm concerned, asking these questions is answering them. That you can contribute to restoring the wonder of nature is a great opportunity. Everyone said it was impossible until someone came along who didn't know. For me, it's not so much about whether it succeeds, but whether I did everything I could. That is why I will close with the wise words that former President of the United States Theodore Roosevelt uttered in 1910 at La Sorbonne, the University of Paris. The quote, for me the ultimate description of true leadership, is called 'The Man in the Arena', yet perhaps it would be better translated into today's language as 'The Woman in the Arena':

> It is not the critic who counts ... The credit belongs to the man/ woman who is actually in the arena, whose face is marred by dust and sweat and blood; who strives valiantly; who errs, who comes up short again and again, because there is no effort without error and shortcoming; but who does actually strive to do the deeds; who knows great enthusiasms, great devotions; who spends him/ herself in a worthy cause; who at the best knows, in the end, the triumph of high achievement, and who at the worst, if he/she fails, at least fails while daring greatly ....

Epilogue

Chaos is the word of our time. It represents an order that we do not yet know. People struggle with this: time seems to have no direction and there is a lack of insight and overview. Where is the world going? People are losing a grip on their existence and our leaders seem to have lost that grip as well. Chaos is a symptom of crisis and in today's world, we stumble from crisis to crisis. Many people feel that way.

Chaos is also a good sign. Chaos is in fact a prerequisite for substantial change. Without chaos, there is no breakthrough in a transition. Chaos is therefore a sign that we can say goodbye to the old. Something new may be born. A new world. A new system.

If we recognize this, we can embrace chaos. It is not easy, and I expect that with the crises still to come – covid was just a taste of what is to come – chaos will only increase in the next 10 years. As a result, the contradictions in society will become even greater than they already are, and the lack of peace will also grow. Even more protests, even more lawsuits, and even more conflicts. We must go through the pain of transition and embrace the chaos.

This is also a book of hope. The greater the chaos, the closer we come to the solution. We learn from crises, and in doing so, we stumble along. Until we reach the tipping point, and, in my view, we are approaching that point in this decade. After that, things can go (relatively) fast because we will experience exponential development. The chaos will diminish, and we will be in calmer waters.

I wanted a different kind of book this time. More personal. More accessible. Simpler. For a wider audience. But also, a kind of magnum opus, an overview of the insights I have acquired over the past decades and which I would like to share with you. That is why I called on the help of a journalist as ghostwriter, Mischa Verheijden. Mischa interviewed me a few times and wrote down his interview so well and aptly that it reflected the core of my thinking. So first of all, I would like to thank Mischa Verheijden for the excellent work he has done. Well done Mischa; through your valuable contribution more people will enjoy this book! Gijs van den Boomen, Arjen de Groot and Michael de Beer of KuiperCompanons have done a fantastic job. Together with them, I worked on a vision of the future for the Netherlands for the next 100 years. Many thanks also to my publisher Nathalie Doruijter of De Geus publishers for all her efforts to make this book possible. And to Thomas Coenraads, the desk editor, who went through the text very sharply and critically, which made it even more compact and fluent. To my colleagues at DRIFT and to my assistant Shifra for all her editing and organizing work for this book. And finally, to my dear wife Inge, for her endless patience and for helping me to endure the necessary stress that this book, even during the holidays, brought with it.

References

Introduction: The Turmoil in Ourselves and in the World

Avelino, F. (2011). *Power in transition: Empowering discourses on sustainability transitions*. PhD Thesis, Erasmus University Rotterdam.

Avelino, F., & Rotmans, J. (2009). Power in transitions: An interdisciplinary framework to study power in relation to structural change. *European Journal of Social Theory, 12*(4), 543–569.

Centola, D. (2021). *Change: How to make big things happen*. New York, NY: Little, Brown Spark.

Giddens, A. (1984). *The constitution of society; outline of the theory of structuration*. Berkeley, CA: University of California Press.

Han, B.-C. (2014). *De vermoeide samenleving*. Amsterdam: Uitgeverij van Gennep.

Morin, E., & Kern, A. B. (1999). Homeland earth: A Manifesto for the new millennium. In *Advances in systems theory, complexity, and the human sciences*. Cresskill, NJ: Hampton Press.

Rotmans, J. (2012). *In het oog van de orkaan: Nederland in transitie*. Boxtel: Uitgeverij Aeneas.

Rotmans, J. (2014). *Een verandering van tijdperk: Nederland kantelt*. Boxtel: Uitgeverij Aeneas.

https://www.edelman.com/trust/2020-trust-barometer, Edelman trust barometer 2020.

https://www.welingelichtekringen.nl/cultuur/2910349/toegejuichte-zomer-

https://www.nieuweleiders.nl/in-gesprek-met/jan-rotmans/

https://www.breakoutteam.nl/

https://www.breakoutteam.nl/manifest

1 Transition Lenses: Seeing Things in a Different Way

Braudel, F. (1976). *The Mediterranean and the Mediterranean World in the age of Philip II*. New York, NY: Harper & Row.

Braun, D., & Kramer, J. (2018). *The corporate tribe: Organizational lessons from anthropology*. Abingdon: Taylor & Francis.

De Haan, H., & Rotmans, J. (2011). Patterns in transitions: Understanding complex patterns of change. *Technological Forecasting and Social Change, 78*(1), 90–102.

De Haan, F., & Rotmans, J. (2018, March). A proposed theoretical framework for actors in transformative change. *Technological Forecasting and Social Change, 128*, 275–286.

Lodder, M., Roorda, C., Loorbach, D., & Spork, C. (2017). *Staat van transitie: Patronen van opbouw en afbraak in vijf domeinen*. DRIFT, Erasmus University Rotterdam.

Lokale Energie Monitor. (2020). Een initiatief van klimaatstichting HIER en RVO. Retrieved from https://www.hieropgewekt.nl/

Loorbach, D. (2007). Transition management: New mode of governance for sustainable development. PhD Thesis, Erasmus University Rotterdam, International Books.

Peres, C. (2002). *Technological revolutions and financial capital: The dynamics of bubbles and golden ages.* Cheltenham: Edward Elgar Publishing.

Piketty, T. (2014). *Capital in the twenty-first century.* Cambridge, MA: Harvard University Press.

Piketty, T. (2020). *Capital and ideology.* Cambridge, MA: Harvard University Press.

Rotmans, J. (2017). *Omwenteling: Van mensen, organisaties en samenleving.* Amsterdam: Uitgeverij De Arbeiderspers.

Rotmans, J., & de Vries, B. (1997). *Perspectives on global change: The TAR- GETS approach.* Cambridge: Cambridge University Press.

Rotmans, J., Kemp, R., & van Asselt, M. B. A. (2001, April). More evolution than revolution: Transition management in public policy. *Foresight, 3*(1), 15–32.

Rotmans, J., & Loorbach, D. (2009). Complexity and transition management. *Journal of Industrial Ecology, 13*(2), 184–196. Special Issue on Complexity and Industrial Ecology.

Sloterdijk, P. (2011). *Du muβt dein leben ändern.* Berlin, Deutschland: Suhrkamp Verlag.

2 Crisis as Opportunity

Beck, U. (1992). *Risk society: Towards a new modernity.* London: Sage.

Break Free From Plastic (BFFP). (2019). *Brand audit 2019, branded: Identifying the World's Top Corporate Plastic Polluters, vol. II, USA.* Retrieved from https://www.break-freefromplastic.org/globalbrandauditreport2019/

Center for International Environmental Law (CIEL), e.a. (2019). *Plastic & climate: The hidden costs of a plastic planet,* May 2019, UK. Retrieved from https://www.5gyres.org/publications

De Film Albatross. Retrieved from https://www.albatrossthefilm.com/

De Waal, S., & Rotmans, J. (2020). Dankzij de crisis kunnen we meer in balans komen, Opiniestuk Trouw, 2 August 2020.

Eurostat. (2020). Renewable energy statistics. Retrieved from https://ec.europa.eu/eurostat/cache/infographs/energy/bloc-4c.html

Gorissen, L. (2020). *Building the future of innovation on millions of years of natural intelligence.* Tunbridge Wells: Wordzworth Publishing.

Hermsen, J. (2019). *Het tij keren, met Rosa Luxemburg en Hannah Arendt.* Amsterdam: Uitgeverij Prometheus.

Holland, J. (1995). *Hidden order: How adaptation builds complexity.* New York, NY: Basic Books.

IPBES, Intergovernmental Science-Policy Platform on Biodiversity and Ecosystem Services. (2019). *The global assessment report on biodiversity and ecosystem services.* Bonn. Retrieved from https://ipbes.net/global-assessment

Kaufmann, S. (1995). *At home in the universe: The search for the laws of self-organization and complexity.* Oxford: Oxford University Press.

Moore, M., & Gibbs, J. (2019). Planet of the humans documentary. Retrieved from www.pla-netofthehumans.com

NRC. (2020, March 26). Risico van pandemie was reëel. *Dutch Newspaper NRC Handelsblad.*

Prigogine, I., & Stengers, I. (1984). *Order out of Chaos: Man's new dialogue with nature* Boulder, CO: New Science Library.

Rotmans, J. (2020). En toch heeft Michael Moore een punt met Planet of the Humans, Opiniestuk in Trouw. 8 mei 2020. Retrieved from https://www.trouw.nl/nieuws/en-toch-heeft-michael-moore-een-punt-met-planet-of-the-humans~b639b0b4/

Rotmans, J., & en anderen van het Break-out Team. (2020). Manifest voor een veer-krachtig en evenwichtig Nederland. Retrieved from https://www.breakoutteam.nl/manifest

Rotmans, J., & Loorbach, D. (2010). Towards a better understanding of transi tions and their governance: A systemic and reflexive approach, Part II. In J. Grin, J. Rotmans, & J. Schot (Eds.), *'Transition towards sustainable development', KSI-book series part I.* Abingdon: Routledge Publishers.

See the first chapter of In het oog van de orkaan

Taleb, N. (2007). *The black swan: The impact of the highly improbable.* New York, NY: Penguin Books.

Van den Bergh, J. (2019). Agrowth instead of anti- and pro-growth: Less polarization, more support for sustainability/climate policies. *The Journal of Population and Sustainability, 3*(1). Retrieved from https://jpopsus.org/full_articles/van-den-bergh-vol.3-no.1/

https://www.edelman.com/trust/2021-trust-barometer, Edelman trust barometer 2021.

3 Civil Servants Can Make the Difference

De Moor, T. (2013). *Homo Cooperans. Instituties voor collectieve actie en de solidaire samenleving*, Oratie, 30 augustus 2013. Universiteit Utrecht.

De Moor, T. (2015). *The dilemma of the commoners: Understanding the use of common-pool resources in a long-term perspective.* Cambridge: Cambridge University Press.

Hagens, K. (2014, April 16). De terugkeer van de commons: weg met staat en markt. *De groene Amsterdammer.*

Ministerie BZK. (2020, September). Essaybundel Ruimte in Regels. Den Haag. Retrieved from https://kennisopenbaarbestuur.nl/rapporten-publicaties/essaybun del-ruimte-in-regels/

Roorda, C., Verhagen, M., Loorbach, D., & en van Steenbergen, F. (2015, February 2015). *Doe-democratie: Niche, visie of hype, DRIFT-onderzoeksrapport.* Erasmus Universiteit Rotterdam.

Rotmans, J. (2018). Omgevingswet als Transitieopgave, G40 Stedennetwerk, essay. Den Haag, Mei 2018. Retrieved from https://www.g40stedennetwerk.nl/files/2018-04/Omgevingswet-essay-Jan_Rotmans.pdf

Rotmans, J. (2019). Verandering van Tijdperk: Wat betekent dat voor Waterschap Zuiderzeeland? Essay in opdracht van het Waterschap Zuiderzeeland, Juli 2018, Lelystad.

Rotmans, J. (2020). Verandering van Tijdperk: Wat betekent dat voor het Open- baar Bestuur? Essay in opdracht van het Ministerie van Binnenlandse Zaken, Januari 2020, Den Haag.

Tjeenk Willink, H. (2019). *Groter denken Kleiner doen: Een oproep*. Amsterdam: Prometheus.

WNF. (2020). *Living planet report 2020*. Wereld Natuur Fonds. Retrieved from https://www.wwf.nl/globalassets/pdf/lpr/lpr-2020-full-report.pdf

4 How Can You, as a Business, Survive the Next Crisis?

Bezos, J. (1997). Brief aan aandeelhouders van Amazon. Retrieved from https://www.sec.gov/Archives/edgar/data/1018724/000119312513151836/d511111dex991.htm

DNB. (2016). *Tijd voor Transitie: Een verkenning van de overgang naar een klimaatneutrale economie*. Amsterdam: De Nederlandsche Bank. Retrieved from https://www.dnb.nl/media/henflz5b/tijdvoortransitie_tcm46-338545.pdf

Engelen, E. e.a. (2020, April 25). Bedrijven die het alleen gaat om geld verdienen, hebben geen bestaansrecht, *Volkskrant*. Retrieved from https://www.volkskrant.nl/columns-opinie/bedrijven-die-het-alleen-gaat-om-geld-verdienen-hebben-geen-bestaansrecht~bf5a48bc/

Kahneman, D. (2012). *Thinking, fast and slow*. New York, NY: Penguin Books.

Klimaatrechtszaak Shell. (2021). uitspraak rechter op 26 mei 2021. Milieudefensie wint rechtszaak tegen Shell. Retrieved from https://nos.nl/artikel/2382398-milieudefensie-wint-rechtszaak-tegen-shell-co2-uitstoot-moet-sneller-dalen

Loorbach, D., Rotmans, J., & Lijnis-Huffenreuter, R. (2014). Ondernemen in transitie: Bedrijfstransities als innovatief model voor duurzaam ondernemen, Stichting Maatschappij en Onderneming (SMO), Den Haag.

Loorbach, D., van Bakel, J., Whiteman, G., & Rotmans, J. (2009). Business strategies for transitions towards sustainable systems. *Business Strategy and the Environment*, *19*, 133–146.

NN Investment Partners. (2019). Onderzoek naar impactbeleggen onder 15.000 beursgenoteerde bedrijven. Retrieved from https://www.nnip.com/nl-NL/professional/insights/articles/een-vijfde-van-de-beursgenoteerde-bedrijven-heeft-een-positieve-impact

5 Palette of Transitions: Challenges and Solutions

Andrijevic, M. e.a. (2020, October 16). COVID-19 recovery funds dwarf clean energy investment needs. *Science*, *370*(6514), 298–300. Retrieved from https://science.sciencemag.org/content/370/6514/298

Avelino, F. (2017). Power in sustainability transitions: Analyzing power and (dis) empowerment in transformative change towards sustainability. *Environmental Policy and Governance*, *27*(6), 505–520.

Change.inc. (2020). Vijf opvallende voorbeelden die de weg vrijmaken voor de circulaire economie. Rianne Lachmeijer, 2 januari 2020. Retrieved from https://www.change.inc/circulaire-economie/circulaire-economie-33047

Circulairinbedrijf.nl. (2020). Gerecycled plastic in de verbrandingsoven? Retrieved from htt-ps://www.circulairinbedrijf.nl/gerecycled-plastic-in-de-verbrandingsoven/

Citigroup. (2015). Energy Darwinism II: Why a low carbon future doesn't have to cost the earth. Retrieved from https://www.citivelocity.com/citigps/energy-darwinism-ii/

Correspondent. (2016, December 13). Dit is de succesvolste klimaatcampagne ooit (en jij kunt meedoen), over de Divestment Beweging. Retrieved from https://decorrespondent.nl/5852/dit-is-de-succesvolste-klimaatcampagne-ooit-en-jij-kunt-meedoen/644943068–c619cd85

Correspondent. (2020, July 3). Niemand weet welk probleem the Ocean Cleanup eigenlijk oplost. Retrieved from https://decorrespondent.nl/11379/niemand-weet-welk-probleem-the-ocean-cleanup-eigenlijk-oplost/2128503726591-df5d997c

https://foodhub.nl/

Documentaire. (2021). Financiering van de Circulaire Economie. Retrieved from https://www.duurzaam-beleggen.nl/2021/02/01/documentaire-financiering-van-circulaire-economie/

DRIFT. (2018, April 10). *Rapport roadmap next economy – Greenport West-Holland 2050, rapport.* Retrieved from https://drift.eur.nl/publications/rapport-road-map-next-economy-greenport-west-holland-2050/

DRIFT. (2020, June 18). Hydrogen for the Port of Rotterdam in an international context: A Plea for leadership Erasmus Universiteit Rotterdam. Retrieved from https://drift.eur.nl/nl/cases/hydrogen-and-port-of-rotterdam-2/

DRIFT. (2015). Doe-democratie: Niche, visie of hype, DRIFT-onderzoeksrapport, Roorda, C., Verhagen, M., Loorbach, D. en van Steenbergen, F., February 2015, Erasmus University Rotterdam.

Duurzaamheid.nl. (2018, February 22). Afgedankte telefoons uit Afrika en Azië zijn goud waard. Retrieved from https://duurzaamheid.nl/artikelen/afgedankte-telefoons-uit-afrika-en-azi%C3%AB-zijn-goud-waard/

EASAC European Academies Science Advisory Council. (2019, February 19). Forest bioenergy, carbon capture and storage, and carbon dioxide removal: an update. Brussels, Belgium. Retrieved from https://easac.eu/publications/details/forest-bioenergy-carbon-capture-and-storage-and-carbon-dioxide-remo-val-an-update/

Egmond, K., & Fransen, J. (2021, August 10). Klimaatbeleid: Geef alle CO_2-uitstoot dezelfde prijs, NRC. Retrieved from https://www.nrc.nl/nieuws/2021/08/09/klimaatbe-leid-stop-met-onderhandelen-geef-alle-uitstoot-dezelfde-prijs-a4054191

Eindadvies van het Adviescollege Stikstofproblematiek over een structurele aanpak van stikstof op lange termijn. (2020, June 8). *Niet alles kan overal, rapport van commissie o.l.v. Johan Remkes.* Retrieved from https://www.rijksoverheid.nl/documenten/rapporten/2020/06/08/niet-alles-kan-overal

Eindrapport van het Adviescollege Meten en Berekenen Stikstof. (2020, June 15). *Meer meten, robuuster rekenen, rapport van Commissie o.l.v Leen Hordijk.* Retrieved from https://www.rijksoverheid.nl/documenten/rapporten/2020/06/15/meer-meten-robuuster-rekenen

Eurostat. (2020). Renewable energy statistics. Retrieved from https://ec.europa.eu/eurostat/statistics-explained/index.php?title=Renewable_energy_statistics

FD Financieele Dagblad. (2018, February 4). Als de Rotterdamse Haven geen pretpark wil worden, moet ze CO_2 radicaal aanpakken Pieter Lalkens en Hans Verbraeken. Retrieved from https://fd.nl/ondernemen/1234069/als-de-rotterdamse-haven-geen-pretpark-wil-worden-moet-ze-co-radicaal-aanpakken

Goldschmeding Foundation. (2021, February 1). Deltaplan Belastinghervorming, the Ex Talks Project. Retrieved from https://goldschmeding.foundation/deltaplan-belastingen-voor-een-circulaire-en-sociale-economie/

IEA International Energy Agency. (2020, May). *World energy investment 2020*. Paris. Retrieved from https://www.iea.org/reports/world-energy-investment-2020

IEA International Energy Agency. (2021, April). *Global energy review*. Paris. Retrieved from https://www.iea.org/reports/global-energy-review-2021

IEA International Energy Agency. (2021, May). *The role of critical minerals in clean energy transitions*. Paris: IEA. Retrieved from https://www.iea.org/reports/the-role-of-critical-minerals-in-clean-energy-transitions

Inspectie van het Onderwijs. (2021). Staat van het Onderwijs, Ministerie Onder-wijs, Cultuur en Wetenschap. Retrieved from https://www.onderwijsinspectie.nl/onderwerpen/staat-van-het-onderwijs/archief

IPCC Intergovernmental Panel on Climate Change. (2019). *2019 refinement to the 2006 IPCC guidelines for national greenhouse gas inventories*. WMO/UNEP, Geneva, Switzerland. Retrieved from https://www.ipcc.ch/report/2019-refinement-to-the-2006-ipcc-guidelines-for-national-greenhouse-gas-inventories/

IPCC Intergovernmental Panel on Climate Change. (2021). *Climate change 2021: The Physical science Basis*. WMO/UNEP, Geneva, Switzerland. Retrieved from https://www.ipcc.ch/report/ar6/wg1/

IRENA International Renewable Energy Agency. (2020). *Global landscape of renewable energy finance 2020*. Masdar City, Abu Dhabi. Retrieved from https://www.irena.org/publications/2020/Nov/Global-Landscape-of-Renewable-Energy-Finance-2020

Kracht in NL, versterk sociale initiatieven. Retrieved from http://krachtinnl.nl/. Our World in Data: Trust. https://ourworldindata.org/trust. World Values Survey. https://www.worldvaluessurvey.org/

KuiperCompagnons. (2021). Atlas van Nederland 2021. Rotterdam: Natuurrijk Nederland: Budgetneutraal naar een Nederland met 50% natuur. Retrieved from https://natuurrijknederland.org/

Metabolic. (2021). Financing circular economy innovation in the Netherlands: The need for an ecosystem approach. Retrieved from https://www.metabolic.nl/publications/financing-circular-economy-innovation-netherlands/

Metabolic, Copper8, Quintel, Polaris. (2021). Een Circulaire Energietransitie: Verkenning naar de metaalvraag van het Nederlandse energiesysteem en kansen voor de industrie, Amsterdam, Nederland, Juni 2021, Amsterdam, Nederland. Retrieved from https://www.copper8.com/circulaire-energietransitie/

NOS. (2018). Het Nederlandse onderwijs glijdt af: Al 20 jaar daalt niveau, zegt inspectie. Retrieved from https://nos.nl/artikel/2226821-het-nederlandse-onderwijs-glijdt-af-al-20-jaar-daalt-niveau-zegt-inspectie

NOS. (2021). Wereldwijd steeds meer rechtszaken over het klimaat. Retrieved from https://nos.nl/artikel/2382278-wereldwijd-steeds-meer-rechtszaken-over-het-klimaat

PBL Planbureau voor de Leefomgeving. (2013). Vergroenen en Verdienen: op zoek naar kansen voor de Nederlandse economie, Den Haag, Nederland. Retrieved from https://www.pbl.nl/publicaties/vergroenen-en-verdienen

PBL Planbureau voor de Leefomgeving. (2021). Integrale Circulaire Economie

PBL Planbureau voor de Leefomgeving. (2021, July 5). *Stikstofcrisis vraagt afgewogen keuze stikstof-, natuur- en klimaatdoelen voor landbouw, rapport*. Retrieved from https://www.pbl.nl/nieuws/2021/stikstofcrisis-vraagt-afgewogen-keuze-stik-stof-natuur-en-klimaatdoelen-voor-landbouw

Porcelijn, B. (2017). *De verborgen impact, Alles over eco-neutraal leven.* Amsterdam: Volt.

Porcelijn, B. (2021). *Het happy 2050 Scenario: Alles wat je kunt doen voor een gelukkige wereld.* Amsterdam: Volt.

Rapportage. (2021). Den Haag, Nederland. Retrieved from https://www.pbl.nl/publicaties/integra-le-circulaire-economie-rapportage-2021

Reneweconomy. (2015, August 25). Citigroup sees $100 trillion of stranded assets if Paris succeeds. Retrieved from https://reneweconomy.com.au/citigroup-sees-100-trillion-of-stranded-assets-if-paris-succeeds-13431/

Rotmans, J. (2020). Zeeland vanuit een Transitiebril, essay in opdracht van ZB| Planbureau en Bibliotheek van Zeeland, Januari 2020, Middelburg.

RTV Rijnmond. (2011). Hoogleraar EUR voert actie tegen bouw kolencentrales. Retrieved from https://www.rijnmond.nl/nieuws/8247/Hoogleraar-EUR-voert-actie-tegen-bouw-kolencentrales

SER Sociaal-Economische Raad. (2020). Biomassa in balans: een duurzaam-heidskader voor hoogwaardige inzet van biogrondstoffen, Advies, Juli 2020, Den Haag, the Netherlands. Retrieved from https://www.ser.nl/-/media/ser/downloads/advie-zen/2020/biomassa-in-balans.pdf

SER Sociaal-Economische Raad. (2021). Naar duurzame toekomstperspectieven voor de landbouw. Retrieved from https://www.ser.nl/-/media/ser/downloads/adviezen/2021/duurzame-toekomstperspectieven-landbouw.pdf

SER Sociaal-Economische Raad. (2021). Gelijke kansen in het onderwijs: Structureel investeren in kansengelijkheid voor iedereen, juni 2021, Den Haag, Nederland. Retrieved from https://www.ser.nl/nl/Publicaties/gelijke-kansen-onderwijs

Stanley, S. K. e.a. (2021, March). From anger to action: Differential impacts of eco-anxiety, eco-depression, and eco-anger on climate action and wellbeing. *The Journal of Climate Change and Health*, *1*, 100003. Retrieved from https://www.science-direct.com/science/article/pii/S2667278221000018

Tegenlicht. (2019, October 28). Boyan Slat wil nu rivieren plasticvrij maken. Retrieved from https://www.vpro.nl/programmas/tegenlicht/lees/artikelen/ocean-clean-up-gaat-rivieren-opruimen.html

True Price Movement. Retrieved from https://trueprice.org/

UNEP United Nations Environment Programme. (2020, December 9). *Emissions gap report 2020.* Retrieved from https://www.unep.org/emissions-gap-report-2020

V & VN en FMS. (2021). Nationaal herstelplan voor de zorg is noodzakelijk, beroepsvereniging voor verzorgenden en verpleegkundigen V&VN en de Federatie Medisch Specialisten (FMS). Retrieved from https://www.venvn.nl/nieuws/v-vn-en-fms-nationaal-herstelplan-voor-de-zorg-is-noodzakelijk/

Van der Linden, M., Toxopeus, H., & Rotmans, J. (2014). *Hoe kunnen we de financiële sector laten kantelen, Hoofdstuk 5 in Verandering van tijdperk: Neder land kantelt.* Boxtel: Uitgeverij Aeneas.

Van Reybrouck, D. (2013). *Tegen Verkiezingen.* Amsterdam: de Bezige Bij.

Van Reybrouck, D. (2013, October 4). Europa gelooft steeds minder in democratie, De Correspondent.

Van Reybrouck, D. (2013). Terug naar Athene: Democratie 2.0 volgens David Van reybrouck. Retrieved from https://orpheuskijktom.com/2013/12/12/terug-naar-athene-demo-cratie-2-0-volgens-david-van-reybrouck/

Volkskrant. (2011). Steeds meer hoogleraren tegen bouw kolencentrales. Retrieved from https://www.volkskrant.nl/economie/steeds-meer-hoogleraren-tegen-bouw-kolencentrales~b9ad391c/

Volkskrant. (2020, February 18). Hoe de groene landbouwambities van de EU verwaterden. Retrieved from https://www.volkskrant.nl/kijkverder/v/2020/hoe-de-groe-ne-landbouwambities-van-de-eu-verwaterden~v91159/

VPRO Tegenlicht. (2015, November 25). Fossielvrij: de invloed van de divestment beweging. Retrieved from https://www.vpro.nl/programmas/tegenlicht/kijk/afleverin-gen/2015-2016/fossielvrij.html

VPRO Tegenlicht. (2020). Op deze vier plekken hebben burgers écht invloed. Retrieved from https://www.vpro.nl/programmas/tegenlicht/lees/artikelen/2020/Vier-voorbeel-den-burgerparticipatie.html

Weston, B. H., & Bollier, D. (2014). *Green governance: Ecological survival, human rights, and the law of the commons.* Cambridge: Cambridge University Press.

https://www.vitaalvechtdal.nl/

https://zorgeloos.care/

https://www.duurzaam-ondernemen.nl/op-black-friday-stunt-eerste-super-markt-ter-wereld-met-echte-prijzen/

https://350.org/category/topic/divestment/

https://www.urgenda.nl/https://theoceancleanup.com/VPRO

6 Personal Transition: the Journey Inwards

Bass, B. M. (1999). Two decades of research and development in transformational leadership. *European Journal of Work & Organizational Psychology, 8*(1), 9–32.

Bos, S. (1999). Nieuwe Dag, nummer van de CD 'Zien'. Retrieved from https://www.stefbos.nl/page/Liedteksten/detail/1332/Nieuwe Dag

Grin, J., Rotmans, J., & Schot, J. (2010). Transitions to sustainable development: New directions in the study of long-term transformative change, KSI book series part I, Routledge Publishers, Great Britain.

Hermsen, J. (2015). *Kairos. Een nieuwe bevlogenheid.* Amsterdam: De Arbeiderspers.

Horvat, S. (2021). *After the apocalypse.* Cambridge: Polity Press.

Lips, R. (2021). *Wie kies je om te zijn: Gesprekken en gedachten over een nieuwe tijd.* Amsterdam: Uitgeverij Ambo/Anthos.

Lips, R. (2021). Retrieved from https://www.nieuweleiders.nl/

New Scientist. (2021, January 12). Doen vrouwelijke leiders het nu wel of niet beter tijdens de coronacrisis? Retrieved from https://www.newscientist.nl/nieuws/deden-vrouwelijke-leiders-het-nu-wel-of-niet-beter-tijdens-de-coronacrisis/

Oosterling, H. (2013). *Eco3: Doendenken.* Prinsenbeek: Uitgeverij Jap Sam Books.

Sloterdijk, P. (2011). See Chapter 2.

Smit, J. (2019). *Het Grote Gevecht & het eenzame gelijk van Paul Polman.* Amsterdam: Uitgeverij Prometheus.

Telegraaf. (1963). Zij die het gelag moeten betalen, artikel over de omslag van kolen naar aardgas die veel mensen op kosten zou jagen, June 1963.

Windsor, L. C., Yannitell Reinhardt, G., Windsor, A. J., Ostergard, R., Allen, S., Burns, C., et al. (2020). Gender in the time of COVID-19: Evaluating national leadership and COVID-19 fatalities. *PLoS One, 15*(12), e0244531.

Printed in the USA
CPSIA information can be obtained
at www.ICGtesting.com
JSHW011634110124
55239JS00003B/14